WIFE KILLER

Detective Tom Le Noir took an instant liking to the four young Filipino women who had asked to meet with him and his partner Buddy Evans. The women were obviously distressed and worried over the sudden disappearance of their friend Emelita Reeves.

"I've paged her and paged her, but she doesn't call. She always calls when I page. I've tried her cell phone. She doesn't answer." Mona Pate said as tears ran down her cheeks.

The other women told the detectives that Emelita was never without her pager or cell phone. Rarely a day went by without all of them having some form of contact with Emelita. None of them had heard from her in almost a week.

"Emelita told us if she ever failed to respond to her pager in thirty minutes it meant she was in danger and that Jack had done something to her," Carolina Mansor said.

Another woman told the detectives, "We all told her to leave her husband. Jack's controlling and jealous. But Emelita was afraid of him. She refused to go with him on his weekly camping trips anymore. She was afraid he would kill her, like he killed his other wives."

Le Noir shot a glance at Evans.

"Like he killed his other wives?" he repeated. The women nodded.

"One died from a shotgun wound and the other drowned. Emelita was sure Jack was responsible," they told Le Noir. "He used to dig a hole when they went camping without saying what it was for. Emilita always thought it was meant to be a grave for her."

She was right.

Other books by Patricia Springer

BLOOD RUSH

FLESH AND BLOOD

MAIL ORDER MURDER

Patricia Springer

Pinnacle Books
Kensington Publishing Corp.
http://www.pinnaclebooks.com

Some names have been changed to protect the privacy of individuals connected to this story.

PINNACLE BOOKS are published by

Kensington Publishing Corp.
850 Third Avenue
New York, NY 10022

Pinnacle and the P logo Reg. U.S. Pat. & TM Off.

First Printing: April, 1999
10 9 8 7 6 5 4 3 2 1

Printed in the United States of America

To Carol and Steve,
with love

ACKNOWLEDGMENTS

My very sincere thanks to Detectives Tom Le Noir and Buddy Evans, the true heroes of this story. Without their unfaltering belief in justice, their tenacity, and compassion for the families left behind, this story would not have had the same conclusion. I appreciate their humor, honesty, integrity, and answering my pages whenever I called.

No writer can survive without the cooperation of many people. I thank Sandy Gately, attorney-at-law; Wes Ball, attorney-at-law; the staff at the Tenth Court of Appeals in Waco, Texas; Bridget Bronstad, district clerk of Bosque County; Tina Church of TC Investigations; Larry Kennedy of the Gatesville Messenger; and Greg Miller, attorney-at-law.

My special appreciation goes to LaRee Bryant, who keeps me on track, as well as Karen Haas, who gives me space, but always with a watchful eye.

It is surmounting difficulties
that make heroes.
—Louis Kossuth

Prologue

Detectives Tom Le Noir and Buddy Evans sat at Le Noir's desk in the Criminal Investigations Division (CID) of the Arlington, Texas, Police Department. They stared at the photos of three women spread across Le Noir's desk. Each dark-haired. Petite. Beautiful. And dead.

They were the wives of Jack Wayne Reeves:

Sharon, wife number two, killed by a shotgun blast to the heart within days of divorcing Jack.

Myong, wife number three, drowned only a few feet from the shores of Lake Whitney in North Central, Texas. She had planned to leave Reeves.

Emelita, wife number four, missing. No one knew where Emelita was. Her friends were concerned, convinced that Reeves had killed her.

As the detectives looked from one photo to the next, they asked themselves: Was Jack Reeves unlucky in love, or a cold-blooded killer?

One

October 12, 1994

"You need to call nine-one-one," Monalisa Pate blurted out, rushing past her friend Arnold Bowlin as he opened the front door of his Arlington, Texas, apartment. Tears streamed down the face of the pretty almond-eyed woman.

"What are you talking about?" Bowlin asked, noting the urgency in his friend's voice as he closed the door.

Pate spun around, shouting, "It's Emelita, she's missing. I've called everybody we know. No one has seen her. No one knows where she is."

Bowlin's narrow eyes widened, filling with concern.

Emelita's friends consisted of a close-knit Asian community. Arnold and Mona, as she preferred to be called, had been friends for years. They had met through Pate's older sister while in Cebu City, Philippines, where they had lived before moving to the United States. Emelita Reeves had resided in Cebu City, as well, until marrying the older American, Jack Reeves.

Like nearly twenty thousand pretty Filipino girls a year, marrying a financially secure American was Emelita's family's passport out of poverty. Cebu City, more than eight thousand miles and twenty-four hours by plane from Texas, is a tropical, hilly, volcanic island lined with rows of shanties and open sewers.

Eleven of Emelita's family members lived in a two-room, second-floor hut, where temperatures often reached more than one hundred degrees. Ramona, Emelita's older sister, occupied the only small bed in the dwelling.

Emelita was her family's only hope for a better life. By marrying Jack Reeves, they would receive $250 a month, a small fortune compared to the average five dollars a day made by most laborers in Cebu. The money received would pay for Emelita's elderly mother's medicine, electricity, and food for the ten remaining family members.

Emelita hadn't loved Jack Reeves when they married, but she believed over time she could make the most of her marriage, while simultaneously helping her beloved family. It was the only way to ease their burdens. She would have done anything for them . . . including marrying a much older stranger and moving thousands of miles away.

Her new friends: Mona Pate, Lynn Combs, Dita Hayes, Maria Langston, Carolina Mansor, April Browning, Arnold Bowlin, and Tony Dayrit helped to make life in Arlington, Texas, enjoyable. They all saw each other often, and Mona and Emelita never missed a day communicating.

Pate, however, had no telephone at her apartment. Thanks to Emelita's possessive husband, who'd given his mail-order bride a pager and cellular phone so he could keep tabs on her, Pate had been able to keep in almost constant contact with Emelita for the past four months. They were close friends. More than friends. Now her dearest companion was missing.

"I've paged her and paged her, but she doesn't call. She always calls when I page. I've tried her cell phone. She doesn't answer. Where could she be?" Pate paced the room nervously.

"When did you last see Emelita?" Bowlin asked quietly, knowing he needed to calm his frantic friend.

"She was supposed to come over yesterday, but she was late. Finally, about six o'clock, she got there. I asked her why she was late, and told her I hadn't eaten lunch because I was waiting for her." Pate dropped her head, her black bangs falling across tear-reddened eyes.

As she wept, Pate thought back to the previous night. "Emelita drove me to work at the Jack in the Box. We talked in the car for a while, then I went in to work. It was about eight o'clock. That was the last time I saw Emelita." She paused to inhale deeply before continuing. "At ten o'clock I took a break and called Emelita at home. She told me she couldn't pick me up after work because she was waiting for a long-distance call from her mom in the Philippines. She told me she would see me today. She said she had a present for me."

What could Emelita have been giving me? Pate asked herself. Afraid she'd never know, she put her face in her hands and wept harder.

"Then what happened?" Bowlin prodded.

"About eleven o'clock I called Emelita again. No one answered. At twelve I called once more," Pate said through her sniffles. "A man said, 'Hello.' It must have been Jack. I hung up. I didn't want to talk to Jack Reeves."

Pate didn't have to tell Bowlin why; all of Emelita's friends had heard the stories of the verbal and physical abuse Jack Reeves had waged on Emelita. The young Filipino wife had described episodes of sexual perversion, forced drug usage, and virtual bondage. Fearing for her life, Emelita's friends had encouraged her to leave the fifty-four-year-old Reeves, whom she had dubbed "grandpa." Emelita had recently confided that she and Reeves had discussed separating and that he had agreed to pay her thirty thousand dollars and set her up in her own apartment. Emelita had told Pate she was only waiting for the promised money, then she would be free. Pate and Emelita had even planned a vacation to the Philippines—once Reeves handed over the money.

Now it had been twenty-four hours with no word from Emelita. Pate was anxious, fearful that something terrible had happened to her friend.

"Call the police," Pate again demanded of Bowlin.

"Do you know where she lives?" he asked, running his fingers through his jet-black hair, trying to think of what to do next.

"Yes, I do."

"Well, you called and there's no answer. You beeped and she doesn't call back. Let's go around to the neighborhood and see if her car is parked at home," he suggested.

Consumed with fear, Mona Pate was ready to try anything.

The Asian couple climbed into Bowlin's car and headed to Emelita's Arlington, Texas, house on Iberis Drive.

Bowlin drove slowly past the single-story, multicolored brick home, its brown and yellow trim barely distinguishable in the dark. Reeves's white four-door dual Ford truck was parked in the side yard, the lights on the running board glowing in the dark. His white Dodge Ram pickup truck was parked in the drive. There was no sign of Emelita's Nissan Pathfinder. Bowlin pulled to the curb, cut the engine, and the two friends sat staring at the unpretentious house across the street.

From the gleam of the nearby streetlight that faintly lit her paper, Pate nervously scribbled what she and Arnold observed. The dimly lit house, the truck in the driveway, the truck with lights burning in the side yard, and Theo, Emelita's son, watching television in the living room.

"Let's go inside. Knock on the door and see if she's at home," Bowlin suggested.

"No!" Pate blurted. "I'm afraid of Jack Reeves." She sank farther down in the seat. "I don't know what he'd do if he saw us."

The pair sat transfixed in the hushed darkness for several more minutes, just watching the house.

Suddenly Pate saw movement inside the darkened garage. A flash of light, then the return to darkness.

"Look!" she commanded.

Bowlin jerked in surprise.

Pate pointed to the windows at the top of the double garage doors. "There's a person inside the garage. I don't know who it is." Her voice quivered.

Almost an hour passed with no further movement from inside the garage. No sign of Reeves. No sign of Emelita.

"I can't stop thinking about what Emelita said to me once,"

Pate whispered in the dimness of Bowlin's car. "She said, 'If you page me and I don't call you back, just call the police because something's happened to me.' " Pate's soft sobs filled the air.

"You're right," Bowlin said. "We need to call nine-one-one. They can have an officer check inside—to see if she's home."

Officer Doug Hirschman and Officer Chip Oxedine, a rookie, of the uniformed division of the Arlington Police Department (APD), arrived at Jack and Emelita Reeves's residence on Iberis Drive at 11:05 P.M. It was just a routine response to a welfare check.

"These things can be anything from someone being late for a dinner date to a child playing on a balcony," Oxedine said as he and his partner exited their car.

The officers casually, but cautiously, approached the midsized, well-kept brick home. The only illumination was a bright light shining from behind the right side of the house. The officers' dark navy-blue uniforms blended into the darkness as they moved away from the puddle of light. They noted a white pickup parked in the drive, but no other vehicles were obvious from their position at the front of the house. Officer Hirschman knocked on the door.

The officers flinched slightly as loud barking suddenly erupted from inside the darkened house. Hirschman and Oxedine waited, but no one responded to their knock.

Hirschman continued to knock on the front door while Oxedine walked over to take a look into the garage that jutted out several feet past the front entrance.

Oxedine stood on his tiptoes, stretching the full-length of his five-foot-eleven-inch, two-hundred-plus-pound frame to shine his flashlight through the high windows, just below the roofline. He noticed a large sports utility-type vehicle parked inside. It was too dark to distinguish colors, except to note the interior appeared darker than the outside paint.

Oxedine continued along the width of the garage, illuminating the windows all along the way. The garage seemed to be clear. As he moved around to the right side of the house, he noticed a bright light shining through the planks of the stockade fence.

Meanwhile, Hirschman, who stood six-three, left the front door to also peer through one of the eight garage windows that spanned the width of the double overhead door. His flashlight caught a reflection.

"Arlington Police, we need to talk to you," Hirschman shouted loudly to a man he spotted crouched in a corner.

Oxedine immediately returned to his partner, who was still standing in front of the garage windows, but he could see nothing.

Hearing the front door open, the officers returned to their original positions at the front of the house.

As the officers rounded the corner, a tall white male was slipping through a small opening between the front door and the door facing. The man had opened the door only wide enough to squeeze his large frame through, shutting the door quickly behind him. Dogs barked from the other side of the closed door.

"I'm Jack Reeves," the man told the officers.

"We're here on a welfare check," Hirschman said.

Oxedine watched Reeves closely, noting the sweat on the man's face, his trembling hands, and the way he breathed in small gasps. *This guy seems very nervous,* Oxedine thought.

Oxedine looked at Reeves questioningly. It seemed odd that he carried a pair of work gloves in his hand, especially at eleven o'clock at night.

"What have you been doing?" Oxedine asked.

"I've been moving a couch in from my trailer in the backyard."

Oxedine decided not to ask why he was moving a sofa into his house that late at night, or how he was managing the task alone. They were there to check on Emelita.

"We need to know if Emelita Reeves is here," Hirschman said, getting to the point of their call. "We'd like to check inside the house."

Suddenly, the muscles in Reeves's neck tightened. He pressed his lips tightly together.

"Well, I'll be honest with you guys, she's a fuckin' lesbian," Reeves blurted out angrily. Waving his arms around in a fit of rage, he added, "She goes out and sleeps with her friends and then comes back and sleeps with me. She disappears for days at a time and I don't know where she is. She left last night at eleven-thirty with her lesbian lover, Lisa Monet. All I care about is, she better show up in the morning. I have to go to work and she has to take care of our son."

Hirschman and Oxedine had no idea that "Lisa Monet" was the nickname of Monalisa Pate, one of the complainants responsible for reporting Emelita's absence to police in the first place.

Straightening to his full strapping stature, Hirschman took a deep breath and explained, "Mr. Reeves, we've had a call about the welfare of Emelita Reeves. We just want to do a walk-through to make sure she's not here. We aren't looking for contraband."

"No, I don't want a bunch of people tromping through my house," Reeves snapped bitterly.

"Sir, that is not our intention. We just need to see who's here," Hirschman said, attempting to reassure Reeves.

Reeves pressed his back firmly against the front door. It was obvious he wasn't going to budge.

Since they had no warrant, the officers backed off.

Oxedine took the portable radio from his utility belt and called dispatch.

"Recontact the person who initiated the report on Emelita Reeves and find out if they could give us any additional information," Oxedine instructed. "Also tell them we were unable to locate Emelita at her residence."

"Mr. Reeves," Officer Hirschman said sternly, "a written report will be completed and forwarded to the investigative division. If anything has happened to Emelita you will be considered a suspect. We need a form of positive identification from you."

Reeves slipped back inside the house, again only partially opening the door, allowing only minimal space for him to fit through. Moments later Reeves returned, accompanied by a small boy.

"This is Theo, my son," Reeves said as he removed his Texas driver's license from a leather wallet and handed it to the officers. "Do you know where Mommy is? Tell them where Mommy is," Reeves said, nudging the boy.

The three-year-old child stared at the officers blankly through huge brown eyes. He did not speak, could not speak because of his severely retarded social development, a fact Reeves neglected to tell the officers.

"Emelita's not here," Reeves barked, continuing to block their entry into the house.

Without probable cause to make a nonconsensual entry, the officers turned and left Jack Reeves standing on the porch of his home, still clinging to his small son.

October 12, 1994

"Jack, this is Mona," Emelita's friend said nervously to Jack Reeves over the telephone.

Reeves's voice bellowed over the wire. "Mona, why did you call the police?"

"I am just worried about Emelita. Do you think she's okay?"

"Yes, she's okay."

"Where's Theo?" Pate's voice reflected as much concern for Emelita's son as for her friend.

"He's here."

"Can I talk to Theo?" Although at three Theo was still unable to form understandable words, Pate recognized the familiar background sounds being made by the boy.

"No," Reeves said flatly.

"Where's Emelita?" Pate persisted. Jack Reeves made her uneasy. She didn't like talking to him, but Pate had to find Emelita.

"She's with Dita," Jack said sharply.

Dita Hayes was another of Emelita Reeves's good Asian-born friends. Pate carefully considered whether Emelita might have gone to Hayes's for the night. Maybe. But one mystery remained.

Why hadn't she answered her pager? Why hadn't she called back? Pate quickly ended the conversation with Jack Reeves and immediately telephoned Hayes.

Hayes had not seen Emelita, nor had she talked with her. Pate's concern for Emelita mounted. Where could her friend be? Pate was frantic with worry. She tried Emelita's pager again, carefully inserting her special code of "55" following the number where she could be reached. She waited. Waited for a call from her friend—her lover.

Pate's anxiety was combined with confusion. She and Emelita had made plans—plans to vacation in the Philippines, plans for a long-term relationship. They both looked forward to sharing a life—once Emelita left Reeves.

October 13, 1994

Maria Langston and Monalisa Pate pulled into the HyperMart parking lot, just south of I-20 and Cooper Street in Arlington. Only two miles from Jack and Emelita Reeves's house. There they planned to meet with Lynn Combs, who worked at the superstore and who was another friend of Emelita's, to try and make sense of Emelita's perplexing disappearance.

As Langston pulled her car into one of the hundreds of parking slots in the expansive parking area, she was shocked to spot Emelita's Pathfinder. The vehicle was legally parked right in the middle of the immense parking lot, facing south. The two women hurriedly rushed to meet Combs outside the HyperMart entrance, their short slim legs moving at above normal speed.

"Lynn, we found Emelita's Pathfinder," Mona said breathlessly.

"Where?"

"Here! Here, in the parking lot," Langston answered.

The three women rushed to Emelita's vehicle.

Lynn Combs stopped just short of reaching the champagne-colored vehicle.

"Something's not right," Combs said. She carefully opened the driver's door with a napkin covering her hand. *I don't want my fingerprints in the car,* she thought.

"Emelita always puts the steering wheel up before getting out. She locks the doors, and sets the alarm. It never matters where she is, she always does that." Combs knew Emelita's habits well.

But the driver's door was not locked. Her alarm had not been set. Her steering wheel was in the down position. Theo's car seat was gone. And, most interesting of all to the three women, was the position of the driver's seat. It was pushed all the way back. The petite Emelita, at only five-three, always had her seat set as far forward as it would go in order to reach the foot pedals. Someone had been driving Emelita's vehicle.

Someone much taller than Emelita.

Pate and Langston kept watch over the Pathfinder while Combs went into the HyperMart to call more of Emelita's friends—and the police.

Pate's work schedule from the Jack in the Box rested on the dashboard of Emelita's vehicle. She had left the schedule there the night Emelita dropped her off at work. Pate quickly glanced at the schedule, then laid it back on the dash.

Within minutes, most of the Asian-born band of friends had congregated at the parking spot, along with two police officers.

Officer Vasteenberg circled the abandoned vehicle while Officer McElwain scanned the parking lot. It was not unusual to be called to the area; it was, after all, the busiest place in Arlington, perhaps all of Tarrant County. The twenty-four-hour store, which featured everything from electronics to eggs, was a customary place to dump stolen cars.

This vehicle is immaculate. There's no soil on the carpet. In fact, the whole interior is spotless. Looks like it may have just been detailed, Vasteenberg thought as he visually inspected the Pathfinder.

Emelita's friends all began talking at once.

"The car belongs to Emelita Reeves," one said hastily.

"Emelita is missing," another added. "Something must have happened to her."

"When was the last time you saw Emelita Reeves?" Vasteenberg asked.

"The last time we saw her was at the Lotus Restaurant day before yesterday, about one o'clock," Lynn Combs answered.

The young woman appeared to be in charge, so Vasteenberg directed the majority of his questions to her. He needed basic information, and she was cooperating.

As far as Officers Vasteenberg and McElwain knew, no crime had been committed, therefore no fingerprints were taken, no evidence collected.

Once Vasteenberg learned where Emelita Reeves lived, he drove the short distance to the house on Iberis, followed by his trainee, Officer McElwain. With luck, Emelita would be sitting in the living room, watching TV, and snacking on a bowl of hot buttered popcorn.

There was no answer at the door of Reeves's house, so Vasteenberg began walking the perimeter, peering in the windows.

Maybe someone is inside, lying on the floor injured, Vasteenberg thought.

But everything looked in order. He swung open the gate on the northwest side of the house and checked the backyard. A large area of grass was flat—smashed. The officer stooped to feel the thin blades of saint augustine sod. It looked as if there'd been some type of heavy vehicle parked on the grass, one that had recently been moved. Maybe that morning, or even the night before.

"What's going on?" a neighbor of the Reeves's asked.

"I'm looking for Jack Reeves," Vasteenberg answered.

"He pulled his camper out of here early this morning."

Officer Vasteenberg had asked Lynn Combs to assist him in contacting anyone who might know where Jack Reeves could be. He returned to the HyperMart to check with her. Maybe she had been able to reach someone in Reeves's family.

Randall Reeves, Jack's older son, pulled into the HyperMart

just behind the Arlington officers. With him was his wife, Debbie.

"I'm Randy Reeves," he told the officers. "I received a call that my stepmother's car was located in the parking lot. There seems to be some concern about her whereabouts."

"That's exactly why we're here," Officer Vasteenberg said. "We were called because of the car."

Randy Reeves, at five eight, was decidedly smaller than the Arlington officer. The slightly built Reeves walked with Vasteenberg to the abandoned Pathfinder.

"Can you impound the vehicle to see if you find anything that might help in finding out where Emelita is?" Randy asked.

"Well, it's legally parked, and there doesn't appear to be any evidence of foul play. Just take it home," Vasteenberg said.

"I'll have to go to the house to get the keys."

With the Arlington Police officers following, Randy and Debbie made their way to Jack's house on Iberis, a short five-minute drive from HyperMart. Randy immediately went to the laundry room, where brass hooks affixed to the wall held a variety of dangling keys. Randy pushed his glasses up on the bridge of his nose as he searched for the right one. No key to the Pathfinder.

As Randy busied himself with the keys, the officers made a quick walk-through of the house to determine if anything was out of place. All seemed in order.

"We need to locate your father," Vasteenberg told Randy.

"My father went camping at Lake Whitney. He goes there quite often. He isn't planning on coming home until tomorrow."

"Well, we need to talk to him as soon as possible," the officer said with some degree of urgency. "We need to have him pick up the vehicle."

"I know where he is. I'll tell him. I'll have to get the keys to the Pathfinder from him, they aren't here."

As Randall Reeves drove away to fetch his father from his favorite camping site at Lake Whitney, Officer Vasteenberg reviewed his notes on the Pathfinder, making mental memos. *The vehicle was legally parked. Only the driver's door was unlocked.*

The area where the vehicle was abandoned is an extremely congested and populated business district. The shopping center is regularly patrolled by on-duty APD officers and APD auto-theft task force officers. He flipped his notebook shut.

The situation was inconsistent with an abduction. However, because of the position of the driver's seat, it seemed obvious that the car had been parked at the HyperMart by someone other than Emelita Reeves. But who?

And where was Emelita?

TWO

October 13, 1994

Randy Reeves left Arlington and headed southwest toward the Hillsboro area of Lake Whitney. He was sure he would find his father at his favorite campsite, one he frequented about once a month.

Randy drove along the two-lane blacktopped road leading to Lake Whitney. He passed only an occasional motorist, mostly locals who were in no hurry to get where they were going. He thought about the conversation he'd had with his father earlier that morning. Jack Reeves had called his son to let him know that the police had been at his house the night before.

"I didn't let them in," Jack had said. "They pissed me off. I was moving furniture into the house. I bought a couch at Levitz." His father had almost sounded remorseful when he said, "I wish I had let them in now. I'm going to the lake to camp with Theo. Emelita knows I'm going. She left the house to pick up a friend. She's just out having fun," Jack had said nonchalantly. "Nothing's happened to her. I'm going to go ahead and take Theo camping."

Now Emelita's car had been found abandoned, and the police wanted to talk to his father. Randy was confused. What had happened to Emelita? And why, if Emelita was missing, had his father left town?

Randy, with his wife, Debbie, on the pickup seat beside
him, turned off the rural road that had been dotted with abandoned cars, rusted tractors, and dented trailers and drove
through the natural rock entrance with cascading jasmine into
the Lake Whitney State Park. It was a serene place. The
brown frame park information building was deserted, lighted
only by the ice and Dr Pepper machines just outside the front
door. The rustle of the American and Texas flags flying on
the tall pole in the front of the building was the only sound
breaking the peacefulness of the park.

Randy followed the tree-lined road past the small airstrip
to the full-hookup area. Driving through a canopy of trees,
past darkened trailers and a scattering of bicycles and ice
chests near concrete picnic tables, he found his father's familiar trailer nestled in a stand of live oak trees. It was just
after midnight.

Randy knocked on the door of the white Nomad trailer.
No answer. He knocked again. No answer. Finally, unable to
rouse his father or Theo, Randy began banging on the side
of the metal camper.

Jack Reeves staggered to the door. *He looks drunk,* Randy
thought.

"What's wrong, Dad?" Randy asked with concern.

"I've taken Valium," his glassy-eyed father responded.
"With a scotch."

From the way his father was stumbling around the trailer,
Randy guessed that he had taken a significant amount of the
dangerous combination. "Dad, Emelita's Pathfinder was
found in the HyperMart parking lot. They still don't know
where Emelita is. Her friends are very worried about her.
They think something's happened to Emelita," Randy said,
hoping his father understood.

Jack Reeves's face wrinkled with apparent concern.

"You pick up Emelita's car and take it to my house,"
Reeves slurred, leaning against the wall for support. He
handed Randy the keys to the Pathfinder. "I'll drive home

tomorrow." Since he'd arrived at the park after five o'clock in the evening, Jack hadn't checked in and paid his twelve-dollar permit-holder fee. He would take care of it when the office opened, then head back to Arlington.

Randy knew his father was in no condition to drive home. Jack and Theo would remain in the trailer at the state park, but Randy's wife did not want to stay the night. Several months pregnant, Debbie wanted the comfort of her own bed, and she wanted to avoid the embarrassment of morning sickness in front of her father-in-law. The young couple left the Lake Whitney State Park in the wee hours of the morning and headed back to the metroplex. The late night, the drive to Lake Whitney to find his father, and the emotional turmoil over Emelita's disappearance had sapped Randy's energy. He could barely keep from falling asleep at the wheel. As he drove into the Hillsboro city limits, he steered his vehicle into the parking lot of a Burger King. He parked and then he and Debbie slept soundly.

About nine o'clock, after a quick breakfast at the fast-food restaurant, Randy and Debbie returned to Arlington, picked up Emelita's Pathfinder, and returned it to his father's house.

Randy parked the champagne-colored vehicle in the drive, then walked to the backyard.

What's that? Randy asked himself.

On closer inspection he realized that the metal frame sitting near the open gate was the internal section of the brown hide-a-bed sofa that had been in his father's living room. The same sofa his father had mentioned the previous day.

"I cut through the fabric of the sofa to remove the arms," Reeves had explained when telling his son how he had managed to get the excessively heavy piece of furniture out of the house by himself. "Then I dropped it off at a Goodwill drop-off spot at I-20 and Green Oaks Road in Arlington."

Randy wondered why his father would buy a new sofa, when the old one seemed perfectly good to him, and why he had discarded the sofa and kept the matching brown chair.

It didn't make sense. The couch was of no use without the bed frame.

Randy and Debbie went inside the house to wait for Jack. They stopped momentarily to inspect the new couch, sitting exactly where the old one once sat. "That sofa's as ugly as sin," Randy muttered out loud, again wondering why his father had replaced the old one.

October 15, 1994

Homicide detective Tom Le Noir leaned back in his chair as he flipped through an incident report his supervisor, Sergeant Dixie Stout, had asked him to review. From the reports submitted by Officers Hirschman and Oxedine, something didn't seem right. Jack Reeves's behavior set off alarm bells.

Swiveling his chair around, Le Noir no longer faced his desktop computer but a color photo of himself with Hulk Hogan, pinned to the back wall of his cubicle. As Le Noir read through the file, the initial report of a missing person was beginning to take on the characteristics of a homicide. The detective asked himself a number of questions: *Why had Reeves been confrontational? Why was he uncooperative? And why had Jack Reeves left on a camping trip during the initial urgent stages of his wife's disappearance?*

Only one man could answer those questions—Jack Reeves.

Three days after Emelita Reeves's apparent disappearance, Detective Le Noir telephoned Emelita's husband.

"Mr. Reeves, this is Detective Le Noir with the Arlington Police Department. I've been trying to reach you in connection with the disappearance of your wife." His voice was strong and authoritative.

"I just got back from a camping trip at Lake Whitney," Reeves said casually, seemingly undaunted by the call. "I haven't heard from Emelita. She refused to go camping with me, she wanted to be with her lesbian friends. Theo, my little boy, went with me."

"I'm curious, Mr. Reeves, why didn't you initiate a missing-person report?"

Jack Reeves's voice instantly changed from calm to irate. "She runs off all the time!" he shouted. "Sooner or later she'll come back."

"When was the last time you saw your wife?" Le Noir asked.

"About eleven-thirty P.M. on October eleventh. She went to visit Mona, one of her lesbian lovers," Reeves sarcastically replied.

Le Noir listened curiously as Reeves began to share portions of his personal life with the detective. Reeves briefly described his and Emelita's sexual relationship and how he put up with her homosexual encounters.

"In fact," Reeves shared, "I wanted to watch Emelita in sexual acts with other women. I also suspect Emelita is having an affair with a man named Tony. I warned her that I would never tolerate her having sex with another man."

Reeves's demeanor was calm, almost matter-of-fact while discussing the intimate aspects of his relationship with his wife, yet his attitude noticeably soured when he spoke of Emelita with another man. Le Noir found the confidences distasteful, and curious. *Why is he telling me this?* Le Noir thought. His high forehead wrinkling from his light eyebrows to his sandy-brown hair as he considered the implication. *And if there's been foul play, he just gave me a motive.*

"Why wouldn't you let the officers in to check the house?" Le Noir asked, getting back to the reason for his call.

"They pissed me off with their accusations," Reeves snapped. "I had taken Theo to Fort Hood that morning, four-wheeling in my Dodge four-by-four. I got home later that evening after purchasing a new sofa. It was a surprise for

Emelita. I was unloading the sofa from the pickup when the officers came to the house."

"Can you give me an example of the officers' accusatory nature?" Le Noir asked, digging for answers.

"Well, they wanted to come into the house and look around," Reeves said irritably.

"Officers Hirschman and Oxedine were merely following routine procedures in an attempt to determine the welfare of your wife," Le Noir explained.

Reeves took a deep breath. "I'm sorry," he apologized. "The officers can come look inside the house if they want to."

But the offer was too late. Three days had passed since the initial contact with Reeves—ample time for him to prepare the house for an inspection.

What good would it do for us to search the house now? Le Noir thought. *His thinly veiled offer is no more than an audacious attempt to con us and to manipulate the investigation.*

Le Noir interpreted Reeves's lack of concern for his wife and his insincerity in his offer to assist in the investigation as a blatant and easily detected smoke screen. But a new question arose in the detective's mind. *What did Jack Reeves have to hide?*

"This is an ongoing investigation," Le Noir told Reeves, "pending the discovery of your wife."

Again Reeves lambasted his wife's character. Then, noticeably calming himself, Reeves casually informed the detective that Emelita would return soon, and everything would be all right. He and Emelita would continue to live together and continue to raise their young son. "I love my son dearly. I would do anything to keep him," Reeves said.

The conversation was a roller coaster of emotions.

Le Noir hung up the phone. He immediately ordered an entry be made on the national criminal database concerning

Emelita's disappearance. Hopefully, his gut feeling was wrong. Hopefully, Emelita Reeves was still alive.

Meanwhile, Emelita's friends could not sit idly by and do nothing. They were desperate to find their friend, and fearful that they would never see her again.

Carolina Mansor, one of the close-knit circle of Filipinos that rallied to help locate Emelita, headed an all-out search effort. She made up fliers and asked friends to help distribute them. She was putting together a reward fund when she contacted Jack Reeves for help.

Reeves quickly took over the search. Displeased with the photo Mansor had selected, he offered another, insisting that a color photo would bring much better results. He pledged twenty-five thousand dollars for a reward and carefully worded the fliers to read, "For The Safe Return Of Emelita Reeves."

October 18, 1994

Detective Le Noir teamed with Detective Buddy Evans of the missing persons division of the Arlington Police Department to work the Emelita Reeves case temporarily. Once another homicide detective was freed up, Evans would return to the missing persons division. It seemed an odd match. Le Noir, a sandy-haired, jovial, "let's catch the bad guys" kind of cop was a distinct contrast to the dark-haired, soft-spoken Evans. But they had a common goal: to find Emelita Reeves.

Le Noir and Evans were not strangers. In 1986 Le Noir had investigated an attempted murder on Evans's life.

Evans had been a rookie cop at the time, on routine patrol. He had spotted a woman sitting in her car on the side of the road, apparently distressed. As Evans had leaned in her driver's-side window to see if he could be of help, she had pumped a bullet straight into his chest. Evans had gone down. He had been saved only by the concealed bulletproof vest he had been wearing.

Le Noir had been assigned the case and had interviewed the suspect, a former junior-high classmate.

"Pam, remember me, we went to junior high together," Le Noir had begun, hoping to build rapport. "Why did you shoot that officer?"

"I was in the store the other day and I was trying to find some Frescas, you know the drink? I didn't think they made them anymore and I wanted a case of Frescas," she had said calmly.

Le Noir had been confused. What did soft drinks have to do with shooting an officer? He had leaned closer to the suspect.

"What were you going to do with them?" Le Noir had asked.

"I was going to take them to the police station and put them in the Coke machine."

Le Noir was had begun to get the idea. Pam was not mentally balanced. Softly he had asked, "That's nice. Why were you going to do that?"

"Well, that way, when I shot one of you, I could watch it spew out of your stomach."

That had been it. Le Noir had his confession.

Pam had been prosecuted and convicted, Le Noir had continued to work in the homicide division, and Evans had been promoted to detective. They had gone about their separate duties until the disappearance of Emelita Reeves had brought them back together.

The detectives met with Carolina Mansor, Maria Langston, April Browning, and Mona Pate at Mansor's Arlington home. The four black-haired, petite, similar-looking women were very close to Emelita, and rarely had a day gone by that they didn't have some form of contact with their friend. The women appeared to have genuine concern for Emelita's safety. They were unquestionably distressed.

Le Noir took an instant liking to the four Filipinos who had all taken American names. He could see that they were true friends, and each had an honest desire to help find Emelita. He understood the bond probably better than Evans.

Le Noir understood the closeness of the four Filipino women sitting before him. As a fourteen-year-old boy, Le Noir, a Louisiana Cajun, had moved to Texas when his father had been transferred by Bell Helicopter. Other families had been uprooted to Texas at the same time. They had bonded, forming their own support system. Their friendships had transported them back to Louisiana when they had felt homesick. Some friendships had endured over the years. He recognized the same loyalty in the four Filipino women. He knew that each of them brought to the other a little piece of home. He admired their loyalty.

"We told Emelita to leave Jack," Pate said, interrupting Le Noir's thoughts. The other women concurred. "She was fed up with the mental and physical abuse. She told us she planned to leave Jack and take Theo with her, regardless of an offer by Jack to pay her thirty thousand dollars and a trip back home to the Philippines if she wouldn't leave him until December."

The woman's anxiety was obvious to Le Noir and Evans.

"That was nothing more than a way to stall her from leaving," Mansor interjected. "Once Jack knew of her plans to leave him, we told her to take Theo and leave."

"Was Emelita having an affair?" Le Noir asked.

Pate admitted that Emelita was indeed having a homosexual liaison with her, but no one else. The other women, all happily married and living heterosexual lifestyles, seemed unaware of any sexual relationship between Mona and Emelita. They knew of no men involved with Emelita, although Emelita had admitted that Reeves was suspicious of her having an affair with a man named Tony Dayrit.

The women barraged the detectives with stories of Jack Reeves's compulsive control of Emelita. She had a new car, a cell phone, a pager, and cash to spend, but he refused to let her have a credit card or put her name on his bank account. He virtually made certain that she lacked the financial resources to leave.

These are smart women, Le Noir thought.

They showered the detectives with their feelings about Emelita and her volatile relationship with Reeves. They mutually concurred that they believed Jack Reeves was responsible for Emelita's disappearance.

"I understand what you're saying," Le Noir said, trying to calm them. "But I have to have facts. Sit down and give me facts."

"Jack was controlling and jealous. Emelita was afraid of him. She refused to go with him on his camping trips to Lake Whitney. She was afraid he would kill her, like he killed his other wives," one of the women said fearfully.

Le Noir's pulse quickened. Shooting a quick glance at Buddy Evans, he shifted forward in his chair.

"Like he killed his other wives?" he prompted.

Three

Le Noir listened eagerly for Carolina Mansor's response.

"Jack had been married twice before. Both women died and Emelita always suspected that Jack had killed them," Mansor said somberly. "She was very afraid of Jack. Emelita told us that he would sometimes dig a large hole in the wooded area of Lake Whitney near their camp. He never explained why he dug the hole, but Emelita thought the hole was a grave for her."

"But why would she stay with a man she feared?" Le Noir asked as he rubbed his deeply dimpled chin.

The answer was easily understood by the four Filipino women. Many of their friends back home had left for the same reason: financial security. Emelita lived in fear of Reeves, to insure the economic assistance he provided her family in the Philippines. The family was very poor. They drew water from a well with the aid of a bucket tied at one end and counterbalanced at the other end by a worn-out rubber tire. Raw sewage ran in the streets. The eleven members of the Villa family bunched together at night on the floor of their cinder-block dwelling. Her father's meager income as a street vendor came nowhere near being adequate to support his family. At eighteen, Emelita had been handing out free samples of shampoo at a grocery store. Everyone who could work in the family, did. The few hundred dollars Jack sent each month would help them live very well. Emelita loved her family, and it was her responsibility to help them in any way she could. They agreed, encouraging her to stay with Reeves, even after she confided in them about her experiences of physical and emotional abuse. She was trapped. Emelita felt she had no choice but to live with danger.

"Would Emelita have any reason to simply leave without notifying anyone?" Le Noir asked, watching Pate carefully. As the last known person to have seen Emelita Reeves, Pate had to be considered a suspect.

"Never," she said emphatically, shaking her head, her short black hair swinging from side to side. Her almond-shaped eyes narrowed. "She would never leave without her vehicle, her pager, her cellular phone, and, most importantly, her son."

Le Noir believed Mona Pate was right. From their description of Emelita's habits, and her family devotion, Le Noir suspected that Emelita Reeves had met with foul play.

"Emelita would always respond to her pager," she continued, tears moistening her dark eyes. The other women concurred. All feared the worst.

"If she doesn't answer her phone, she is probably dead," Mansor said softly. "She told us if she ever failed to respond to her pager within thirty minutes, it meant she was in danger and that Jack had done something to her."

Le Noir and Evans pondered Mansor's sobering statement. Although Jack Reeves was a strong suspect in the disappearance of his wife, they had to pursue every possibility.

"Does she have any enemies or problems that would account for her disappearance?" Le Noir asked.

The four friends looked at one another and shook their heads slightly. They were in agreement. Emelita did not socialize outside their immediate circle of friends. Emelita had no adverse relationships—other than with Jack Reeves.

"He was sexually perverse," they all agreed. "Jack is the only person who ever hurt Emelita."

The women told stories of how Reeves had forced Emelita to perform obscene sexual acts while he photographed her. How she was never allowed to use the bathroom without leaving the door open. And, how he would bring home men from his paint-contracting job to be with Emelita, although she always refused.

"Emelita is a loving and caring person," Pate said sadly, almost in a whisper.

The description was contrary to the depiction of Emelita given by Jack Reeves.

Le Noir and Evans stood to leave. "I want to assure you that we have a great interest in this case. We share your concerns for Emelita's welfare and will do all we can to find your friend." *These are neat ladies,* Le Noir thought. *They want to find their friend, and so do I.*

All four women pledged to give their complete cooperation during the investigation. A fact that did not go unnoticed by Le Noir and Evans.

According to the initial report given Le Noir, Lynn Combs and Cecilia Zenk had met with Emelita at the Lotus Restaurant off Little Road in Arlington on the afternoon of her disappearance.

When Le Noir met with Lynn she explained that Emelita had been late for their twelve-thirty lunch date, keeping her and Zenk waiting more than two and a half hours.

The women had sat patiently in the Asian-styled dining room, sipping green tea and occasionally filling a plate from one of two long serving isles in the center of the red-carpeted restaurant.

They laughed and talked while enjoying the steamed rice, egg rolls, and a bevy of other delectable foods. Fragrant vapors rose past the artificial flower arrangements atop the steam tables, up toward the red and gold dragon-encrusted lamps hanging above. The delicious aromas permeated the women's senses, beckoning them back for additional helpings.

Amid the other diners, mostly overweight patrons with plates piled high with ribs and fried chicken, Combs and Zenk ate their lunch while growing increasingly more anxious. They kept asking one another, "Where's Emelita?"

Combs recalled the relief she felt as Emelita walked through the gold carved archway flanked by red columns and a plastic ficus tree. But as Emelita pulled out one of the red-cushioned mahogany chairs, Combs and Zenk became alarmed.

"What happened to your face?" Combs asked, staring at Emelita. Her normally pale slender features looked puffy and swollen.

"I've been crying. Jack and I were fighting all night. Jack got mad when I told him I planned to leave him. He pulled my hair and tried to choke me," Emelita said, pressing her hand to her throat. "He thinks I'm having an affair. He thinks it's Tony Dayrit."

The two women tried to comfort Emelita, but fear visibly gripped her as tears coursed down her cheeks.

"He told me he would kill both me and any man I was having an affair with if he ever found out for sure." Emelita took a long deep breath. "Jack promised to give me thirty thousand dollars, pay for an apartment for six months, and leave me alone if I would stay with him till December. He wants one last Christmas together. But tomorrow I'm going to see my lawyer. I'm going to take Theo and the dog. I'm going to divorce Jack Reeves."

"Why wait?" her friends asked. "Get out of this, now."

"I have to wait. Besides, Jack won't do anything to me. He loves me." The women weren't sure if Emelita was trying to convince them, or herself. Then she added, "But, if you ever call my beeper and I fail to respond within a half hour, call the police."

Combs and Zenk knew they weren't going to persuade Emelita to leave immediately; all they could do was try to take her mind off the unpleasant confrontation with Jack Reeves. At four o'clock Zenk suggested, "Let's go to the mall. Shopping always makes us feel better."

The women drove the short distance down Interstate 20 to the Parks Mall, just north of Cooper Street. Emelita regularly spent hours at the mall only minutes from her home. Perhaps to pass the time. Perhaps to buy "things" that made her life with Jack Reeves palatable.

The women strolled through the two-story enclosed atrium-styled shopping center, then took the glass elevator to the second floor. Emelita spotted the Wilson's Leather shop nestled between a hip clothing store and a fine jeweler.

"Let's go in. I've been wanting a leather jacket," she said.

Standing in the leather-goods store was like sitting in a brand-new car. The essence of rich leather filled their nostrils.

Emelita tried on jacket after jacket. Her mood improved with each garment she slipped over her narrow shoulders. A broad smile accentuated her high cheekbones and deep brown eyes when she made her final choice.

"I'll put fifty dollars down and get the rest of the money from Jack. I can pick it up tomorrow."

As Emelita was completing the store layaway form, her cell phone rang.

"Hello," Emelita said. After a brief conversation she turned to her friends. "I have to go. Jack wants me to come right home." The smile on Emelita's face only moments before was gone. Fear returned to her eyes.

"That was the last time we saw Emelita," Lynn Combs told Le Noir.

Combs had met Emelita Reeves on September 18, 1993, while Emelita had been shopping at the HyperMart store where Combs worked. Spotting a similar face in the crowd, Combs approached Emelita and began a conversation, hoping they would have something in common. The two Filipino women became fast friends.

"Emelita told me how she met her husband," Combs told Le Noir. "Her parents had placed an ad in a mail-order bride magazine in hopes that Emelita would meet a rich American, who would marry her, and help them financially. She married Jack Reeves for the sole purpose of financial security and residency in the United States. It was a loveless marriage. Emelita often spoke of their sexual relationship. She frequently complained of Jack's impotence and his failure to sexually gratify her. She told me, 'I have to get drunk to have sex with Jack. Otherwise I'd puke.'"

Le Noir pondered this latest revelation. From Combs's description of the Reeveses' union, Emelita may have decided putting up with Jack wasn't worth the price for her family's security. Could she have just run away?

"Jack is extremely possessive. He refused to treat Emelita with the dignity and respect of a wife," Combs explained. "He refused to allow Emelita to get a Social Security card, therefore she couldn't work. Jack gave her a cash allowance but refused to let her have a checking account or credit cards. He completely controlled her. He wouldn't let her have the slightest bit of independence from him."

It had been Combs who introduced Emelita to other Filipinos. All the women were happily married but continued to enjoy evenings at the Baja Club, a popular Arlington disco.

"She told Jack that all her girlfriends were bisexual and that she was having a lesbian fling with them," Combs said in explanation of why a possessive Jack Reeves would allow his wife to go clubbing without him.

The ploy worked. So well that Reeves asked Emelita to take his dildos and porn tapes with her on her encounters. Combs smiled as she told Le Noir how Emelita would show up at her house with a purse full of sexual paraphernalia. And how she and Emelita would have a good laugh.

Combs shared information given by Emelita's other friends regarding her usual habit of returning pages. "Jack gave Emelita the cellular phone and pager in order to keep a constant monitor on her whereabouts. He would become extremely irritated if Emelita failed to call him back immediately after he paged. That possessiveness is what programmed Emelita to immediately call anyone who had paged her. That's why I knew something was wrong when I never got a response," Combs said. "I talked to Tony Dayrit, another one of our friends, who was worried about Emelita when she failed to show up for their scheduled date on the evening of October eleventh. She didn't answer Tony's pages, either."

"Was Emelita having an affair with Tony?" Le Noir asked.

"Emelita told me she and Tony were having an affair," Combs said. "But Tony denies it. He has a fiancée back home."

Combs took a long breath and looked squarely at Le Noir.

"I'm convinced that Jack Reeves killed Emelita," she said. "He used to strut around the house with a revolver tucked in his pants. Emelita told me he kept one under his pillow." She took a deep breath. "The only way of getting information or evidence to prove he's responsible for Emelita's disappearance will be for me to pretend to sympathize with him. To side with him."

"Lynn, you can't do that," Le Noir insisted, alarmed by her statement. "It's too dangerous."

"I've already talked to him. I told him Emelita was having an affair with a man. I told him I felt sorry for him. I wanted to gain his trust, then maybe he would slip up and tell me something about what happened to Emelita. But he said horrible things about her," Combs said angrily.

"For your safety, I urge you to stop talking to Jack Reeves. You can continue to cooperate with the investigation, I just want you to cease any covert endeavors," Le Noir cautioned.

Reeves's controlling behavior, the obvious lack of concern over his wife's disappearance, and Reeves's curious trip to Lake Whitney during the early stages of the investigation set alarms clanging in Le Noir's and Evans's minds. Though Reeves couldn't be considered the sole suspect, the experienced detectives had strong suspicions. It was time to meet face-to-face with Jack Reeves.

October 20, 1994

Jack Reeves arrived at the Arlington Police Department at noon. He identified himself and asked to speak to Detective Le Noir. The uniformed officer relayed the information to the third-floor CID offices via telephone, and within minutes Le Noir was shaking hands with Reeves in the lobby of the APD.

"Come on up," Le Noir said as he led Reeves through the standing metal detector to the station elevator.

As the men exited the elevator, Buddy Evans introduced himself to Reeves. "We need to have a positive identification," Evans said. "Do you have a license?"

Reeves produced a Texas driver's license identifying him as a white male, born June 25, 1940.

"Do you understand that this interview is strictly voluntary?" Evans asked. "You are free to leave at any time."

"I understand," Reeves assured the detectives. "I'll be glad to talk to you about Emelita's disappearance."

Le Noir led Reeves through the glass door leading into the third-floor criminal investigation area and ushered him into a large conference room. This wasn't a formal interrogation. The detectives just wanted to feel Reeves out. Find out what he knew.

Le Noir and Evans had prearranged for Le Noir to conduct the interview. Tom Le Noir was a cagey Cajun, who had grown up in the bayous of Louisiana, and he had twelve years of homicide investigations behind him. His philosophy was, if you love what you're doing, you'll enjoy your work. He loved being a homicide cop.

"Where are you from, Jack?" Le Noir began with a routine background question, hoping to set Reeves at ease.

Reeves leaned forward, resting his elbows on the desk that separated him from the detectives, revealing a panther tattoo on his right forearm.

"I went to high school in Sulpher, Oklahoma, then moved to Wichita Falls, Texas. I was in the military for twenty-five years. I retired from the U.S. Army in 1985 as an E-eight and moved to Arlington. I bought the home I'm in now. I'm an independent paint contractor at Vandervort," Reeves said. He appeared relaxed.

Then, for reasons unexplained, Jack Reeves suddenly began to brag about his sexual attributes and went into detail about how Emelita used sexual aids.

"Emelita used dildos, you know, a simulated penis. She had

ones with different designs ranging from normal size to great big ones," Reeves said, a large grin covering his face as he moved his hands in and out to indicate the sizes of the dildos.

As Reeves continued to carry on regarding his sexual preferences he unexpectedly bragged, "I love to eat pussy," and ran his fingers through his dyed black hair.

Le Noir and Evans sat quietly. They would allow Reeves to continue with the outburst. The more he babbled, the more they learned about the man who was quickly becoming their chief suspect.

As rapidly as Reeves had shifted the interview from Emelita's disappearance to his sexual pleasures, he redirected the discussion to his financial status. Handing the detectives copies of his bank statements, Reeves bragged, "I have a one-hundred-thousand-dollar CD and a seventy-five-thousand-dollar CD. I have lots of money. I have several other CDs worth thousands of dollars." Reeves leaned back in his chair, obviously proud of his accumulated wealth.

"How do you account for these large sums of money?" Le Noir asked.

"My elderly father carried large sums of money around in a bag. He gave me the money to invest," Reeves explained.

Le Noir made a mental note, *Run a financial check.*

Although Reeves's outbursts concerning his sexual appetites and his financial situation were interesting, Le Noir resumed control of the interview.

"You know, we've interviewed a number of Emelita's friends," Le Noir said. "They are suspicious of you, Jack."

"I'm not surprised," Reeves shot back sharply.

"Have you ever been married before, Jack?"

"Yes, I was married to a woman named Myong I met in Korea. She died by drowning in 1986 at Lake Whitney while we were on a camping and fishing trip," Reeves said, having regained his composure. Then, as if an afterthought, Reeves rubbed his eyes and seemingly began to cry.

Le Noir watched carefully. No tears.

"She didn't deserve to die that way," Reeves added.

Strange, Le Noir thought, *just as quickly as he became emotional, he returned to a clear-eyed, calm state. And why did he say, "to die that way?"*

"Myong was relaxing on a float next to our docked boat. I went to gather crickets for fishing bait. She must have slipped off while I was gone. It was only about ten feet of water, but Myong couldn't swim. I immediately sold the boat because the memories of her death haunted me too much. I got rid of everything that reminded me of Myong's death," Reeves said while nervously tapping his fingers on the desktop.

"But you still camp at the same spot, is that right?" Le Noir questioned.

"Yes," Reeves admitted after a brief hesitation.

The interview was getting more interesting with each query. Reeves remained calm and answered each of Le Noir's questions as Evans observed. It was a cat-and-mouse game between Le Noir and Reeves. A game Reeves couldn't possibly win. He was far outclassed by his opponent.

"Were you married prior to Myong?" Le Noir asked, not for information but for emotional reaction.

Reeves's demeanor quickly changed from calm and cooperative to defensive.

"What do my past marriages have to do with anything?" Reeves demanded.

The cunning Le Noir decided to level with Reeves and calculate his reaction. "Emelita's friends suspect you of Emelita's disappearance because they believe you killed your other wives. I'm simply trying to determine whether or not their suspicions are warranted," Le Noir said frankly.

Reeves shifted uneasily in his chair. As though he felt the gray walls of the room closing in on him, he unconsciously pushed his chair back and into the corner farthermost from the questioning detective.

He feels trapped, Le Noir thought.

"Okay," Reeves said reluctantly, "I'll talk about my past

wives. I was married to Sharon Delane Reeves. Sharon committed suicide in Copperas Cove, Texas in 1978." Anger edged his voice.

Either this guy is very unlucky in love, or he's a cold-blooded killer, Le Noir thought.

"I refuse to discuss the deaths of my wives any further," he said forcefully, with a flash of hostility in his eyes. "I'm here to talk about Emelita's disappearance. Just keep your questions to that subject."

Le Noir agreed and let Reeves jump from one subject to another at will.

"I intend to change the title for the Nissan Pathfinder from Emelita's name to mine, and give the car to Randy, my older son," Jack said.

Le Noir looked questioningly at Reeves but said nothing. Changing the title from his wife's name within eight days of her disappearance was extremely premature. It defied logic—unless he had knowledge that Emelita was not going to return.

Le Noir refocused. "I understand, Jack. Do you have a problem with providing a written statement to account for your last known contact with Emelita?"

"No, I don't object, but on my terms," Reeves said, crossing his arms across his chest in a defiant manner. "I'll only answer questions I'm comfortable with, and I want a copy of the statement after it's done."

Interesting. He's putting limitations on the information he's willing to provide, Le Noir thought as he watched Reeves closely. *And, his behavior grossly deviates from the expectations of a person whose spouse is missing and unaccounted for.*

"Have you ever been arrested and charged with a crime?"

"No, I'm a law-abiding citizen," Reeves said, looking Le Noir in the eye.

"Jack, I'm going to Mirandize you—read you your rights before we can take your statement."

Jack Reeves sat quietly as Detective Tom Le Noir read from a small card retrieved from his pocket. Reeves could remain silent. He could consult an attorney. Reeves waived his constitutional rights and voluntarily agreed to provide a written statement and to discuss the disappearance of his wife—again, only within his terms.

Le Noir sat in front of a CID typewriter and began pecking at the keys as Reeves answered questions posed to him by the detective. Le Noir made certain the statement was brief, and questions were nonaccusatory.

Jack Reeves began his statement by telling detectives that he was born June 25, 1940 and that he currently resided on Iberis Drive in Arlington, Texas, along with his Filipino wife Emelita. Reeves claimed that he and Emelita had lived in the house on Iberis Drive since they had married in 1987, except for a separation period of twenty-three months.

Reeves then addressed the issue of his wife's disappearance, stating that Emelita had gone out about 11:30 P.M. on October 11th to her friend Dita's house. Reeves claimed he had not seen Emelita since that time, nor had he seen her Nissan Pathfinder until it was recovered by the police on October 14th.

Nervously Jack Reeves began telling Le Noir about the night police officers arrived at his house, searching for Emelita. He admitted that he was upset with the police and refused to allow them to search the house. "I had nothing to hide," Reeves added quickly, explaining that the officers had upset him by saying he looked suspicious and accused him of hiding in the garage. But Reeves insisted he was in the garage only to look out the window to see who was ringing the doorbell.

Reeves continued to explain that he told officers that Emelita and her Pathfinder were not at the house, insisting that only his motorcycle was parked in the garage when officers arrived.

"I wish I had cooperated with the police," Reeves told Le Noir, adding that he wanted to find Emelita and would help in any way he could with the investigation.

As though an afterthought, Reeves added that this was the third time Emelita had disappeared and that was why he hadn't reported the incident to police.

Jack Reeves signed his statement at 1:23 P.M. on October 20, 1994.

Le Noir typed Reeves's statement and handed it to him. He leaned back in his chair as he watched his suspect carefully study each sentence for a lengthy period. During his inspection of the document, Reeves's brow wrinkled and his jaw tensed. Displeased with portions of his statement, Reeves picked up a pen from the desk and meticulously began making corrections.

Reeves carefully inserted "In August 1985" after the phrase "when I retired from the military." In paragraph one, beside the explanation of his separation from Emelita while she was pregnant, Reeves wrote, "Emelita lived in the Philippines for the twenty-three months." Midway through the statement, he carefully underlined the phrase, "I did not know where she was at," and printed in the paper's margin, "she was at Mona's house."

Once Reeves was satisfied that the document accurately stated his version of the facts, he handed it to Detective Le Noir.

Le Noir read aloud the statement he and Reeves had prepared. Reeves was listening for accuracy, Le Noir and Evans for discrepancies. Reeves signed and dated the paper.

While reading, Le Noir had noted that in Reeves's written statement he claimed that on the date and time Officers Hirschman and Oxedine were at his residence there was no vehicle parked in the garage and that he didn't own another vehicle similar in color or body style of the Pathfinder. That was in direct opposition to the observations made by the officers. Unknowingly, Reeves had provided evidence to support the suspicion that Emelita's 1993 Pathfinder was, in fact, concealed in the closed garage on the date and time in question.

Reeves also provided a different account as to why he was in the garage at the time Officers Hirschman and Oxedine were at his residence. Now Reeves claimed he was in the garage for the sole purpose of seeing who was at the door. He never mentioned moving a sofa in from the backyard. But Reeves had been unable to provide a reasonable explanation for his paranoia at the mere presence of someone ringing his doorbell. Rather than simply answering the door or looking through the peephole, which would have revealed the police at the door, he claimed he had gone into the garage to look out the window to see who was ringing. A window that didn't even provide a view of the front door.

Reeves's discrepancies made no sense. Furthermore, Reeves contradicted himself when he claimed that Emelita was with her friend Dita, then later scribbled in the margin that she was with Mona.

Le Noir made a mental note. Reeves's story was inconsistent.

Le Noir spent a lengthy period of time informing Reeves of the investigative procedures that would be used in attempting to locate his missing wife. The lead detective made certain he avoided direct accusations. It was premature to point an accusing finger at Jack Reeves, and he wanted to keep the suspect cooperative. He wanted to maintain the positive rapport they had established.

Reeves appeared comfortable with the investigative procedures Le Noir spelled out. He seemed relaxed, almost as though he were in control.

"We eliminate persons from suspicion through the use of a polygraph examination," Le Noir said matter-of-factly. He noticed Reeves's slack posture become rigid. "There is nothing to fear, and the examinations should not be a cause of apprehension. It is simply an investigative tool, which can expedite answers to certain issues." In a further attempt to set Reeves more at ease, Le Noir added almost offhandedly, "Polygraph examinations are inadmissible in a court of law, and therefore they cannot be used as incriminating evidence."

But Reeves wasn't buying what Le Noir was selling. He had no intentions of taking a lie-detector test.

"I'm naturally nervous and I'm afraid I would do poorly," Reeves said, shifting uneasily in his chair.

"Mere nervousness will not affect the determination of truthfulness or deception, and will easily be detected by the polygraph operator, preventing a false reading," Le Noir explained.

"I'd be too nervous," Reeves said, looking down and shaking his head.

"I can assure you of the credibility and integrity of the polygraph examination," Le Noir said, hoping to push Reeves to comply.

"I just don't know. What kind of questions would be asked?"

"The questions will be predetermined. You'll have an opportunity to know the questions in advance. My primary questions will be: Do you know the whereabouts of Emelita? Do you know the status of her welfare? And, are you concealing information from the police that would lead to the whereabouts of Emelita and the discovery of her welfare?"

Le Noir studied Reeves carefully.

"I need to speak with an attorney," Reeves announced.

At that point the interview was over. The detectives had learned very quickly that Reeves was not receptive to questioning of an accusatory or confrontational nature.

"I want you to search Emelita's Nissan Pathfinder for fingerprints or other evidence," Reeves insisted.

"We'll do that, Jack," Le Noir said. "Why don't you bring it by the station. You know, Jack, something may be wrong with Emelita. Something may have happened to her. We don't know. I've got to find her. If someone killed her, I'll tell you this, I'll find that person. That's what I get paid to do. The thing about murder investigations is there's no statute of limitations. You never quit. You never give up. I have so many years left with this police department. What I will guarantee you," Le Noir said, pointing his finger at Reeves, "is I will work on this until the day I retire from this department, then someone else will have to pick it up from there. The bottom line is I won't stop. I won't give up."

Le Noir walked to the Xerox machine in the corner of the room to make a requested copy of the written statement Reeves had made and signed. As he lifted the lid on the machine to insert the original copy, he found his attention quickly diverted back to Reeves and the question he directed to Detective Evans.

"Are y'all going to blame me if Emelita's found at Lake Whitney?"

A few minutes later, Evans escorted Reeves downstairs to the main lobby of the APD. When he returned, Tom Le Noir was leaning against the interview-room door, looking like the cat that had swallowed the canary.

"Did you pick up any clues?" Le Noir asked in a humorous, smart-ass manner.

Evans grinned sheepishly, "Do you think we might want to go to Lake Whitney and look around?"

Four

October 22, 1994

The pager affixed to Detective Le Noir's belt interrupted his thoughts. Le Noir checked the number printed on the small screen. Within minutes he was returning the call.

"This is Le Noir," he said curtly.

"Detective Le Noir, this is Jack Reeves. When can I bring Emelita's Pathfinder down to the station?"

A time was set for Reeves to meet Le Noir and Evans at the APD and within an hour he was pulling into the station parking lot.

Le Noir waited for Reeves on the hedge-lined, slanted walkway adjacent to the station. He carefully watched as Reeves exited the Nissan Pathfinder and easily removed the child seat belted into the rear seat of the vehicle. Reeves left the steering wheel in the down position and the driver's seat pushed all the way back.

"I don't ever drive this car so I can't figure out how to set the alarm or door locks," Reeves said as he handed Le Noir the keys.

"You've parked in a secured area. Don't worry about not being able to set the alarm or locks. It'll be okay," Le Noir said as he made mental notes that Reeves had parked Emelita's Pathfinder in the exact same manner in which it was discovered at the HyperMart.

I can't confront him about the incriminating similarities now, Le Noir thought, *he might overreact to the implied accusation.*

"It will take us awhile to process the car. Buddy and I will give you a ride back home," Le Noir said, walking toward his new, white Crown Victoria. The department issued new unmarked vehicles to the detective division, then after a pre-determined amount of mileage was acquired, they were outfitted for patrol.

"You know, I was in Vietnam," Reeves said while en route to his house. "I was a machine gunner on a helicopter. We'd fly over the fields and shoot randomly into spider holes."

"I'm not familiar with the term spider holes," Evans said.

"The Vietcong would dig holes to conceal themselves, then jump out and ambush the approaching enemy. I'd shoot in the holes and take them out," Reeves said with obvious pleasure, becoming increasingly animated as he discussed the number of Vietcong he had killed.

He enjoyed the killing, Le Noir thought.

"Let me buy you guys lunch," Reeves said.

"No, thanks, Jack, can't do that," Le Noir answered. He felt sure lunch wouldn't settle well if he had to share it with Jack Reeves.

October 25, 1994

"Detective Le Noir, I have evidence that will assist you in locating Emelita," Jack Reeves said, continuing to show respect by properly addressing the younger man whenever he called. "Can I bring it in?"

Le Noir agreed to meet with Reeves, then contacted Detective Evans. "Buddy, Jack is coming in with what he claims is evidence. I want you to be here."

About noon Jack Reeves arrived at the police department carrying a cardboard box. Once he made his way past the officer at the front desk, through the metal detector, and up to Le Noir's office on the third floor, he opened the lid.

"This belonged to Emelita," he said, grinning as he pulled a dildo from the container.

That is the nastiest thing I've ever seen, Le Noir thought, staring at the dirty dildo, *and the most disgusting.* Le Noir felt his stomach sour. His nose crinkled as if he had smelled a dead armadillo on a Texas highway.

Both Le Noir and Evans were speechless. They saw no evidentiary value in the sex object.

"Why did you bring us that?" Le Noir finally asked.

"I know you have police dogs that can sniff the dildo and get the scent of Emelita's vagina. Then you can locate her body." Reeves grinned, obviously proud of his suggestion.

Le Noir shut his eyes, shaking his head slightly in an attempt to banish the mental image of a K-9 officer holding the foul sexual instrument for his dog to sniff.

This is the second time Reeves has displayed sexual perversion during this investigation. Le Noir wondered if a pattern was forming. Would there be more?

Still stunned, and finding no appropriate response to the unusual behavior, the detectives thanked Reeves for his help and escorted him from the CID offices. They kept his disgusting "evidence."

Neither Le Noir or Evans believed it was either pertinent or wise to let Reeves know all the measures being taken to locate Emelita. Although Reeves was the husband of the missing person, he was also considered a suspect. The detectives believed Reeves was on a need-to-know basis. And he didn't need to know everything.

A team of trainers and their highly proficient cadaver dogs were called in to assist in the hunt for Emelita Reeves. Minus the dildo Reeves provided, the trainers and dogs were dispatched to the wooded area east of the HyperMart store. Mercy, a black Labrador-Belgian Sheepdog mix, worked the slabs and newly poured foundations in a nearby housing development under construction. Other dogs throughly explored the woods and drainage ditches. Le Noir was hoping there would be some evidence of Emelita found in the underbrush; if not a body, at least a scent that would help them find her. But Mercy found no sign of Emelita Reeves.

Le Noir was frustrated. The investigation was focusing increased suspicion on Jack Reeves, but Le Noir knew from his twelve years of homicide investigations that he couldn't accuse Reeves directly. He would have to work the man, and he had a plan in mind. Le Noir called Reeves and requested he come down to the station to go over the progress of the investigation to that point. Then he went downstairs to Evans's office.

"Some of these guys you can sit down with and you'll get a confession from them during the conversation," Le Noir told Evans as they waited for Reeves to appear. "But Jack's the cagey type. He thinks, 'You're not going to catch me.' We'll give him enough rope and he'll hang himself." Le Noir smiled broadly as Evans looked questioningly, wondering what his new partner was up to.

"You're fixing to hear some weird stuff," Le Noir said with a gleam in his eye. "I've got an idea. Just smile and go with me."

Evans's forehead wrinkled as he wondered just what Le Noir was up to. But he was the junior member of this homicide investigation, still on loan from missing persons, so he yielded to the more experienced investigator, only muttering an affirmative, "Okay."

Jack Reeves was predictably cooperative. Within an hour Reeves was back at the Arlington Police Department. This time Reeves was escorted to a small interview room in the juvenile division on the second floor. Reeves had Theo by his side.

"Jack, I think Emelita may be dead," Le Noir began. Reeves remained expressionless as he appeared to listen attentively.

"If Emelita is in fact deceased, forensic technology, like DNA, can clearly identify the suspect responsible for her murder and the disposal of her body," Le Noir explained.

Reeves leaned forward toward Le Noir, resting his forearms

on the desktop. Le Noir decided to throw out the first of two bluffs. The seasoned homicide detective frequently utilized the tactic to ignite a response from a suspect in determining evidence of suspicion or guilt.

"If Emelita was killed inside the house, even though her body was moved, decomposition would have occurred immediately and dead skin cells from her body would become embedded in the area where her body rested."

Evans glanced over at Le Noir, remembering his instructions to go along with the strange posture his partner was employing. But Evans couldn't help but wonder, *What is he talking about? Dead skin cells? Immediate decomposition?* Evans remained silent.

"The dead cells wouldn't be visible to the naked eye and could only be detected through a microscopic examination," Le Noir added. "They would show up best on a carpeted surface. Conventional cleaning wouldn't even remove the dead cells from carpet."

Evans and Le Noir studied Reeves closely. He fidgeted in his chair, wrung his hands, and nervously stroked his graying hair. He'd obviously given up dying it over the last few weeks.

"But there's no blood on the carpet," Reeves said.

"Emelita may have been choked or smothered, therefore eliminating the probability of blood or trace evidence. If she was dragged across the carpeted floor, she would leave behind undetected DNA evidence. We need to take a look at the carpet, Jack." Le Noir, who was enjoying the cat-and-mouse game, paused for Reeves to respond.

Reeves's confidence seemed to have waned. His head drooped slightly and his voice was weaker. "Ah, I'm in the process of replacing the carpet," Reeves said.

"Jack, I don't want you to do that right now. Let us have a chance to examine the carpet. We can't get to it until later this week, but hold off on replacing it until we get finished with our testing." Evans noted Reeves's shoulders relaxing as Le Noir told him the testing wouldn't be done that day. "The DNA will determine whether or not Emelita was sexually assaulted," Le Noir said, then waited for Reeves's reply to his bluff.

Theo played quietly on the floor with a toy police car he had brought with him to the station. *Window dressing. Nice touch, Jack,* Le Noir thought. *Yeah, you really love the police. There's probably a butchered cop in the trunk.*

Reeves twisted back and forth in his swivel chair. He took short gasps of breath and spoke quickly. "Emelita and I had sexual intercourse only moments prior to her disappearance. If semen is found in Emelita's vagina, it will be mine."

"There's nothing to be concerned about with consensual intercourse," Le Noir said shrewdly. "Forensic technicians will be interested only in evidence of forced intercourse—like sexual assault."

Le Noir was patient. He couldn't confront Reeves directly with a murder accusation, or he could lose him. He had to give him an out. He had to keep him hanging on.

As he had done during the previous interview, Reeves scooted his chair backward toward the corner of the interview room farthest from Le Noir and Evans. *He does that, when he feels trapped,* Le Noir thought.

It was time to initiate the second bluff.

"We got a crime-stoppers tip that a body has been discovered," Le Noir said.

"Was Emelita's body found at Lake Whitney?" Reeves snapped. "If so, am I going to be blamed?"

Evans cut his eyes toward Le Noir. This was the second time Reeves had made a reference to Lake Whitney and the discovery of Emelita's body.

"We'll keep you informed of any discovery."

The interview was over.

Before Jack Reeves had walked through the outer doors of the Arlington police station, Le Noir had assigned a surveillance team to monitor Reeves's residence.

As Le Noir had predicted, it didn't take long for his bluff to pay off. The next morning he received a call from the surveillance team. Jack Reeves was having the carpet in his house removed.

Seven or eight months prior to Emelita Reeves's mysterious disappearance, Jack Reeves had talked with Tom Kirkland about replacing the carpet in his Arlington home.

"Do you install carpet?" Reeves had asked Kirkland, after overhearing a conversation between Kirkland and another employee at the Vandervort Dairy. Reeves and Kirkland were seated at separate tables in the lounge area. Reeves, a paint contractor, and Kirkland, a security officer with Burns Security, were enjoying a cup of freshly brewed coffee during a morning break.

"Yeah," Kirkland replied while blowing steam from the hot Java, "I do carpet as a side business."

"In a few months I'm going to get mine done. I'll give you the business," Reeves said.

Several months passed before Reeves approached Kirkland again. "I'm almost ready for the carpet, do you have any samples?" Reeves asked.

"Yes, but I'll need to go out to your house and take measurements, to see what you'll need."

After work Kirkland followed Reeves to his house on Iberis Drive in South Arlington. He measured the floors, as directed by Reeves, and returned to his truck to retrieve the carpet samples for Reeves's consideration.

"I have a few samples here," Kirkland said, handing the large swatches to Reeves. "I'll be glad for you to look at them."

"I don't know what color," Reeves said, shaking his head in confusion. "Let me get Emelita."

Emelita Reeves, much younger than her graying husband, flipped through the samples, ultimately making a final selection.

"The only rooms I want done now are the dining room, the living room, and the bedrooms. I need to wait on the hallway. I'm having some plumbing problems. My brother-in-law will repair the leak, then I'll get back to you on that," Reeves said.

Kirkland ordered the carpet. The floor covering arrived about two weeks after Emelita's disappearance.

With the Arlington Police surveillance team positioned outside the house, Kirkland and his crew ripped out the worn carpet and replaced it with the newly ordered floor covering.

"Are you going to take the old carpet with you?" Reeves asked. "I don't want it sitting out in my driveway."

"No, the city will pick it up," Kirkland informed him.

"No, they don't do that," Reeves insisted, obviously anxious to have the materials removed from the premises, defying Le Noir's instructions. "I'll pay extra to get rid of it."

Per Reeves's instructions, Kirkland and his crew hauled the old carpet to the city dump. There, pieces of the carpet were cut and salvaged by a couple of the workers for use in their own homes. Except for a couple of spots chewed by the two puppies living at the house, the carpet appeared to be in excellent condition.

Le Noir was angry. Jack Reeves had taken the bait about DNA being detectable on the carpet but Reeves had managed to destroy any possible evidence before a search warrant could be obtained. Still upset at the missed opportunity, Le Noir snatched his phone from its cradle and dialed Jack Reeves's number.

"Why did you remove the carpet, knowing I wanted to examine it?" Le Noir demanded to know.

"Don't worry," Reeves's said in a sly tone, "the person I hired to remove the carpet was told to preserve it for the police. Besides, I only replaced certain sections, not the whole house." Reeves's tone of voice irritated Le Noir. *He thinks he's pulled a fast one.*

"Why the hurry, Jack? Why couldn't you wait to replace the carpet until after we had a chance to examine it?"

Reeves, unable to justify his urgency in replacing the carpet after agreeing to hold off, stammered, stuttered, and maneuvered around the questions.

"Give me the name of the person who's holding the carpet for us," Le Noir demanded.

Reeves quickly turned over the name of Tom Kirkland and how the detective could reach him.

Le Noir made the call to Kirkland as soon as he hung up with Reeves.

"No, Reeves never told me to keep the carpet," Kirkland told Le Noir. "In fact, he paid me thirty-five dollars extra with specific instructions to dispose of it. I took it straight to the landfill."

Le Noir could feel warmth come to his full fair-skinned cheeks. Reeves had blatantly lied to him. Deliberately defied his instructions.

"Reeves even gave me and my workers several pieces of furniture. Let's see, a TV, VCR, and a home-entertainment shelf," Kirkland added.

Interesting, Le Noir thought. *Now, why would Jack be giving away furniture two weeks after his wife disappears?*

One of the two bluffs initiated by Le Noir had obviously worked. Reeves had taken the bait, removed the carpet, then lied about where it was. It was time to test out the second bluff. Could Emelita Reeves's body be somewhere in the Lake Whitney area? Le Noir decided to make an all-out effort to locate any skeletal remains.

Based on Reeves's comments and continuous concern that he would be blamed if Emelita's body were found at Lake Whitney, the detectives ordered an aerial search of the entire area.

Lake Whitney, about seventy-five miles southwest of Dallas, is a winding lake meandering along 23, 560 acres of the Brazos River. With steep, rocky bluffs, Whitney is quite scenic, but the terrain created a major obstacle in conducting a general search. The ground surrounding a great portion of the lake was obscured by trees, rocks, and tall grasses.

No unmarked graves appeared on the aerial photos. No skeletal remains. Le Noir and Evans weren't surprised—only disappointed. Discovery of a body would have cinched an indictment of murder, but Le Noir feared they would never find the body.

Bodies go unfound all the time. There are children's pictures on milk cartons all over the world to prove it. They could only wait. Wait for Emelita to be found.

Le Noir and Evans communicated with county officials and park rangers at Lake Whitney requesting immediate notification pending the discovery of any human remains in their area. In addition, the detectives initiated the distribution of information through state and national channels of communication, requesting an immediate call upon the discovery of human remains consistent with the anatomy of an adult Asian female.

As Le Noir and Evans continued to interview friends of Emelita Reeves, and proceeded with the elimination of suspects, Le Noir decided it was time to look into the coincidental deaths of both Myong and Sharon Reeves. Two young women, both reported to be in excellent health who had met with untimely deaths, both married to Jack Reeves. There were more questions than answers in the minds of the two detectives. The first step was to order death certificates from the Texas Department of Health and Bureau of Vital Statistics.

But there was more information needed. Le Noir decided to contact Myong's and Sharon's families. A little more research provided names and numbers for the family of Reeves's first wife.

Le Noir had no idea how Sharon's brother, Larry Vaughn, or her father, James Vaughn, would react to his questions. Were they close to Reeves? Were they in communication with him? Not knowing the relationship between Jack Reeves and the Vaughns, Le Noir proceeded with caution when he made the first call.

"Hello, Mr. Vaughn, my name is Detective Le Noir. I'm with the Arlington Police Department. Do you know Jack Reeves?"

If he says yes, he was a wonderful son-in-law, I'll just say, thank you, goodbye, Le Noir thought as he waited impatiently for Vaughn's response.

"He was married to my daughter," James Vaughn said, his voice sounding sad.

"When was the last time you saw Jack and talked to him?" Le Noir asked, implying nothing more than a passing interest.

"The last time I saw Jack Reeves was after he murdered my daughter," James Vaughn said, his frail voice breaking.

Le Noir sat straight up in his chair, his feet firmly planted on the floor of his CID office cubicle.

"We really need to talk to you," Le Noir said with an edge of urgency in his voice. "Can we come right over?"

Five

October 29, 1994

With Le Noir behind the wheel of his city-issued Crown Victoria, and Evans in the passenger seat, the duo headed west toward Fort Worth and a meeting with James and Larry Vaughn. The partners, still getting acquainted, chatted idly.

"How did you get the name Buddy?" Le Noir asked.

"I was named for Buddy Holly. I grew up in Lubbock, Texas, where Holly grew up. Our parents were good friends, so my parents named me after him," Evans explained.

Le Noir glanced over at Evans with a degree of surprise. Who would have guessed that the conservative Detective Evans would have been named for a rock-and-roll legend.

"I have Holly's phonograph," Evans added proudly.

Turning the full-sized auto into the short Vaughn driveway, the detectives noted that the house was just as Mr. Vaughn had described. A small frame house, very neat in appearance.

A number of religious objects sprinkled about the small living room indicated to Le Noir that this was a very religious family.

As James Vaughn sat across from the Arlington detectives, his brow wrinkled and his eyes squinted in a narrow line. He waited for Le Noir to speak.

The lead detective watched Vaughn closely. *He seems to be saying, what are you doing here. What do you want?*

Le Noir began the conversation with an explanation of the

disappearance of Emelita Reeves, and his concern that two other of Reeves's wives had met untimely deaths.

James Vaughn and his son, Larry, sat slumped on the sofa, listening intently to the concerns the officers expressed about Jack Reeves.

The timid senior Vaughn finally spoke. "I've been convinced for the past sixteen years that son-of-a-bitch killed my daughter," Vaughn said, staring deep into the eyes of Tom Le Noir, then Buddy Evans. The language didn't correspond with Vaughn's meekness. He truly believed Jack Reeves killed his daughter.

He looks at us like, 'where have you been for the past sixteen years?' Le Noir thought.

Hoping to find the reasons behind why the Vaughns felt suspicious of Reeves, Le Noir encouraged them to talk about Sharon, her relationship to Jack, and her sudden death.

"Sharon was a good girl," Mr. Vaughn said, his voice broken by sadness. "And real smart."

Mr. Vaughn was a frail little man, pale in complexion. He had retained the majority of his dark brown hair through the years, highlighted with only a sprinkling of gray. His daughter, Sharon, had inherited his lean body type and delicate features.

Sharon's younger brother, Larry, shared few of his father's physical characteristics. He was the salt to Sharon's pepper. His blond hair, round face, and stout body were dramatically opposed to the petite darkness of his sister. The common bond they'd shared was love of family. James and Larry Vaughn spoke tenderly of Sharon, but their words turned bitter when discussing her husband, Jack.

The detectives learned that Sharon and Jack Reeves had been married approximately seventeen years at the time of her death in 1978. They had two sons—and a bad marriage.

Reportedly, Jack Reeves had met Sharon Vaughn at the North-side Baptist Church in Wichita Falls, Texas. They seemed oddly matched. At twenty-one, the six-foot Reeves was a college dropout who loved motorcycles and had already been married once. Sharon was a five-foot-one, petite, naive seventeen-year-old member of the church choir. Opposites attract—Reeves and Sharon collided.

From the moment Reeves saw the dark-haired beauty with her bouffant hairdo and deep brown eyes, he knew he wanted Sharon Vaughn. Had to have her.

"Do you want to go to the drag races?" Reeves had asked Sharon.

Perhaps it was the bad-boy biker image, the thrill of a walk on the wild side, or his slick black hair and rugged good looks that prompted her to say yes. But from that moment on, Sharon and Reeves were inseparable. He dominated her attention, keeping even her family at a distance.

In 1961 Reeves convinced Sharon to run away to nearby Gainesville and be married.

Hand in hand the young lovers climbed the steps of the historic 1910 Beaux Arts style Cook County courthouse, with its tall white columns and domed clock tower. Once inside, streams of light from the stained-glass dome highlighted the shine of Sharon's medium-length dark hair. She was a beautiful bride. Reeves and Sharon clung to the iron-rail banister as they ascended the limestone steps to the second-floor office of the justice of the peace.

From the large windows that spanned the spacious room, they could see a small portion of Gainesville's history. Century-old buildings with ornate brick inlays, and a statue honoring the women of the confederacy.

Within minutes they were husband and wife.

Reeves pledged Sharon to secrecy before dropping her back off at her parents' house. He immediately left for Fort Worth, looking for employment and a place to live with his new bride.

The following weekend Reeves returned to take Sharon, along with her belongings, back to Fort Worth. Once there, Sharon called her parents and told them the news of her marriage.

"You stay right there," ordered her father. "I'm coming to get you. We'll get it annulled."

But Reeves was now in charge. He grabbed the phone from

Sharon's hand. "It won't do any good," he taunted. "We'll just do it again somewhere else."

So began the marriage of Jack and Sharon Reeves. Alienated from her family, in a strange new town, friendless except for Reeves, Sharon's dependence on her new husband was already firmly established.

Sharon became pregnant soon after, forcing Reeves to face his obligation of providing for his growing family. Showing few signs of ambition, and yet obsessed with money and what it could provide, Reeves reluctantly enlisted in the Army. Surprisingly, he took to the rigid discipline well. He excelled at marksmanship, and his newest obsession soon became guns.

James and Larry Vaughn shuddered at the memories of Reeves visiting their house, a duffel bag stuffed with firearms slung over his shoulder. Guns made the Vaughn men nervous, but not as nervous as Jack Reeves made them.

Reeves displayed characteristics that overwhelmingly concerned Sharon's father. He refused to eat a meal at his in-laws' house until someone else at the table had tasted all the food first. And, as though his paranoia was not enough, he issued orders to Sharon as though she, too, were in the military. But James Vaughn's biggest concern regarding Jack Reeves was how he had managed to minimize his daughter's contact with her family.

Thirty years later, as he bitterly spoke with Detectives Le Noir and Evans, Vaughn still blamed Jack Reeves for the changes in his sweet, innocent daughter. Rubbing his eyes and smoothing his busy brown brows, he explained how Sharon had transformed from a sin-free church girl to a flashy dresser in short skirts and flamboyant wigs.

Le Noir and Evans felt sorry for James Vaughn. If it were possible for the mild-mannered Vaughn to hate, he must truly hate Jack Reeves. Reeves had stolen his daughter. First her spirit, then her life.

Sharon's brother had no warmer feelings for Reeves than his father. He had considered Reeves a threat to his sister during their entire marriage.

"We were all up visiting my parents' home in Wichita Falls about a week before Sharon died," Larry Vaughn told Le Noir and Evans. "Everybody had gone to bed except for Jack and Sharon. They were in the bedroom I used as a boy, and I was on the sofa in the living room. The living room is right next to that bedroom. They got into an argument. I heard Jack load a gun, and I heard my sister say, 'Put that thing away.' They were talking real loud." The fear that must have gripped Larry Vaughn in the dark of his parents' house still showed in his face.

"What do you mean you heard him load a gun?" Evans asked.

"Well, I could hear a clip being slid in the cylinder of a handgun and clicking into place," Vaughn said. His round face quivered slightly, as though Reeves were in front of him repeating the action.

"What happened after you heard Sharon say, 'Put that away'?" Le Noir asked.

"I got up and I was going to go in there, but about that time the arguing stopped. They were talking in normal voices. I backed off," he said.

It was obvious that the timid, younger Vaughn would have been little match for the aggressive, older, stronger Reeves.

"The next week, Sharon was dead." Larry lowered his head, concealing the tears that moistened his eyes.

The Vaughns lovingly remembered Sharon as the innocent victim of Jack Reeves—a brute the timid Vaughn men feared too much to confront. After her death they discovered incidents of abuse, intimidation, and sexual perversion far worse than they had witnessed or imagined.

The detectives learned that at the time of her death Sharon Reeves was living with her two sons in Copperas Cove, Texas. The small, L-shaped house they shared on Pleasant Lane was nestled in a neighborhood filled with rental homes and transient military families. Jack Reeves was stationed with the U.S. Army in South Korea on what was known in military circles as a command-sponsored one-year tour of duty.

During Reeves's absence, Sharon decided she couldn't live

with him any longer. She was tired of the beatings with a belt that left her arms so bruised she was forced to wear long-sleeved dresses in the Texas heat. Violent episodes that included Reeves trying to run her car off the road, tying her to a tree, and threatening her with a gun. But what gave Sharon Reeves the strength to file for divorce was a newfound love.

Sharon was a real looker. When she walked into a room, every man turned to gaze at her—and even some of the women. Her short skirts, high heels, and striking good looks had drawn the attention of a Fort Hood colonel. They met on base where Sharon was secretary to the base commander. The colonel was a man who made her feel like a woman of worth. A man who was tender, loving, and nonviolent.

Sharon filed for divorce. While still stationed in Korea, Reeves was served with the divorce papers. He was furious, refusing to sign them. Sharon was his. No other man could have her. Divorce was not an option. He flew home immediately.

Within a few days of Jack Reeves's arrival in Copperas Cove, Sharon Reeves was dead. A shotgun blast to her chest. The official ruling—suicide.

"Jack Reeves was the only other person in that house when Sharon died," Larry Vaughn said. "He killed her, then set it up to look like she did it." His face turned red, hot from the emotions evoked by his sister's senseless death.

"Sharon didn't kill herself," James Vaughn said with conviction. "Jack Reeves killed my daughter."

"Well, we want to look into Sharon's death, and the death of his second wife, Myong," Le Noir said. "We think he's responsible for the disappearance of his third wife, Emelita. By looking into the mysterious deaths of Sharon and Myong, we will see if Jack Reeves might have a predisposition for murder."

The skeptical expression faded from the faces of James and Larry Vaughn. Their shoulders relaxed, their eyes brightened. A slight upturned curve of their lips revealed optimism. For the first time in sixteen years, the Vaughns had hope. Hope that Jack Reeves would finally be found responsible for Sharon's death.

Le Noir and Evans drove back to the Arlington police station struggling with a mixture of emotions. The always high-spirited Le Noir was the first to speak.

"Those people came alive in there. They've had this thing bottled up inside them for sixteen years," Le Noir said in rapid Cajun fashion.

Evans smiled broadly. He suddenly felt as though something positive would be gained from Emelita's plight.

"We're going to give them new life. New hope," Evans said with satisfaction.

"Yeah," Tom said, his mood changing from exuberant to cautious, "but we gotta solve it now. If we don't, it will crush them. We can't let them down."

The smile faded from Evans's face. He realized how much the Vaughns would gain if they could prove Sharon's death was murder, but he also knew how much they would lose if they weren't successful.

Going into another jurisdiction and opening up a sixteen-year-old murder case was tricky. The Copperas Cove authorities might think Le Noir was saying, "Hey, you screwed up on this investigation." They might not take kindly to "big-city cops" making such an implied accusation. Le Noir would have to be tactful.

The final decision whether or not to contact the Copperas Cove department wasn't Le Noir's or Evans's. Homicide's chain of command would make the call.

Six

November 3, 1994

As Detective Buddy Evans dialed the number of the Copperas Cove Police Department, the words of Tom Le Noir rang in his ears. "My supervisor, Sergeant Dixie Stout, warned me to exercise extreme discretion in this inquiry," Le Noir had warned Evans. "Chief Pugh is afraid we're going to go to Copperas Cove and ruffle some feathers."

Sergeant David Berry of the Copperas Cove police took Evans's call.

"This is Detective Buddy Evans with the Arlington, Texas, Police Department," Evans began. "We're investigating the disappearance of Emelita Reeves. We suspect that she may have been murdered by her husband, Jack Reeves."

"How can I help you?" Berry asked, somewhat confused.

"Reeves retired from the United States Army in 1985 and had been stationed at Fort Hood, Texas. He had been married to a woman by the name of Sharon Delane Reeves while he was stationed at Fort Hood. During the course of our investigation, we discovered that Sharon Reeves was reported to have committed suicide in Copperas Cove, Texas, back in 1978."

Berry's interest escalated. "Do you doubt the suicide claim?" Berry asked.

"Well, Reeves's second wife, a Korean woman, was reportedly drowned in Lake Whitney in 1986. We believe that Jack Reeves may have murdered all three of his wives," Evans said.

Evans now had Berry's undivided attention. "What can I do for you, Detective?" Berry asked.

"We'd like to meet with you to discuss Sharon Reeves's death."

To Evans's surprise, and relief, Sergeant Berry was extremely receptive. "Sure, we can meet on the eighth," Berry offered.

"If you will, pull the 1978 investigation and attempt to identify the principals involved," Evans requested.

"I'll try," Berry said, "but an original case report that old would have most likely been destroyed. I'll do what I can. We'll see you about ten o'clock on the morning of the eighth."

A flash of satisfaction struck Evans. At least Berry was willing to talk to him and Le Noir. He hadn't slammed the phone down in his ear, called him a crazy cop, and told him to stay out of his town. This was a good sign.

While Le Noir and Evans concentrated on their investigation of the disappearance of Emelita Reeves, Sergeant Berry began searching for the documents associated with the 1978 suicide case. One lone index card remained in the Copperas Cove Police Department Records Section, under the name of Sharon D. Reeves. It read:

Sharon D Reeves
78-1764-Suicide-Victim-7-20-78
W\F Age 34

There had to be more information other than one single index card. Berry contacted Debbie Anderson, custodian of evidence and property, to see if she could locate any evidence or documents pertaining to the Reeves case.

Berry was disappointed to learn that all evidence in the sixteen-year-old incident had been destroyed, except for one old evidence log and two property receipts. The information contained on the pages of the evidence log read:

In Date	Case Number	SN	Description	Disposition
7-21-78	78-1764	020662	Winchester MDL 370 20 gauge	Returned to Bill Ray [Reeves's attorney at the time of Sharon's death] 8-2-78
		LBH-3091	H&R MDL 1873 Cal 45-70	
7-21-78	78-1764	None	2 Notes 1 empty shell 4 loaded shells	8-2-78 Returned to Bill Ray Destroyed

The property receipt that was submitted by Officer Johnny Smith on July 20, 1978, showed several items taken into evidence. Those items included three guns, one gun case, one fired shotgun shell, four unshot yellow gun shells, one piece of white paper with writing by Sharon Reeves, and one piece of white paper with writing by Jack and Sharon Reeves.

Not much to go on. Le Noir and Evans would have their work cut out for them if he expected to build a case on the evidence being held by the Copperas Cove police.

November 8, 1994

Le Noir and Evans enjoyed the peacefulness of the wide open spaces during their two-hour drive to Copperas Cove, a city whose slogan is "The City Built for Family Living."

The landscape, dotted with grazing cattle, stock tanks, and lush trees, was a pleasant reprise from the metroplex's overpopulation and hustle-and-bustle lifestyle. The scenery helped Le Noir relax. He was eager to take a look at the case file on Sharon Reeves, but he'd have to tread lightly not to step on any toes.

Le Noir couldn't help but replay in his mind his promise to Sergeant Stout. "I'm just going down to talk to David Berry. We'll chat just like two cops. We'll talk shop. I'll just feel him out, see how he feels about us looking into the case. If he tells us to get out of his office, we'll leave."

Le Noir parked his car in front of the small police department headquarters. He and Evans gave a slight nod of encouragement to one another and walked into the main entrance. This meeting could either mean a huge break in their case, or it could turn out to be just another road trip leading nowhere.

Sergeant David Berry met them in the lobby. He was a tall man, in his late forties, and a bit thick in the middle. After the introductions Berry said, "Well, they're waiting for you." He turned to lead the Arlington detectives into the secured area of the Copperas Cove Police Department (CCPD).

"Who's 'they'?" Le Noir asked Evans in a hushed tone.

Evans shrugged. They had expected to meet with Berry, no one else. The conference room was filled with unfamiliar faces. The normally talkative Le Noir was momentarily speechless. He and Evans stood before a group of several men and one woman feeling as though they had been caught with their pants down. Who were these people?

Introductions revealed those in attendance included Sandy Gately, District Attorney of Coryell County, and the only female in the group; Fred Cummings, a Texas ranger; Robert McDonald, chief of Police of Copperas Cove in 1978; Johnny Smith, a former CCPD officer who was the first officer on the scene after Sharon Reeves's death; Lieutenant Michael Galiana, a CCPD officer who was on duty that same night; Joe Ebarb, investigator for the DA's office and a former CCPD officer; and Captain Scott Huckabee and Sergeant Danny Austin, currently with the CCPD.

Le Noir and Evans took their seats at the table before Le Noir began to explain the reason for their visit. "There's this man in our town named Jack Reeves. His wife died here in Copperas Cove. Her name was Sharon Reeves."

For the next ten minutes Le Noir tried to be politically sensitive; beating around the bush so that no feelings would be hurt, no insults taken.

Finally the retired chief interrupted, speaking in a thick Texas twang. "Detective, let's just cut to the chase. We messed up back then, didn't we? Something was wrong."

Relief poured over Le Noir and Evans. These were good people.

"Basically, something's not right," Le Noir said, now feeling at ease with the receptive attitude of all the people present. "I think the man got away with murder."

At that point, Le Noir and Evans leaned back in their chairs and began explaining the details of the mysterious disappearance of Emelita and the unusual death of Myong. They related a number of contradictions and suspicious actions on the part of Jack Reeves throughout the course of their investigation, including his initial refusal to discuss the deaths of his past two wives; how Reeves said the memory of Myong's death haunted him, yet he continued to camp at Lake Whitney on a regular basis; and that he had not heard from Emelita since October 11, yet her friends saw her on October 12 and Emelita told them she and Reeves had been arguing.

"I'm planning on filing charges on Reeves for Emelita's death, but without a body I need something to support the charge. I need to show that Jack Reeves had a potential and a history of murder. I can't do that with a suicide and an accidental drowning," Le Noir said.

The faces of the assembled group were fixed on Le Noir. They listened with keen interest.

"If Sharon's death was suicide and Myong's accidental, then that's fine, but I don't believe that's what happened," Le Noir said. He inhaled deeply. He had to lay it on the line. He had to tell them exactly what he needed from them. Le Noir leaned forward, resting his forearms on the large conference table.

"I know that in my business you deal with massive quantities of ego. You have to be confident. You have to be egotistical. But, look, we all need to put our egos in our back pockets. Nobody knows anybody here. I'm not here to prove anything. I'm not here to discredit what happened here in 1978. The bottom line is, we have a man now, in 1994, that I believe has killed his present wife. He probably killed the others. We need to find out if that's what happened. If he did kill Sharon, we need to work together to put him away. That's what it all boils down to." Le Noir was finished. He had said all there was to say. He sat back and waited for their response.

Everyone at the table agreed—an incriminating pattern existed involving the deaths of two wives and maybe a third.

"As Le Noir stated, there are particulars and modus operandi that are similar in the deaths, and now there's a disappearance," DA investigator Ebarb said.

The "round table" discussion lasted for seven hours.

Officers who responded to the death of Sharon Reeves recalled their observations and suspicions.

"I was the first officer on the scene," Johnny Smith said. "I don't remember exactly what time it was. When I walked into the bedroom I saw a white female lying totally nude on the bed with a gunshot wound in the center of her chest. There was a shotgun upright between her legs. She was lying on her back with her arms extended down to her sides. Her legs were bent at the knees, and both feet were dangling off the bed, touching the floor. I walked to the right side of her body, reached down with my right hand, and checked for a pulse on her right wrist. As I took hold of her wrist, her hand reached up and grabbed me. It took me by surprise." Smith's eyes widened as he described the scene. Sixteen years before, the event must have scared him witless.

"It was the first time I ever encountered something like that. At the same time she grabbed my wrist, the last bit of air was expelled from her body. Whether it was the last breath or trapped air, I don't know," Smith said.

The faces that surrounded Smith were solemn. Each person forming a mental image of Sharon Reeves reaching out to Smith. The room was quiet except for the deep voice of the officer.

"While I was trying to pry her fingers off my wrist I noticed Reeves and a small boy were standing in the doorway by the bedroom. Reeves was holding the boy very close with his arms around him. They were both watching me. I told Reeves to get the boy out of the room," Smith said. "I did notice that Reeves showed no emotion at all in relation to what had just transpired. I thought that was peculiar."

Le Noir and Evans glanced at one another, shaking their heads slightly. Both officers were fathers, and neither could imagine why Reeves would have allowed his young son to see his mother in that state.

"There are certain things that come to mind concerning the incident," Smith said. "One being that Reeves had recently come home from Korea. He and his wife were having problems and they supposedly had reconciled their marriage the night before. They had drawn up wills. They had sex. Reeves said he had gone into the kitchen to fix something to eat while she went to take a bath. Within a few minutes he heard a gunshot. He went back to the bedroom and found his wife lying on the bed."

"Anything unusual that particularly stands out in your mind?" Sandy Gately, the Coryell DA, asked.

"Just that Reeves was calm and unemotional," Smith said.

Smith's description had a familiar chime. It was much the same reaction Reeves had exhibited when Le Noir and Evans questioned him about Emelita's disappearance.

"Sometime during our initial investigation of the scene, Reeves produced a suicide note. I remember asking him where he found it, and he said in the china cabinet. I remember the note very well. It read, To My Dearest Big Dick, Sorry things didn't work out the way that you wanted. I loved you and John but I couldn't make up my mind so I thought that I would just end it."

My Dearest Big Dick? Le Noir repeated to himself. The phrase fit the pattern of Reeves's obsession with sex.

"Anything unusual about the body?" Le Noir asked.

"When we turned her over to check for an exit wound, we noticed a big knot on her back. The gunshot did not penetrate completely through the body," Smith explained.

"Galiana, when did you arrive on the scene?" Sergeant Berry asked.

"I was a reserve officer riding with Officer Rick Carson that night. We arrived after Smith. I went inside and looked at the body. I noticed a single gunshot wound to the left breast of the woman. The entry wound appeared to be about the same diameter as the barrel of the shotgun. The wound was a little bloody and it appeared as if the flesh around it had been seared by burning powder from the shotgun blast. I noticed the shotgun pellets were still inside the wound and they had not exited the body. When we rolled her over, there was no exit wounds but bumps where the pellets could be seen behind the skin on her back.

"I remember thinking that, because of her physical stature and the size of the shotgun, I didn't see how the victim could have shot herself. The woman was short and could not have reached the trigger with her hand to shoot herself. And I didn't think it was possible for her to have used her foot to pull the trigger," Galiana said.

"What was your assignment?" Berry asked.

"I was instructed to stand at the front door and secure the crime scene. I was not to allow anybody to go inside other than the officers and those who were permitted to enter. That's when I talked to Reeves," Galiana said.

"What did you talk about?" Berry asked.

"Well, I was trying to keep his mind off of what was happening. I basically just wanted to make him feel at ease, although he appeared very calm under the circumstances. He started talking about Korea. He mentioned that he had just come back from Korea, more or less to save his marriage. I told him I was half-Korean, but that I had never been there. He told me that in Korea you can have sex real easy. He said females would come up to you while you were on duty and give you blowjobs through the fence," Galiana said, deliberately avoiding eye contact with Sandy Gately.

"So while this guy's dead wife's body was lying on the bed inside the house, Jack Reeves stood on the front porch and talked about having sex in Korea," Le Noir said, shaking his head in disgust.

"He also pointed out a dildo in the master bedroom," Smith recalled. "But I can't remember the significance, if any, Reeves placed on it."

"I remember that," Galiana said. "It was a double-headed dildo, depicting a hand showing the middle finger and a penis."

"We've had a similar experience. Reeves brought a dildo to the department, suggesting the K-nine unit could use it to get a scent of Emelita for a search," Le Noir said.

Sandy Gately grimaced. A couple of the men smirked, shaking their heads at the obvious absurdity.

"Another interesting thing," Smith said. "I remember when we interviewed him at the house he held his ten-year-old son in front of him. I asked him if he didn't think the boy should go to a neighbor's until we at least removed the body, but he kept the boy close."

"Yeah, he did the same thing in Arlington. It's like he uses his children as a shield against the police," Evans said.

Le Noir and Evans learned that Reeves's older son, sixteen-year-old Ricky, was at work at the time of the shooting.

"I also saw the suicide note. It had a hand drawn picture of the dildo on it," Galiana said. "And there was a handwritten will that was signed by both Jack and Sharon Reeves. Reeves stated that they had written it out the night before. I remember them because, after seeing both the note and the will, I thought, something's not right. I've thought about this case for years; it just never made sense."

As the officers continued to relate facts about Sharon Reeves's death, Jack Reeves's personality began to emerge. It seemed everybody in Copperas Cove remembered Reeves as the meanest, most cantankerous man they had ever met. The Reeves they described was a tough, contemptible, intimidating individual. Sharon, on the other hand, had been characterized as a fun-loving, outgoing, friendly type who dramatically changed when Jack Reeves returned from Korea. A parallel comparison with the Jack Reeves of 1994 and Emelita.

"I'd like for you guys to document your recollections of the death investigation and give them to Sergeant Berry," Le Noir said. Then looking to Berry he added, "Can you search the files and archives for any photographs taken of the crime scene?"

The response from the Copperas Cove personnel was more than Le Noir and Evans could have hoped for. The personalities of the big-city cops meshed well with the small-town officers.

"We'll do all we can from this end to pull this thing together," Gately said.

Le Noir knew that Sandy Gately would make certain it was done. He'd first met Gately twelve years earlier while he was an undercover cop on loan to the Waco, Texas, Police Department, and Gately was an assistant DA in Waco. She had the reputation of an aggressive, no-nonsense litigator. Le Noir could tell from the intensity in her blue eyes and the set of her thin jaw that Sandy Gately would be a force to contend with in the courtroom. He was glad Gately was on the team.

"Well, I think we're all in agreement that from the information you have discovered during your investigation, coupled with the fact that two of Jack Reeves's wives died under unusual conditions and a third wife is currently missing and presumed dead, that the sixteen-year-old case of Sharon Reeves should be reopened for investigation," Berry said.

A shot of adrenaline was pumped into Le Noir and Evans. They each smiled broadly. They had just taken a huge step forward in proving their case against Jack Reeves.

"I'd like for you to consider exhuming the body of Sharon Reeves and having a pathologist examine the gunshot wound. He can determine if the angle and direction is consistent with the scenario provided to police by Reeves in 1978," Le Noir said. He had been sitting in the conference room for hours cautiously containing his characteristic exuberance. Now, his excitement over working with the CCPD on Sharon Reeves's alleged suicide was unleashed.

"I believe if we can determine the actual cause of Sharon's death it will lead us to evidence in establishing a modus operandi and direct correlation to the death of Emelita Reeves," Le Noir said excitedly.

Sergeant Berry readily agreed to secure a court order for the exhumation, and to procure a copy of Reeves's military record.

Le Noir and Evans returned to Arlington, more than a little hopeful that they would be able to prove Jack Reeves committed murder. But reality reared its ugly head. What if they were wrong? What if Sharon Reeves had pulled the trigger that ended her life? Would that end their case?

Seven

Jack Reeves busied himself by sorting, packing, and storing all of Emelita's belongings. Tucked neatly into boxes stacked in a spare room of their South Arlington home, Emelita's jewelry, clothing, and personal effects were put away. Emelita had only been gone for two weeks. If Reeves expected her to return, as he told the police, why pack her things?

Reeves concentrated on removing Emelita's memory from his house, while police concentrated on the manner in which they believed he had removed Sharon from his life. Reeves was in the dark. He had no idea the investigation had taken such a radical turn.

November 10, 1994

Detectives Le Noir and Evans met with Dr. Jeffrey Barnard, chief medical examiner of the Dallas County Medical Examiner's Office. Le Noir explained his investigative plan and asked Dr. Barnard if it was feasible to exhume the remains of Sharon Reeves to perform an autopsy. Copperas Cove authorities hadn't requested one in 1978.

Dr. Barnard, a studious-looking, slender gentleman with glasses and blond hair, agreed with Le Noir and Evans on the value an autopsy would be to the investigation. He seemed eager to perform the procedure.

Le Noir was energized, Evans pleased. Things were falling into place.

Three days later, Le Noir and Evans, along with Sergeant Berry, Danny Austin, Fred Cummings, and Sandy Gately, met with Dr. Barnard and Dr. Stone, another Dallas County medical examiner (ME).

"The success of the autopsy depends on various possibilities," Dr. Barnard explained. "If a lot of water has seeped into the casket over a period of years, there may not be enough remains available to examine. She could just be soup. Our findings will greatly depend on how preserved Sharon's body is after sixteen years of deterioration. But, there is a good possibility evidence can be obtained if the body is in a mummified state."

"We'd like to have any medical records that were available on Sharon Reeves prior to the autopsy being performed," Dr. Stone said.

"I'll get right on it," Sergeant Berry assured them.

The newly formed team coordinated the exhumation of Sharon Reeves from Burkburnette, Texas, and the transportation of the body to the Dallas Medical Examiner's Office.

"I'll take care of getting the court order," Gately said.

"And I'll coordinate the exhumation and transportation of the body," Berry offered.

"Evans and I will make sure we are present with Dr. Barnard during the autopsy," Le Noir said.

The team was beginning to work like a well-oiled machine.

With preparations for the exhumation of Sharon Reeves under way, Le Noir and Evans continued their investigation into the disappearance of Emelita Reeves. They obtained the park receipt registered in the name of Jack Reeves from Lake Whitney State Park. The receipt verified that Reeves had indeed arrived at the park after hours on October 13, 1994, and checked out sometime on October 14. Park personnel described Jack Reeves as a "regular camper" at the park. But the regular camper had changed his habits.

According to Park Ranger James Karr, Reeves had been camping at Lake Whitney weekly, arriving every Thursday for a number of years. Then after the disappearance of Emelita, he'd suddenly ended the ritualistic routine.

"His change of habit establishes merit to the theory that Emelita's body is likely disposed of somewhere on the perimeters of Lake Whitney," Le Noir said to Evans. His eyes peered deep into the wooded area behind Reeves's usual campsite, wondering if Emelita was buried among the thick foliage. Then, he turned to scan the vast horizon. *Where are you?* he asked silently, wishing Emelita could answer.

November 17, 1994

During a routine background check, it was discovered that Jack Reeves had a half sister, Pat Goodman, who lived in Arlington with her husband Gary. Although Reeves had indicated that he did not want Le Noir and Evans to speak to Pat, a meeting was scheduled for the next day.

November 18, 1994

Evans pulled into the driveway of Pat and Gary Goodman's house about noon. It was a nice brick home, ample enough for the Goodmans and their four children.

Evans and Le Noir were optimistic about the prospect of meeting Reeves's sister. She had indicated in their phone conversation that she was willing to talk to them about Jack's background, and about Emelita's disappearance.

Pat began the conversation by telling the detectives that Jack was born in Paris, Texas, but raised in Sulfur, Oklahoma, where he graduated from high school in 1959. Reeves's parents had

separated shortly after his birth and divorced in 1947 when Jack
was seven years old.

Pat Goodman was sketchy on Reeves's early childhood, perhaps protecting the pleasant memories of her own. But others
who knew the Reeves family claimed that Jack was deprived of
attention by his natural father, who worked eighty hours a week
in a box factory; coddled by his mother, and regularly bull-
whipped by his maternal grandfather—who family members said
killed his own son with a whipping.

Two years after Reeves's divorce, Jack's mother married a career Air Force man, named Curran, and the family moved from
base to base every few months. Three years after his mother
remarried, Pat was born.

Sulfur, Oklahoma, was the only place Jack Reeves ever really
considered home His stepfather was stationed there for five and
a half years, longer than any other assignment. Reeves played
bass horn in the high-school marching band.

Reeves was a dashing young man with slick black hair and a
winning smile. He projected a bit of a bad-boy image, opting for
leather jackets and biker boots over his classmates' cowboy duds.
He was known as a loner.

When Reeves was only seventeen, he married a fifteen-year-
old blond-haired beauty named Amerylys. They had dated for a
while, then gone steady. Reeves was captivated by the vivacious
young girl.

It was later learned that Amerylys had grown tired of Reeves.
She'd tried to break up with him and return his class ring, but he
wouldn't accept her rejection. He had even threatened suicide if
she left him. She feared he would hurt himself with one of his
hunting rifles or the knife he bragged about carrying in one of
his black biker boots. She continued the relationship.

When Reeves and Amerylys eloped in August 1952, she was
pregnant with his child. She miscarried and her mother had the
marriage annulled on grounds that the immature bride was under
age. She sent her daughter to Fort Worth to live with relatives in

order to escape Reeves, who she considered lazy, domineering, and controlling. A real nuisance.

"Jack is an introvert," Pat Goodman said, pushing her auburn hair from her eyes. "He had few, if any, male friends. Jack isn't close with anyone in the immediate family, either, especially his eldest son, Ricky." Pat looked sad when mentioning her nephew's name.

Ricky had little if any contact with his father since the death of his mother. Unlike Randy, who was home at the time of Sharon's death, Ricky was working a summer job during the shooting. The loss of his mother hit him hard. Pat indicated that Ricky and Reeves had several unresolved issues between them, although it did not appear that the death of his mother was one of them.

"Ricky was very close to his mother, Sharon. The relationship between Jack and Ricky deteriorated after her death. Their relationship is simply nonexistent at present," she said, not elaborating further.

"Where's Jack's father?" Evans asked.

"Jack's biological father, Jack Reeves, Sr., is in a veteran's nursing home in Bonham, Texas," Pat replied.

The phone rang and she answered it.

Le Noir could hear the booming voice of Jack Reeves even with the phone pressed to Pat Goodman's ear. "What are they doing there?" he demanded to know. "What are they asking you?"

Reeves's paranoia was growing.

Returning to her conversation with Le Noir and Evans, Pat reflected on what she knew about the relationship between her brother and Emelita. "I remember he sent Emelita to the Philippines when she became pregnant with Theo. Emelita stayed there for about two years, until Jack finally allowed her and Theo to return."

"While Emelita was gone, he had an affair with a Russian woman named Natalie. He met her through the personal ads in the newspaper," Gary said.

The Goodmans first met Natalie when they agreed to have dinner with Reeves and his "friend" at Ryan's Steakhouse in Arlington. "I have someone I want you to meet," he had said. He introduced them to Natalie, yet another attractive, petite foreigner. But Natalie was blond, a sharp contrast to the dark-haired beauties he usually engaged. And Natalie was Ukrainian with a thick accent and bad teeth.

Reeves had met Natalie through a personal ad in the August 31, 1991, edition of the *Fort Worth Star Telegram*. Her ad had read, "Classy Lady, originally from Europe, divorced, petite blond . . . Seeks marriage minded, professional gentleman 45 to 58." A short time later he put Natalie up in the local Ramada Inn, then moved her into the Arlington home vacated by Emelita, who was giving birth to their son in the Philippines. He spent thousands of dollars on dental work and jewelry for his newest "little girl."

Gary Goodman recalled vividly the comment Reeves made during dinner. "I'm gonna pay for her dental work. She's the best lay I've ever had. Fucks my brains out," he'd whispered.

"Jack would bring Natalie up to the plant, where he worked as a paint contractor, and tell the guys, 'She's screwing my brains out; I need some sleep,' " Gary recalled, with some embarrassment.

"Where's Natalie now?" Evans asked.

"Jack said he went home from work early one day and she was packing up some of his things—ripping him off. He claimed Natalie was a gold digger and that she was trying to get to his money, so he sent her away. He never told us where she moved but indicated it was some place up north. Said there was a guy up there that wanted to marry her. She simply disappeared," Goodman said. Gary's speech was flat but his eyes were questioning. Evans wondered if Gary really believed that Natalie had "simply disappeared."

She's a gold digger, Le Noir thought. *That's a motive for murder. Don't take Jack's toys. You take his toys and you die.*

The phone rang again. It was Reeves. "What questions have

they been asking you about me?" he demanded, speaking rapidly. Pat Goodman ignored his question and hung up.

Gary Goodman was a tall man with short salt-and-pepper hair, more salt than pepper at the sides. He obviously cared deeply for his wife, taking her hand as she returned to the conversation.

"Are you familiar with the death of Myong?" Pat asked the detectives.

"We know she drowned at Lake Whitney while Jack allegedly was getting bait for fishing," Le Noir said, not offering too much information.

"We've always been suspicious that Jack may have been responsible for her death," Gary said.

The phone rang a third time. Reeves again. Gary was on the phone only momentarily before returning his attention to the detectives.

"Why does Jack keep calling?" Le Noir asked.

"Jack's concerned that you would find out about the polygraph test he took," Gary Goodman said.

Quick glances shot between Le Noir and Evans confirmed neither had knowledge of a polygraph taken by Reeves.

"But he refused to take a polygraph," Le Noir told the Goodmans.

"We know he refused yours, but he took one through his lawyer. We don't know what the results were, but his son Randy took him to the test, and he probably knows the results," Pat offered.

Le Noir verbalized what Evans was thinking. "Well, I can assure you that Reeves or his attorney would have notified our office if he had passed the polygraph," Le Noir said, rather indignantly.

"You're right. He'd also have told us if he'd passed," Gary said.

On the way back to the station, Le Noir stared out the window as Evans drove. "So Jack took a polygraph. Well, now isn't that interesting?" There was a sarcastic grin on his face and a chuckle in his voice.

* * *

As Le Noir was getting ready for bed that evening, his pager went off. He recognized the number on the digital screen. It was Jack Reeves. *I wonder what Jack wants,* Le Noir thought.

"Jack, how are you doing?" the detective asked after Reeves answered the phone.

"Le Noir!" Reeves's voice blasted over the telephone. His tone of voice was belligerent. In the past Reeves had always treated Le Noir with respect, referring to him as Detective Le Noir. Something had changed. Something had set Reeves off, causing him to be aggressive and combative. Most likely their visit with the Goodmans.

"I'm not talking to you anymore. I've talked to my lawyer and he says not to talk to you. I've got nothin' else to say," Reeves said angrily.

"Okay," Le Noir said calmly. He knew the way to get to Reeves was by never letting him have the last word.

"By the way, I want my dildo back, and I want my other stuff back," Reeves demanded.

"Well, you aren't getting it back, Jack. How's that?" Le Noir said in a caustic tone.

"You gotta give me that stuff back," Reeves said loudly.

"I'm not giving it back to you. How does that grab you, Jack? You aren't getting it back. As a matter of fact, our conversation has ended. I don't want to talk to you anymore," Le Noir said, then hung up the phone. Le Noir sat back and grinned, quite satisfied with his exchange with Reeves. Reeves wanted control, and now he'd lost it. Le Noir snickered softly.

Moments later the detective's pager went off. Reeves's number appeared on the display. Le Noir grinned broadly. He'd just let Reeves sweat it out. The pager went off once more, with Reeves's number showing across the narrow screen. Le Noir laughed out loud.

Le Noir telephoned Evans to tell him about the conversation with Reeves. He, too, was curious as to Reeves's sudden change of attitude.

The next morning, the first call Le Noir received at his office was from Jack Reeves.

"Jack, we're not talking anymore. I don't want to talk to you. You've invoked your rights and I have to protect your rights. We're *not* talking." Le Noir hung up the phone.

His pager immediately rang. He ignored it. It rang again. *He's ballistic,* Le Noir thought. *It's driving him wild.* The cagey detective smiled, leaning back in his office chair. He had Reeves just where he wanted him—for the time being.

The investigations of both Emelita and Sharon Reeves were well under way. Two down—one more to go. It was time to look into the mysterious drowning of Myong Reeves.

Eight

Myong Hui Chong, a young Korean female in her early twenties, was the kind of woman Jack Wayne Reeves just loved to death. Like Sharon before her, and Emelita, Natalie, and others after, Myong was gorgeous and petite. What made her even more desirable was her belief that if you lost your virginity to a man, you had to love him, honor him, and obey him. That made Myong the perfect woman for Reeves.

But as repeatedly Reeves was enjoying sexual pleasures with both his American housekeeper and Myong while stationed in South Korea, his wife Sharon was falling in love with Colonel John Behneman at Fort Hood in Copperas Cove. Reeves lied to both his lovers about being separated from his wife, a lie that shockingly became reality when he received divorce papers. He flew home to Copperas Cove a married man and returned to South Korea a widower.

Reeves resumed his life of dual pleasures until his tour of duty was complete and he returned to the States. He left his housekeeper behind but he didn't return empty-handed. He had brought Myong with him. They were wed on New Year's Eve, 1980, in Jacksboro, Texas.

November 21, 1994

Buddy Evans was again behind the wheel driving himself and Le Noir on yet another road trip in pursuit of information. Only this time it was in connection to Myong.

In Hillsboro, Texas, the detectives interviewed Mike Urban,

the Texas Parks and Wildlife game warden who had responded
to the death of Myong Reeves.

"I remember it well," Urban said. He ran his fingers through
his thick brown hair. "It was real strange. Jack Reeves showed
no emotion during the search for his wife, or when divers removed her body from the waters of Lake Whitney."

Le Noir scanned a water-fatality report filed by the Texas
Parks and Wildlife Service after Myong's July 28, 1986,
death. It disclosed no criminal investigation was conducted
in the drowning death of twenty-nine-year-old Myong
Reeves. Jack Reeves had reported that he left Myong on a
flotation mattress while he gathered crickets as fish bait.
When he returned, the mattress was unoccupied. He then notified the park rangers.

"Was there anything else that was strange about the incident?"
Le Noir asked, placing the report on Urban's desk.

"Yeah, the circumstances surrounding Myong's death were
not consistent with the circumstances that normally accompany
the accidental drowning of an adult. I suspected foul play, however the justice of the peace did not concur. By mere observation
he ruled her death an accident. There wasn't an autopsy."

"Exactly what made you suspicious?" Evans asked.

"There were a number of concerns," Urban said, shifting in
his chair as though to get comfortable for a long session. The
thirty-something game warden spoke from experience. "First,
the flotation device she was reported to have fallen from was
undamaged. It had a full air supply. It's unlikely an adult would
fall off and not be able to retrieve it and hold on.

"Then, Lake Whitney is known for its silence and peacefulness. Noises associated with a person drowning, such as water
splashing and calls for help, would be heard by anyone within
one to two hundred yards. It's also unlikely that Jack Reeves
wouldn't have heard the noises. The area around the drowning
site has limited land space near the cove where the incident occurred. I just don't see how he couldn't have heard her calls for
help.

"And the drowning occurred in ten feet of water, within a few feet of land. The boat was docked nearby, in three feet of water. It doesn't seem feasible that she couldn't have made it to a point where she could merely stand up."

There was a long pause while Le Noir and Evans digested the scene Urban had described.

"I've worked three other drownings where people were recovered from the lake with obvious trauma to the body," Urban said, filling the void of silence. "They should have required an autopsy. But for some reason the same justice of the peace that ruled Myong's death accidental, also ruled those deaths accidental drownings based on his medically untrained observation alone." He shook his head, unable to give any further explanation.

Le Noir recalled Reeves telling him in one of his initial statements that he had sold the boat docked near Myong when the drowning occurred, due to the "horrible memory" of Myong's death. The detectives asked that the Parks and Wildlife Service pull the sale records on Reeves's boat.

Records indicated that Reeves had not sold the boat immediately at all, but in fact had waited two years before he transferred the title to his son Randall Reeves. Randall's address was listed as the same Iberis Drive address in Arlington where Jack Reeves resided.

Le Noir's face began to redden as he read further. The boat was not actually sold to another party until March 11, 1993, seven years after Myong's death. "There's a big difference between immediately and seven years," Le Noir quipped. "Just another one of Jack's little lies."

November 30, 1994

On the road again, Le Noir and Evans headed north. They stopped to eat lunch, then drove to Ron Barr's house on Princeton Avenue in Wichita Falls.

Emelita's cousin Cristi had met and married Ron Barr

in much the same manner Emelita and Jack had gotten together. Cristi was also a mail-order bride, but far more successful than her cousin. Ron and Cristi appeared happily married, and they remained close to her family back in the Philippines. Ron possessed a fierce devotion to family and a keen sense of duty.

"I have recently returned from a visit to the Philippines," Barr told the detectives. "I tape-recorded conversations with the family about their recent calls from Emelita." Limping from an old war injury, he crossed the room to hand Evans the box of micro-cassette tapes.

Barr, whom Evans described as a "by-God Texas boy," explained the tapes were in Filipino, but that the family had revealed that Emelita was very much afraid of Reeves. She told them he was sick and perverted. He forced her to use dildos and vibrators. She wanted to go home, but had been encouraged to stay with Reeves, for the sake of the family.

"Listen, Jack has been calling me on a regular basis since the disappearance of Emelita. I think he may be responsible for her disappearance, and maybe her death. During a recent call he attempted to convince me that he was not to blame for her disappearance or her murder," Barr said.

How fascinating, Le Noir thought. *He used the term "murder." We've never mentioned murder.* He eyed Evans, who by the puzzling look on his face was thinking the same thing.

"You know, Jack called me about you, too," Barr said, looking at Le Noir. "He said he had talked to his attorney and had done some checking on you. He said you're one of the best, even referred to you as Columbo. He said if anybody can find Emelita, solve the case, and get the killer, it will be you."

Le Noir took note of the reference to "the killer." And by putting emphasis on Le Noir as one of the best, Reeves had just put an air of importance on himself. *You're not important, Reeves,* Le Noir thought. *You're nothing but another murderer we'll get off the streets.*

Barr interrupted Le Noir's thoughts. "Jack's been asking me

to do something that really disturbs me," Barr said, frown lines wrinkling his brow. "He keeps asking me to assist him in bringing a female from the Philippines to live with him. He prefers a direct family member of Emelita's."

Emelita had been missing just over a month. Reeves was already looking for her replacement, just as he had done with Sharon and with Myong. *A pattern consistent with foul play,* Le Noir thought.

December 6, 1994

The documentation on Myong Chong Reeves requested from the Immigration and Naturalization Service by Detective Evans arrived at the APD. As Le Noir leafed through the file he noted that Myong was the daughter of Pyong and Sun Choi Chong, who resided in Korea. Then Le Noir found a possible address for Myong's sister Sue who lived in Michigan.

Le Noir made the call. The address was that of Sue's former mother-in-law, Mrs. Vanzo, and although her son and Sue had been divorced for some time, she and Sue remained in contact.

"Did you know Myong and Jack Reeves?" Le Noir asked.

"Yes, Myong came to live with me after she left Jack. However, Jack Reeves drove from Texas to Michigan and took her back with him," Mrs. Vanzo said. "Jack Reeves appeared to be an abusive and very possessive man.

"After Myong's death, Sue called to talk with me. She said Jack had convinced her to take her two small daughters to Arlington and live with him. I was very concerned for Sue and the girls," Mrs. Vanzo said, a hint of fear still tainting her voice. "Sue only stayed with Jack two or three days before coming here. She told me that she had feared for her life and the safety of the girls. Evidently, they left Jack's house in the middle of the night, taking his car without his knowledge."

"Do you know why Sue was so afraid of Jack?" Le Noir nudged.

"She didn't say exactly what happened in Arlington that scared her so much, but it was an intense fear. Sue did say she suspected Jack Reeves had murdered her sister Myong."

After learning that Sue had remarried and was living in another state, Le Noir made contact.

"This is Detective Le Noir with the Arlington, Texas, Police Department," he began. "I'm investigating the disappearance of a woman married to Jack Reeves. I'd like to talk to you about Myong, and her relationship to Reeves."

Sue let out a little screech. "Oh, yes," she said excitedly. "I think Jack killed my sister Myong. I've thought so for eight years."

"What can you tell me about Myong and Jack's relationship?" Le Noir asked, pressing the record button on the tape recorder. It was important to insure the accuracy of their conversation.

"Myong and I were very close. We wrote to one another often during her marriage to Jack Reeves. Jack was very abusive to my sister," Sue said, bitterness edging her voice. "He was extremely possessive and controlling of her, but the sexual behavior Myong described was alarmingly perverted. Myong was afraid of Jack."

She told Le Noir about receiving a letter from Myong only days prior to her death in which she had made allegations of physical and sexual abuse by Reeves and told her sister of her plans to leave him. The letter was steeped in fear and desperation. Her outcries for help were tormenting to the distant sister. Unfortunately, this was the last communication Sue had with her sister Myong.

Sue agreed to fax a copy of the original letter, written in Korean, along with a translated version, to Le Noir's office.

Le Noir stood by the fax machine reading page one of the transmittal as page two was coming over the wire.

The detective felt pangs of anger as he read the painful words

Myong had written to her sister. She wrote of frequent fights with Reeves, how her eyes were red and swollen from crying, and there was a wound on her thigh. The young Korean's letter was filled with confusion. Myong failed to understand why Reeves blamed her for their marital discord, accepting no responsibility himself.

The distressing words, which were arduously sprawled across the page, indicated Myong's anguish over her failure to gain citizenship and Reeves's lack of concern about her paperwork. She felt trapped. Captive. Reeves wouldn't even allow her to call her sister.

Le Noir felt the desperation, the despair of the woman who had penned the letter. Myong spoke of distress, worry, and helplessness. Obviously, Myong Hui Reeves had been a woman snared in a relationship of physical and emotional bondage.

Le Noir looked at the copy of the original letter in Korean. It had been scripted by a delicate hand. Flowers adorned the bottom left-hand corner of the paper.

Le Noir felt his chest tighten. *This was a sensitive, loving human being,* he thought. *Jack Reeves had no right to do what he did to this caring woman.*

In speaking further with Sue, Le Noir learned that she had been in Arlington for Myong's funeral.

"I noticed bruising to Myong's head and other parts of her body," she said bitterly, recalling how her sister appeared in the cold casket at the Moore Funeral Home in Arlington. "I told Jack that an autopsy should be performed but he said he was going to have Myong's body cremated. I protested, but Jack ordered the cremation be done immediately. I was very upset and very suspicious of Jack. I felt completely vulnerable and powerless. I was convinced that Jack murdered my sister. I agreed to stay with him only in an attempt to gain evidence of his guilt. But, my plan backfired," she said, her voice fading away.

Sue was convinced that Reeves had killed Myong, telling Le

Noir that her sister was very frightened of the water, and couldn't swim. Even when the two Korean women would go to the beach, Myong would stay on land, far from the water. She even refused to wade in the shallow end. Because of that fear, Sue just couldn't believe that Myong would have lain on a plastic float in the lake, especially with no one else around.

"I was surprised to hear she had even ridden in a boat, but she was submissive to Jack and did everything he told her. We all did. He scared us all." Sue's voice revealed a slight quiver.

What could have frightened her so much? Le Noir wondered. "What happened, Sue?" the detective asked with genuine concern.

"I was scared to death of Jack. He was very strange, sexually perverted, and extremely possessive. My two small daughters were with me and Jack completely ruled their lives. He demanded that they sleep in his room and that he be allowed to bathe and dress them," Sue said, her words filled with fear, even after eight years. Sue recalled times when Reeves would insist on rubbing lotion on the children, an act that made the young mother cringe.

Jack Reeves was a man obviously obsessed with sex. He preferred small women with small breasts—and young girls. Le Noir and Evans later discussed the possibility of Reeves being a pedophile but decided Reeves's preference was for small adult women, rather than children.

"What about you, Sue? What did Jack Reeves do to you?" Le Noir asked. It wasn't just the answer Le Noir was after, but to console her as well.

Reluctantly Sue answered, perhaps out of embarrassment, perhaps out of shame. "Jack drugged me and then raped me at his home. I was dumbfounded as to how Jack could have sexual intercourse with me, Myong's sister, the day before her funeral."

Sue had stayed in a separate bedroom, with the door locked, but that didn't deter Reeves. She would wake up in the middle of the night, with Jack standing over her.

The native-born Korean spoke of the dominance of Reeves, his refusal to let her get a job at a local bank, and his constant watching over her. She compared her experience with Reeves to that of Myong's turbulent five-and-a-half-year marriage, scared by beatings, drugs, and reenactments of pornographic videos. Myong would run away, Reeves would drag her back. Then, when she made plans to divorce the aging Reeves, she was suddenly dead.

Sue knew she had to escape, and quickly. As soon as Reeves left the house one night, she and her children fled to Colorado, escaping the fear of death.

After speaking with Game Warden Urban and Sue, Le Noir and Evans decided to request that the Texas rangers reopen the investigation into the drowning death of Myong Reeves.

Jack Reeves's troubles had doubled with the inquiry into Sharon's death, and now tripled with the reexamination of Myong's drowning. Le Noir and Evans were digging a hole Jack Reeves would have difficulty climbing out of.

While Le Noir and Evans investigated the suspicious drowning of Myong Reeves, Sergeant Berry of Copperas Cove concentrated on Sharon Reeves. After securing the black-and-white photo of Sharon's lifeless body stretched across her bed, he contacted Sharon's brother, Larry Vaughn.

Vaughn was aware of the joint investigation being conducted by Copperas Cove and Arlington, and was more than willing to help.

"I have a crime-scene photo of Sharon, but I need you to send me a picture of her so I can ensure that the photograph I have is indeed that of Sharon Reeves," Berry explained.

"I'll send you a picture of Sharon right after she graduated, and one of Sharon and Jack together," Larry said.

"Are you aware that we plan to exhume Sharon's body and have an autopsy performed?" Berry asked.

"Yes," Larry replied softly.

"The Arlington PD believes that Jack Reeves may have killed three of his wives," Berry said, attempting to reinforce their need to disturb Sharon's body, hoping to cushion the blow.

"I'm sure that he did!" Vaughn declared vehemently. Berry understood that his anger was directed toward Jack Reeves, not him.

Berry gave Vaughn his name and telephone number and told him to keep in touch.

Berry had agreed to look into the death of Sharon Reeves with some degree of idle curiosity. He was now as convinced as Le Noir and Evans that Sharon Reeves wasn't despondent over choosing between two men she loved; he was now doubly sure that the one she no longer loved had killed her. That man was Jack Reeves.

A check with the local Copperas Cove funeral home produced a folder containing a copy of an autopsy order issued by justice of the peace C. W. Storm, dated July 20, 1978. The order authorized an autopsy be performed at Darnall Army Hospital at Fort Hood. But the autopsy was never completed. Berry also found tucked in the file folder, an inquest form signed by Judge Storms revoking the "Order of Autopsy." Apparently, the judge revoked his own order based on a statement by the chief pathologist at Fort Hood, in which he stated that the gunshot wound appeared to be self-inflicted, triggered by the right toe.

If that autopsy had been performed back in '78 we might not be going through all of this now, Berry thought. But he was committed to the investigation. He ordered more documents, including the death certificate and original petition of divorce between Sharon and Jack Reeves.

Berry slowly stroked his brown mustache as he read the divorce decree. The original petition was filed by Sharon Reeves, on February 8, 1978. On June 21, 1978, a letter was sent to the district clerk of Coryell County with a motion to appoint an attorney for

Jack Reeves. Phil Zeigler was appointed. On July 12, 1978, Sharon Reeves signed an affidavit stating that, on July 11, she had entered into a property settlement and child-support agreement with Reeves. Although Sharon stated that she fully understood that her attorney had advised her against both settlements, she had agreed to divide the custody of the children and refused child support.

She asked for nothing, and was willing to split up her children, Berry thought, rocking back in his chair. *I wonder why she would agree to that, unless Jack somehow persuaded her to do it.* Berry knew there was no way of telling what personal pressure was placed on Sharon Reeves to enter into the agreement, and to disregard the advice of her own attorney. The affidavit was signed July 12, 1978, eight days prior to her death. The divorce was granted July 13, 1978.

The next document gave Berry cause to sit up. Bowed over the paper he had laid flat on the desk, he read carefully. It seemed as though both Sharon and Jack Reeves had made a motion to the court to set aside the divorce judgment and grant a new trial. The grounds: their desire to change their position in regard to the expectation for reconciliation.

It didn't make sense. She loved another man. She had her divorce. Yet, she asked the court to reconsider. Berry could only imagine the type of persuasion Jack Reeves must have used to convince her to file such a petition.

Then Berry looked at the date the "Motion For New Trial" was signed—July 20, 1978. Why would Sharon Reeves file such a motion citing reconciliation, then commit suicide that same evening?

While Berry continued to ponder the inexplicable coincidence of asking that her divorce be reversed the same day of her alleged suicide, another oddity emerged. Sharon Reeves had signed a will on March 7, 1978, four months prior to her death. The will was filed with the county clerk on August 7, 1978, eighteen days following Sharon's death. Yet, Lieutenant Galiana had reported that he recalled seeing a handwritten will signed by both Jack and Sharon Reeves on the day of the shooting. It had been written and dated the night before. Now it seemed that will was nowhere to be found. Jack Reeves had the March 7th will probated as Sharon's "Last Will and Testament." *Strange,* Berry thought, *that a handwritten will would have been prepared a day before Sharon committed suicide. Maybe Jack hadn't known about the prior will.*

The veteran cop thought there were just too many coincidences.

Meanwhile, Le Noir and Evans decided it was time to speak to Jack Reeves's mother and father. Perhaps they could shed some light on their daughters-in-law's mysterious deaths. And on what made their son tick.

They first headed to Bonham, Texas, and the Veteran's Administration hospital where Jack Reeves, Sr., resided.

Dressed in dark suits, white shirts, and conservative ties, the detectives approached an ailing Jack Reeves, Sr., with caution.

"Mr. Reeves, I'm Detective Le Noir, and this is Detective Evans," Le Noir said warmly.

"I've been waiting for you," the frail, gray-haired Reeves replied.

Le Noir was bubbling inside with excitement. *He knows something about Jack's wives and he wants to tell us,* Le Noir thought.

The elder Reeves began handing stacks of papers to both detectives. "I've been waiting for you to come. I've been writing you, and calling you," the elder Reeves said anxiously.

"What are these?" Le Noir asked, referring to the papers Reeves had given him.

"That's what he took from me," Reeves said, sadness in his voice, sorrow in his eyes.

"Wait a minute. Do you know why we're here?" Evans asked.

"Yes, you're the FBI. I've been waiting for you."

Le Noir and Evans were confused. Why would Jack Reeves, Sr., think they were the FBI?

"No, my name is Tom Le Noir, this is Buddy Evans, we're here investigating a homicide for the Arlington Police Department," Le Noir explained.

The sad, tired eyes of Jack Reeves, Sr., began to fill with tears. "Emelita's dead, isn't she?" he asked. "He killed her, didn't he?"

Tom Le Noir sat down beside the elder Reeves and gently asked why he would make such a statement.

"The other ones were killed, too," Reeves said, dropping his head.

The detectives encouraged Jack Reeves, Sr., to elaborate on his speculation that his son had killed Sharon, Myong, and Emelita.

"He likes killing," Reeves offered. "He's a killing machine. It started in Vietnam. He liked the killing."

As Le Noir and Evans continued their conversation with Jack's father, they learned that the money Jack had bragged to the detectives about having in CD accounts in Arlington had been, in essence, stolen from his father.

Jack Reeves, Sr., was a decorated war veteran who had been part of the U.S. forces that landed in Normandy. He didn't believe in the safety of banks and had hidden his money in WW II shell canisters in his backyard.

The elder Reeves was in the midst of divorcing his second wife. According to him, Jack's advice was that women couldn't be trusted. He convinced his father to give him the money to hold until after the divorce. The money would be returned, and his father would not have lost half of his holdings in divorce court. The plan seemed like a good one to Reeves, Sr.—until Jack refused to return the money to him.

Had Jack Reeves yielded the money his father had amassed, the elder Reeves would probably have lived out his days on a sunny piece of Texas ranch land. Instead, the old war hero was condemned to a solitary life in the VA hospital.

Jack Reeves, Sr., had been writing to the FBI for months in

an attempt to gain help in recovering his money from Jack. The disappointment cloaked his face as he realized Le Noir and Evans were unable to help him in his efforts.

The situation angered Le Noir and Evans. They both wished they could help in some way.

Jack Reeves, Sr., shuffled along the corridor of the VA hospital as he walked Le Noir and Evans to the front entrance.

"Jack's been wanting me to come stay with him for a while," Reeves said.

"Why haven't you?" Le Noir asked.

"I'd be dead in a week."

Next Le Noir and Evans headed for Wichita Falls and the home of Bennie Curran, Jack Reeves's mother. Evans found it extremely interesting, even poignant, that dozens of family photos were scattered about the house—but not one was of her son, Jack.

Bennie Curran was an attractive woman in her mid-to-late seventies, well-groomed with a bouffant hairdo. In typical motherly fashion she was initially loyal to her son, and complimentary to her daughters-in-law.

"She was so pretty and so cute," Curran said of Emelita.

But as her conversation with the detectives proceeded, she began to remember things about Jack that were disturbing. By the end of the visit, even Jack Reeves's own mother conceded that he could very well be responsible for the deaths of Sharon, Myong, and Emelita.

December 12, 1994

Sergeant Berry of Copperas Cove informed Le Noir that he had been able to locate one lone crime-scene photo of Sharon Reeves. He would be mailing it to Le Noir's office that day. And the best news of all, arrangements had finally been scheduled for the exhumation of Sharon Reeves on the fourteenth. Le Noir was excited, he couldn't wait to see what condition Sharon's body was in. Would an autopsy be possible? Would they be able to prove *murder*? In two days he'd know.

Nine

December 14, 1994

The single crime-scene photograph of Sharon Reeves arrived on Le Noir's desk. He anxiously ripped open the envelope flap and slid the eight-by-ten glossy black-and-white photo out of the manila mailer.

He stared at the nude, blood-splattered body sprawled across the rumpled bed. Sharon Reeves lay on her back, her arms bent at the elbows, palms up on each side of her body. Her head was turned to the side, facing away from the camera. Her short, dark brown hair was neatly cropped. Just to the left of her left breast was a hole the size of a gun barrel. Little blood was visible on the right breast. From just beneath where her bra would normally rest, to the top of her bikini line, blood was splattered in a dense, nonuniform manner. The same splatter pattern was on her right leg. Her left leg showed long lines of blood drips, with light splattering. A long gun barrel rested between her legs, which were bent at the knees and hanging loosely off the end of the bed. The bed was unmade, the sheets crumpled.

Le Noir's trained eyes were immediately drawn to several discrepancies. *It is blatant that this scene has been staged,* Le Noir thought as he continued to study the photo.

The sheet underneath Sharon's body was pulled forward, the accordion folds more narrow at the bottom and wider at the top, near Sharon's head. Le Noir's best guess was that Sharon had been at the top of the bed, but had been pulled to the end along with the sheets. Supporting his assumption was evidence of blood smearing to the body, consistent with the body being moved or tampered with after being shot. The gun appeared to have been placed between her open legs.

I wish we had all the sheets to see the splatters, Le Noir thought. But he didn't have the sheets. All he had was the one lone photo. He continued to study it in great detail.

Sharon Reeves's dark suntanned skin was contrasted by the paleness of her bikini outline. Le Noir looked closely. Just below her panty line a trickle of blood ran from just left of her belly-button sideways to the bed sheet. The line of blood indicated that the blood was pocketed, then released, allowing it to flow out. *He must have taken off her panties,* Le Noir thought. *That's the only way that blood could have run like that.* The absence of significant amounts of blood in the pubic area when there was a good deal of blood on her stomach was another indication that her underwear had been removed.

Something else bothered Le Noir. The blood spatter didn't look right. Over the twelve years he had been in homicide, he had seen more crime-scene photos than he'd like to remember. The blood on Sharon Reeves's body was inconsistent with normal blood spatter. Then it dawned on him, it looked watered down. It was runny and thin. Had she been wet when she was shot? The spatter wasn't nearly consistent with what Reeves claimed happened that night.

Le Noir's concentration moved to the fatal wound itself. He knew that if Sharon had shot herself in the heart she would have died instantly. Her heart would have stopped pumping. She would have stopped bleeding. If she had been sitting up and shot herself, her heart may have given one or two more pumps, but then it would have stopped. The blood-spatter pattern on Sharon's chest, similar to those on her pubic area, indicated that blood was pocketed before it started to flow. Streaks of blood were visible from the breast to the sheets. The pattern was consistent with a bra being worn when the shot was fired, then taken off after her death, allowing the blood to flow freely. That scenario would account for the absence of significant blood splattering on her breasts. But why? Why would Jack Reeves remove his wife's bra and panties after she died?

Le Noir gazed at Sharon's open arms. Had Sharon shot herself, and held the weapon in the normal manner, blood spatter would be on the outside of her arms—not the inside. Just one more inconsistency.

But the major, most blatant discrepancy was the gun barrel between her legs. It screamed staging. A blast from the shotgun would have repelled the gun away from the body, it would not have fallen between her legs. The gun was obviously placed there.

Le Noir was thrilled with the crime-scene photo. Of course, he would love to have more pictures, from different angles, and color would be good, but one was all he needed if the photo was good. And this one was.

Detective Evans arrived a few minutes after Le Noir called him to his office. Without saying much, Le Noir handed his partner the picture of Sharon Reeves. Evans studied the photo in silence. Within minutes Evans concurred with Le Noir's analysis of the positioning of the body, of the blood-spatter patterns, and the placement of the weapon.

"I think we need to let someone better trained in evaluating blood spatters than we are, take a look at this," Evans suggested.

Le Noir agreed. He took the photo to APD crime scene technician Greg Scarborough. Scarborough concurred with their assessment of the crime scene and urged them to search for experts in the field of blood spatter for more detailed interpretations.

Le Noir contacted Ronald Singer of the Tarrant County Medical Examiner's Office. Then he drove the thirty minutes to Singer's office. It didn't take long for Singer to agree that the blood-spatter patterns were inconsistent with the victim shooting herself. He kept the photo so he could make a full written report of his findings.

Le Noir was confident that Singer's final analysis would indicate that Sharon Reeves had not committed suicide, rather Sharon Reeves had been murdered.

Final preparations were being made to exhume Sharon Reeves's body. Sergeant Berry had acquired her medical records, as requested by Doctors Barnard and Stone. No dental records were available. They had been destroyed sometime during the sixteen years since Sharon's death.

Berry arranged with David Newton of the Wichita Falls Embalming Service to perform the actual exhumation.

"It will take about two hours," Newton told Berry.

"As soon as the casket is retrieved, Sergeant Austin and I will follow you to the Southwest Institute of Forensic Sciences in Dallas," Berry said.

"Anything special I need to know?" Newton asked. He wanted to make certain that everything was done to the state's specifications.

"The Texas Department of Health statute states that a disinterred body must be transported in a container, which insures against the seepage of fluid or the escape of offensive odors," Berry informed him. "Just make sure you comply."

On December 14, 1994, at 8:45 A.M., the disinterment began with the roar of the backhoe and the breaking of the ground over Sharon Reeves's grave. Scoop by scoop, earth was dug away from the grave site and piled high on a nearby vacant plot. Finally, metal touched metal and the engine of the gas-driven digging tool was quieted. The casket was lifted from its resting place at 10:30 A.M.

Thirty minutes later Newton raised the lid on Sharon's casket. Sergeant Berry peered inside. Sharon Reeves's body was mummified and covered in a white mold. Berry removed his hat and leaned in closer to the body to identify a small picture held in Sharon's hands. It appeared to be Sharon and two small boys, probably her children.

"The body seems to be in good shape for an autopsy. Go ahead and transport it to the Medical Examiner's Office," Berry instructed. "We'll follow."

Once Sharon Reeves's body was safely delivered to Dr. Barnard, Sergeants Berry and Austin returned to Copperas Cove. Their job was done. It was now up to Doctors Barnard and Stone to determine if Sharon indeed took her own life, or if she was murdered.

December 15, 1994

Le Noir and Evans were emotionally charged as they drove to the Southwest Institute of Forensic Sciences (SWIFS) to view the autopsy of Sharon Reeves. Somewhat like two rookie cops on their first day of patrol, they felt a little bit of nervousness and a lot of excitement.

The detectives were greeted in the morgue by the foulest odor imaginable. It was worse than any road kill on a hot Texas day. Encased in the morgue were twelve to fifteen bodies lying on gurneys and in various stages of decomposition and autopsy. As Dr. Barnard greeted them, Evans noticed that the putrid smell didn't seem to faze the doctor. Evans tried hard to only breathe through his mouth.

The detectives covered their street shoes with paper booties, and Evans donned a mask. The shield that covered his nose and mouth did little to filter out the rank odor.

A broad smile, from his upturned lips to the wrinkles at the corners of his eyes, crossed the face of Dr. Barnard as the lid to the blue metallic coffin was removed. There before him was an almost perfectly mummified body. He was as excited as a kid with a new toy. He had the perfect specimen.

"She's in great condition," Dr. Barnard said, not really speaking to anyone.

"Yeah, we can thank Jack for that," Le Noir said. "I understand he insisted on only the best for Sharon. He made certain that she had the best waterproof, airtight casket money could buy. He did us a real favor."

Sharon's head, her brown wavy hair still neatly coiffed, rested on an off-white satin pillow. A wilted corsage was neatly pinned to the left-hand side. A plastic cover protected the photograph she held in her hands. A Bible was at her waist. Rings adorned the third finger of her left hand; one containing six clear stones; the other four small clear stones surrounding one large central stone. On her right hand was a white metallic ring with a blue stone and smaller clear stones on each side. She wore a gold bracelet on her right wrist and a gold necklace with an amber stone at her throat. On her left wrist was a white metallic watch with clear stones. She wore gold loop earrings.

Sharon was fully clothed in a one-piece navy and white knit pants outfit. She had on panty hose, a bra, and platform shoes.

After removing her clothing and jewelry, the white mold that covered the extremities of Sharon's body was washed away with Clorox bleach and a rag. Then photos were taken of Sharon from top to bottom, front to back.

The sutures that closed the wound in Sharon's chest were still intact. The pellets and wadding from the shotgun blast were still lodged in her back. It was amazing. The corpse was in better condition than either Le Noir or Dr. Barnard could have hoped for. Sharon's own body would be able to tell them if she had taken her life.

Dr. Barnard began the autopsy by removing the sutures and cutting open the wound. He was able to see how the wound traveled from the front to the back of the body where the wadding still rested. The charge went sharply from right to left, and nearly horizontal with a very minimal downward slant. Next, he cut along Sharon's left side. The wound track was clearly visible. Dr. Barnard took a steel rod, inserted it in the chest wound, and pushed it back to the wadding. The straight line gave a clear picture of the angle of the shot, both horizontally and vertically.

Dr. Barnard moved from the fatal wound to a cut on the right big toe. He knew immediately that it had been cut with a sharp instrument.

"If you'll notice," Dr. Barnard said to Le Noir and Evans, "the cut is smooth. On an impact wound, such as the recoil from a gunshot, the skin will be torn. It will have jagged edges. This cut is smooth with the flesh laid open."

"Jack must have cut it," Le Noir commented, as he took a closer look. "And the cut is on the underside. If the toe was injured during recoil it would have been on the top of the toe, from the kickback."

Even more interesting was the direction of the cut. Rather than a round or semicircle incision, indicating the toe had been used to pull the trigger, the cut was vertical. The incision went from the top of the big toe, near the nail, directly downward toward the foot. *Jack just didn't quite think this through,* Le Noir thought. *Just another example of a moron implementing what he thinks is a stroke of genius.*

Sharon's big toe was amputated and placed in a jar of formaldehyde solution. "Sandy Gately may want this for evidence," Le Noir said, holding up the specimen.

Evans shuddered slightly as he visualized twelve jurors passing around a jar with a big toe in it.

The initial autopsy took about four hours to complete. Le Noir and Evans left Doctors Barnard and Stone to complete the remainder of the autopsy, which included examination of the brains and other internal organs. Dr. Barnard would submit a complete report to them later.

The detectives had the information they needed to proceed with the investigation. Sharon Reeves had not pulled the trigger with her toe and, from the angle of the entry wound, was not likely to have pulled the trigger at all.

The case against Jack Reeves was mounting. But the joint case of the Arlington and Copperas Cove Police Departments was far from complete. They needed more information before an arrest warrant could be issued.

Le Noir sent the crime-scene photo to Tom Bevel, an internationally regarded blood-spatter expert from Oklahoma City, for his evaluation. Wanting Bevel to arrive at his findings without prejudice, Le Noir gave Bevel no details of the case. With the aid of a female APD employee, Evans and Scarborough prepared to re-create the shooting. Meanwhile, Sergeant Berry ordered the military record of Jack Reeves.

Mid-February 1995

"Tom, I might have something here," Berry told Le Noir by phone. "I got Reeves's military records. Seems as though he killed a man while stationed in Italy. An alleged Peeping Tom."

Reeves's death toll appeared to be increasing.

Ten

It was the second week of February 1995, Emelita had been missing for four months. Le Noir was anxious to hear what Sergeant Berry had to say about another possible Reeves killing.

"Who did Reeves kill in Italy?" Le Noir asked Sergeant Berry.

The Copperas Cove officer explained that Jack Reeves had been stationed in Verona, Italy, with the United States Army when he shot and killed a man on September 9, 1967.

"It appears Reeves shot and killed an Italian citizen who had been window-peeping. Reeves reportedly confronted the man after hearing noises outside of his quarters," Berry said.

"How did he kill him?" Le Noir asked.

"Evidently, he retrieved a twenty-two-caliber Marlin rifle from his residence and went outside. The twenty-five-year-old Italian man supposedly saw Reeves and attempted to jump over a railing near the Reeveses' quarters. Reeves shot him, and the Italian apparently died at the scene. He was found with his trousers' zipper open, and his penis was protruding from his pants," Berry explained.

"Can you send me a copy of the report?" Le Noir asked.

"Sure," Berry agreed.

The report indicated that Jack Reeves stood trial in an Italian courtroom with an Italian attorney retained at the U.S. government's expense. Reeves was found guilty of voluntary homicide; that ruling was slightly modified, and he was sentenced to two years, eleven months, and twenty days. Reeves's attorney immediately filed an appeal, claiming the act was self-defense.

With the help of a new Italian law broadening the definition of self-defense, the intervention of then-President Lyndon Johnson, U. S. military officials, and petitions signed by hundreds of Wichita Falls, Texas, residents at the requests of both Reeves's and Sharon's parents, Reeves was exonerated. The higher appeals court overruled the lower court's decision and declared the incident self-defense. Reeves had served less than four months of his sentence.

The Court of Assizes of Appeal of Venice stated in its brief that they believed the lower court did not consider sufficient medical, legal, and technical reports. The prevailing question of the justices was how the bullet ended up in the body of the victim.

Reeves claimed he hadn't intentionally killed the victim, but fired only to scare him off. The victim, however, had been shot in the back, as if fleeing the scene.

The defense's expert witness pointed out that the hole caused by the entrance of the bullet into the body was exaggeratedly big. He claimed the initial trajectory of the bullet was due to the victim sitting astride the balcony rail.

The president of the appeal court agreed, claiming that the bullet could have ricocheted off the balcony rail before striking the victim.

Reeves's lawyer added that Reeves acted under the continuous impression that he was worried for the safety of his pregnant wife, Sharon, and his young son. "The elements clearly showed the existence of self-defense," he told the court.

The April 23, 1971, the Supreme Court in Rome affirmed the appeal court's decision, and the case of Jack Reeves was closed.

Le Noir stared at the report. *Sure,* he thought, *a bullet that hits a narrow iron rail and just happens to land in the back of someone fleeing. That doesn't make sense. Jack shot that man in the back.* Le Noir believed that the Italian was just one more victim of Jack Reeves. One more murder he got away with.

* * *

Detective Le Noir recruited crime scene technician Greg Scarborough to help with the reenactment of the shooting death of Sharon Reeves. Scarborough obtained the exact measurements of Sharon Reeves, along with the direction and angle of the wound from Dr. Barnard. He also acquired a gun that closely approximated the weapon used to kill Sharon Reeves, since Reeves claimed he no longer owned the shotgun. Now all they needed was a model.

Le Noir assigned Evans to work with Scarborough. By now Le Noir and Evans had meshed as partners. Le Noir had been so impressed with the work that Evans had done that he asked his supervisor to have Evans reassigned to homicide until the case of Emelita Reeves was concluded. As far as Le Noir was concerned, Buddy Evans was a homicide cop. He respected his abilities and work ethic. The respect was mutual. Evans laughingly referred to Le Noir as Batman, the ultimate crime fighter, and himself as Robin, his trusty sidekick.

Evans and Scarborough looked around the offices of the APD for a woman the approximate size and shape of Sharon Reeves. Dana Para, a pretty Hispanic receptionist in the narcotics division, was finally recruited. Actually, Para had a little longer reach and longer legs than Sharon Reeves, but the officers wanted to give the benefit of the doubt on the side of suicide. They bent over backward to make the test as fair as possible.

Through the crime scene investigation division Scarborough had access to still-photographic equipment, as well as video cameras. They were set to begin.

In theory, based on their knowledge from the autopsy, a suicide wasn't possible—not with the angle of the wound track. The reconstruction would help to support, or to challenge, the probability of a suicide. Either way, they would have some answers.

Evans, Scarborough, and Para met in one of the juvenile-interview rooms on the second floor of the APD. They talked at length about how the reenactment would be performed.

The situation was simulated as closely as possible, but with Para dressed in a black leotard, rather than nude as Sharon Reeves had been on the night of her death. The leotard was marked with tailor's chalk on the front where the shot entered, and on the back where the wadding had been lodged. Para gripped the gun so that the barrel rested against the chest mark and projected toward the back in the angle described by Dr. Barnard.

Scarborough announced each procedure on tape before each reenactment was performed.

Para sat, stood, and lay down. Every possible body position was re-created. Evans had even obtained the dimensions of the bed Sharon Reeves had died on so that the exact height was duplicated. Once again, Reeves had helped them out. He kept the bed his second wife died on in his storage shed at the rear of his Iberis Drive house.

It was difficult for Dana Para to hold the gun. It was heavy. Also, the weight of the gun made it difficult for her to maintain the angle. Even when she did maintain the angle of the projection, she was unable to pull the trigger. Not with her finger. Not with her toe.

"It doesn't make sense that she would kill herself with a shotgun anyway," Evans said as the trio took a short break. "Women normally don't use guns for suicide—it's too messy. An overdose of sleeping pills is far more likely. Besides, if she had wanted to shoot herself, why hadn't she used the small Smith and Wesson that was found in the drawer of the nightstand next to the bed?"

After two and a half days of reenactments, the law of physics prevailed. The reconstruction established evidence that challenged the probability of Sharon Reeves having the ability to position the firearm in the exact direction and angle consistent with her wound and pull the trigger with her big toe, while maintaining the weapon in that position. Furthermore, Dana Para could not maneuver a vertical positioning of her big toe into the trigger guard.

Le Noir was exhilarated by the results of the reenactment. He had been looking for a break in the Emelita Reeves case for four months. The reenactment was a large piece of the puzzle that would help to establish that Jack Reeves did indeed have a history of violence, a history of murder.

Le Noir sent the documented findings to Dr. Barnard's office, at his request. On February 21, 1995, Dr. Barnard contacted Le Noir.

"Upon reviewing the reconstruction, blood-spatter analysis, and circumstances surrounding the death of Sharon Reeves, I'm comfortable in refuting the original ruling of suicide. I've ruled the death as undetermined—suggestive of a homicide," Dr. Barnard said.

Le Noir couldn't wait to meet with Sandy Gately and Sergeant Berry. He recognized a successful prosecution of Jack Reeves for the death of Sharon would help to establish evidence of an ongoing modus operandi by Reeves in relationship with all three wives.

February 21, 1995

The divorce petition filed by Jack Wayne Reeves against Emelita Villa Reeves was final. In the statement of evidence Jack claimed the marriage had become insupportable because of conflict of personalities between him and Emelita.

Emelita was appointed an attorney ad litem, Debra Yaniko Dupont, by the court to represent her in her absence. Dupont filed a general denial on behalf of Emelita, which read:

On February 1, 1995, Ms. Dupont spoke with petitioner, Jack Wayne Reeves, to discover what knowledge he had of where the Respondent could be located. Mr. Reeves indicated that his wife had run away and that he was afraid she would come back and take their minor child. Mr. Reeves stated that the last time he saw his wife was on Tuesday, October 11, 1994. He stated that she left that evening to visit friends. The following day Mr. Reeves left for a camping trip to Lake Whitney and was not concerned that his wife had not returned as she often spent several days with the girlfriends. Mr. Reeves does believe that his wife is still alive and that she may return and try to take away their minor child.

On February 1, 1995, Ms. Dupont contacted Emelita Villa Reeves's cousin, Cristi, who lives in Wichita Falls, Texas. She was told by Cristi that the last time she saw Emelita was late September, 1994, right before her trip to the Philippines to visit other family. Emelita had given her some things to take to her parents in the Philippines. Cristi explained that it was impossible to contact Emelita's family in the Philippines as they did not have a telephone and only could call from a pay phone.

On February 3, 1995, Ms. Dupont spoke with Detective Tom Le Noir of the Arlington Police Homicide Unit. Mr. Le Noir stated that Ms. Reeves is still listed as a missing person and that he felt sure that she is deceased.

Ms. Dupont stated that she has exhausted all of her resources in attempting to locate the Respondent.

Reeves was granted sole custody of Theo, all personal property, all cash, bank accounts, and retirement or pension plans, all life insurance, and all motor vehicles. Jack Reeves got it all.

The decree was signed by Jack Reeves and Debra Yaniko Dupont, attorney ad litem.

Through the courts, Jack Reeves had managed to establish that Emelita had abandoned him—giving credibility to his claim.

March 7, 1995

The combined team of Le Noir, Evans, Berry, and Gately met at the Copperas Cove Police Department to discuss the status of the investigation. Based on the medical examiner's report and the reenactment videos, Sandy Gately was optimistic for a successful prosecution of Jack Reeves for the murder of Sharon Reeves. Her enthusiasm was only surpassed by that of the always hyper Le Noir. Gately's blue eyes danced as she agreed that Sergeant Berry would assume the responsibility of drafting an arrest warrant. Le Noir would be responsible for the evidentiary search warrant for Reeves's residence. She could smell the courtroom battle. It was her arena. It was where she was most effective. If the detectives gave her the evidence, she felt certain she could put Reeves away.

Although the body of Emelita Reeves had not been discovered, Detectives Le Noir and Evans were still confident that her body was concealed somewhere around Lake Whitney. They remained optimistic that she would soon be found. However, they concentrated their efforts in assisting Coryell County in the prosecution of Jack Reeves for the death of Sharon. If they could get him on Sharon's murder, they felt certain they'd get him for Emelita's.

March 17, 1995

"Tom, this is Berry," the sergeant said over the phone. "The warrant has been issued out of Coryell County to arrest Jack Wayne Reeves for the charge of murder."

Le Noir couldn't repress a broad smile. *We've got you, Jack,* he thought. *You're goin' down.*

Eleven

Jack Reeves was lonely. He didn't like being alone. Emelita was gone and he needed a wife, a mother for Theo, and a lover. Desperate, Jack called Emelita's family and asked if Marisa, their twenty-one-year-old daughter, could come and live with him. He claimed that he wanted someone from the family to help him raise his son, but the family was not about to lose another daughter to Jack Reeves.

Not to be discouraged, Reeves renewed his subscription to *Cherry Blossoms Magazine,* the same magazine where he found Emelita. He began sending out letters.

20, January 1995

Dear _____,

   Hi, I saw your picture in the _____ issue of *Cherry Blossoms.* I think you are a very beautiful lady with a beautiful smile. I know that you will have a lot of men write to you and I hope you will take the time to read my letter and correspond with me.

   My name is: Jack Reeves, I am a very young 54 years of age, black hair and brown eyes, 6 feet tall and weigh 170 pounds. So you can see that I am not fat or overweight. I am retired from the military and have a very good pension for life. I also have my own business and other financial investments. Because of all these things I make a very comfortable living and do not have to work unless I want to. I do not smoke or drink and I believe in God.

I am divorced with a handsome 3 year old son. My son lives with me and like I said before I am a very young 54. I like to exercise and can do more than a lot of men half my age. Most people I meet for the first time think that I am in my early 40s. I like eating out, movies, boating (I have my own boat), fishing, motorcycling, traveling and camping. I have a 5th wheel camping trailer for camping and traveling.

I am a Christian man and I do not believe in divorce. My marriage lasted for seven years and I divorced my wife because she was a Tomboy (Author's Note: Filipino slang for lesbian). She deserted my son and I, so I had to file for divorce to get custody of my son. His name is Theo and he is a very wonderful young man and I love him very much. I am a devoted family man and I really tried to make my previous marriage work, but was unable to do so because of her desire for other women.

I feel that I have a lot to offer the right woman. An older man is more established and can support a wife in a more comfortable life style than a younger man. I am a very romantic man and I want a woman who believes in God to be my life partner. I do no want a servant or a slave, but an equal partner for life. To share love with and to be a family together. I do not believe in cheating or being dishonest with my wife. During my 7 years of marriage I supported my wife's family and I believe that I am a very responsible person. I want a wife who is honest and is not afraid to show her love for her husband and who has a strong belief in family ties.

I have my own home in Arlington which is located between Dallas and Fort Worth, Texas. Six Flags is located here and it is a lot like Disney Land. I like to take my son there and he really enjoys it. My son and I also like to go camping in the trailer. Camping in a trailer is

nice and comfortable because it has all the comforts of
home. The trailer has a shower, toilet, stove, refrigerator,
couch, queen size bed, television and an air conditioner.

After I am married and my wife arrives in Texas I
would like for her to go to driving school and get her
driver's license. After that I will buy her a new car. That
way if she wants to go to the grocery store or the shopping
mall she can do so. I want my wife to be very happy and
I want to spoil her with everything I can. My pension
alone is more money than most people make working in
Texas and we can live a very comfortable life together.

Enclosed is a photo of my son and I. I hope that you
like it and will write to me. I will be very happy to help
you with the postage for the letters that you write me. I
hope that we can become friends with each other through
our correspondence and maybe much more. I am very
marriage minded and I am looking for my life partner. I
plan to come to the Philippines during the month of July
1995 to get married. I look forward to receiving your
letters.

Best Regards to You and Your Family

Reeves received responses from several women but it was
twenty-two-year-old Amy that caught his eye. Her first letter to
Reeves was dated February 8, 1995, just shy of four months from
the date Emelita was reported missing.

Amy was another petite Filipino, only four feet, ten inches,
weighing just ninety pounds. She had the same deep dark eyes
and shiny black hair as Emelita. The same innocent smile.

Amy was a two-year-college graduate. She wrote of the jobless
rate in her country and how her family had little more than their
love for one another. Amy told Jack that his age was not a big
deal, but that most of all she wanted a man who would love,
accept, and respect her for who she was.

"I believe that age doesn't matter to those people in love,"
Amy wrote. "I prefer a man older than me—because like what

you've said, they are more established and know how to take care of his wife and children, and knows the responsibility and commitments of a husband to his family. It's not hard for a woman to fall in love with a man—if a man is worthy to be loved."

She thanked him for the money he sent and signed her letter "Sincerely, Amy."

Jack was thrilled to hear from Amy. He responded to her first letter on February 16, 1995, describing how he had read the young Filipino woman's letter over and over again. He exclaimed he was certain that they were meant for one another, pleading for her to wait for his arrival in the Philippines and begging her not to marry anyone else. "It would hurt real bad," Jack told Amy, indicating how he would feel if he lost her love to another. To help express his sincerity, and to insure her loyalty, Jack sent along a cashiers check in the amount of $250.00. In return he expected Amy not to write to any other men.

Jack Reeves poured on the charm, telling Amy not only how beautiful she was but how wealthy he was. "I'm not telling you this to brag, but to let you know that I can take very good care of you . . ." Reeves said of his financial status.

Reeves assured the young woman he hoped would soon be his bride, that he did not believe in divorce but that Emelita's desertion had forced him to file for divorce and gain custody of Theo. He assured Amy once more that he was sincere, honest, patient, and understanding and that he did not want to be her boss, but rather her equal. He concluded by telling Amy how much he longed to hold her in his arms. The letter was signed, "Love You Forever and Ever, Jack and Theo."

Jack had found the next Mrs. Reeves. He made plans to fly to the Philippines, just outside Cebu City where Emelita's family resided, in July, and make Amy his wife. But in the meantime, this "one-woman man" continued to write to other women.

* * *

On March 21, 1995, Jack Reeves wrote to Vilma, yet another Filipino woman expressing his love for her, as well as his displeasure. Vilma had not responded to Jack's letter as expediently as he had hoped. He expected his correspondents to answer immediately. Jack told the young beauty that he was a very romantic man and that he loved sex, expressing his desire to buy some good X-rated videos while in Manila. He requested photos of Vilma in a bathing suit, photos larger than the ones she had sent with her last letter. ". . . besides having beautiful legs it looks like you also have beautiful breasts," Reeves wrote, adding that he longed to kiss her all over her body. He ended his letter by writing, "I am a one-woman man and I want a one-man woman." Again he signed his letter with both his and Theo's names.

Jack Reeves sealed the letter to Vilma and left his Arlington home, along with Theo, for the Bardin Street post office. He hadn't noticed the surveillance team that had been positioned across the street from his house since eight o'clock that morning. He didn't see them pull into the post office parking lot behind him.

As Reeves and Theo stood in line to mail the letter to Vilma, uniformed police officers executed the Coryell County arrest warrant without incident. Reeves was handcuffed, Mirandized, and transported to the Arlington Police Department. Theo accompanied him to the police station.

Jack Reeves was in shock. His heavy jaw sagged with the weight of disbelief. His eyes drooped at the corners. Reeves suddenly looked much older than his fifty-four years.

Le Noir, Sergeant Berry, Sandy Gately, and Texas Ranger Fred Cummings stood at the far rear of the judge's area, out of Reeves's sight. They wanted a front-row seat to the arraignment.

It's fixing to crumble for you, Mr. Reeves, Gately thought, a slight smile on her lips.

Standing stoop-shouldered before the judge, Reeves raised his head slightly, asking, "Why am I under arrest?"

"For killing your wife," the judge answered solemnly.

"I didn't kill Emelita. I told Le Noir I didn't kill Emelita," Reeves protested.

From the darkness Le Noir responded loudly, "Jack, this isn't Emelita." Jack Reeves looked around to find Le Noir, but he was concealed from view.

"Which one is it?" Reeves asked.

Sandy Gately stared at Le Noir and Berry as she mouthed silently, "Which one?"

Le Noir stepped forward. He wanted Reeves to see his face. "This is Sharon."

All the color in Jack Reeves's face drained. He appeared stunned and confused. He glanced at Le Noir as if to ask, "what do you mean Sharon?" The investigative team had successfully kept Reeves in the dark. He was totally unaware of the Copperas Cove investigation, the exhumation of Sharon's body, or the autopsy.

"We haven't gotten to Emelita yet. We're doing this systematically," Le Noir said with authority.

A faint glimmer of understanding lit Reeves's tired, sad eyes. His expression of confusion turned to a scowl of hatred directed at Le Noir. He clenched his teeth, and narrowed his eyes. The man he had toyed with during the investigation was getting the last laugh. Jack Reeves was furious.

Once the arraignment was over, Tom Le Noir approached Theo, who was being held in another area of the Arlington station while he waited for his aunt and uncle Pat and Gary Goodman to pick him up.

"Hi, Theo," Le Noir said to the boy. Theo turned his back to the detective.

"Can I get you a drink?" Le Noir asked. Theo shook his head no.

Maybe the kid just doesn't like me, Le Noir thought. He asked Sandy Gately to come over and talk to Theo.

Sandy squatted down, getting on the child's level. She attempted to converse with Theo, but he refused to talk. He would only shake his head no.

"I think he's been coached not to talk to anyone," Le Noir said. "He's afraid."

Theo was taken home by the Goodmans, and it was time for Reeves to leave, as well. Gately, Berry, and Cummings took custody of Reeves to transport him to Coryell County. Seated in the backseat of the CCPD car, Jack Reeves began to give directions to Berry on how to get to Copperas Cove.

"It's best to take I-thirty-five down to Waco," Reeves said as they pulled out of the sally port at the Arlington Police Department.

Gately shook her head, her short brown hair swinging from side to side. *This guy always needs to be in control,* Gately thought. But she was in control, and she had no intention of relinquishing it to Jack Reeves.

Gately, Cummings, and Berry were hungry. It was midafternoon and none of the three had had lunch. Just outside of Waco, Texas, the group decided to stop for a cold drink. They bought Reeves one, as well.

"Let me out of the cuffs so I can drink my soda," Reeves said.

"No way," Cummings answered. "You can drink it in the cuffs."

"If I try to escape, just shoot me," Reeves suggested.

Fred Cummings looked at Reeves with disdain. "I don't have to," Cummings said, sizing the aging Reeves up against his own tall, well-developed body. "If I can't take down a guy like you, it's time to retire."

Reeves remained handcuffed in the backseat of the cruiser for the balance of the trip.

By the time Le Noir and Evans arrived at Reeves's residence at 2:30 P.M., the area was saturated with news media. The patrol division had done their job by quartering off the property and keeping unauthorized personnel away. At 3:10 P.M., standing on the red doormat, Le Noir unlocked the brown front door. He,

Evans, and the search team entered to make a preliminary inspection of the house.

For all of Jack Reeves's bragging about money and possessions, the house was quite plain. There were no expensive paintings or furnishings. It was no more than average.

The search team entered the living room first. A light-blue and mauve sectional sofa took center stage. A large television occupied the opposite wall, along with a reel-to-reel tape player. A cheap pink ceramic lamp was on the end table, which also held a number of *Penthouse* magazines. Additional magazines were stacked under the coffee table, which was in front of the sectional sofa. A number of videos lay on the coffee table and around the room. Videos with titles such as *Anal Recall, Deep Inside the Orient,* and *Oriental Explosion.*

The dining room contained a cloth-draped table and a dark wood buffet with a large ornate gold mirror hanging above it. The hutch, on the opposite wall, was scattered with inexpensive knickknacks and a number of decorative liquor bottles—the kind you get as Christmas gifts from people who don't know you very well.

The kitchen Emelita was so proud to be mistress over was quite plain, too. No ornamental trappings, no countertop appliances. On a low breakfast bar adjacent to the kitchen was a tape recorder hooked up to the telephone. A number of cassettes were scattered on the counter.

The laundry room, with its gold appliances, was neat and tidy. The keys on separate gold hooks, where Randy Reeves had searched for the Pathfinder key nearly five months earlier, still hung on a blank wall. The laundry room led to the cluttered garage. A motorcycle and deep freeze piled high with junk was on one side of the double-car garage; on the other, carpet remnants, gun cases, and a bowling ball in a brown case.

Back inside the house, Le Noir and Evans searched the master bedroom. Sheer pink drapes hung over the windows, and a light flowered spread covered the bed. Pink doilies were on top of each of the dark wooden nightstands. A dark brown armoire was across from the bed, along with a TV stand and three shotguns. The closet was filled with only male clothing. Jeans, starched and ironed shirts, and leather jackets hung neatly in a row. Seven pairs of cowboy boots were lined up on the floor. Ammunition was stacked on a shelf, along with more magazines, and dozens of pornographic videos.

In the second of three bedrooms a piano stood against one wall, surrounded by boxes of Emelita's personal belongings. Photos of Emelita and Theo had been placed on top. A desk and chair were pushed against another wall. A typewriter was on top of the desk, a black file cabinet on the floor beside it. The closet was filled with bright orange life vests.

The last room was filled with children's toys. A small red rideable motorcycle, a basketball goal, and a Batman punching bag. Several other toys were scattered about the room. A brown and beige fold-out sleeper-chair was in the corner. A green-topped plastic storage chest held more toys, as did a four-shelf bookcase that also held an oscillating fan.

"All these toys are Jack's way of making Theo dependent on him," Le Noir said. "All the goodies he gave his family were a way to control them and make them dependent. Toys for Theo, a car, cell phone, a pager, and cash for Emelita. It's all about control."

The child's room looked ordinary, nothing unusual, until Le Noir spotted the gun. Resting against a windowsill, was a loaded shotgun.

"What in the world was Jack thinking?" Le Noir asked. "Leaving a loaded gun in the kid's room." The mere presence of the gun made him angry.

The shed at the rear of the property was filled with miscellaneous items, including a five-piece matched set of inexpensive brown vinyl luggage. Name tags bearing the name of Emelita Reeves were attached. Four additional mismatched pieces of luggage were also stored in the shed. *If she ran away, as Jack contended, how did she carry her clothes?* Le Noir wondered.

A tall dark brown wooden bed frame was at the back of the

shed. It was the headboard of the bed Sharon Reeves had been killed on. Le Noir wondered, *Why would you keep the bed your wife died in*? It was disturbing to Le Noir. It seemed almost a trophy.

The entire search of the Iberis Drive residence took two and a half days. Once the crime scene technicians had collected, cared for, and taken custody of the evidence, it was stored. Items found to be of evidentiary value to the Copperas Cove investigation were turned over to them, including letters between Sharon and Colonel John Behneman, the man she wanted to divorce Reeves for. One letter in particular caught the detectives' eyes. It was dated July 15, 1978, and was written by Behneman, who at that time was stationed overseas. He expressed his joy at Sharon's divorce from Reeves. However, he warned Sharon to exercise caution around Reeves. He worried about Reeves's reaction to the divorce. Evidently, his fears were warranted; five days later Sharon was dead.

A paper that appeared to be a New Year's resolution list depicted the type of control Jack Reeves had over Sharon. On the single sheet of lined notebook paper Sharon Reeves promised to do ten things in 1969.

Sharon promised to stop being mean and cranky to her husband; to answer Reeves when he talked to her; to buy him reloading equipment, which evidently she had forgotten at Christmas; to wear panties; to let Reeves get a Colt .45; to not give "it" to anyone but her husband, even while he was in Vietnam; to be nice to Reeves and to let him be the boss all of the time; to abide by all the New Year's resolutions, as well as any additional ones Reeves might think of; and Sharon Reeves promised to try not to rub her "nasties" on Reeves all the time. The degrading list was signed by Sharon Reeves. A humiliating notation appeared under Sharon's signature. The appendage read, "Better known as 'Ass Hole'."

An envelope that was found tucked away in Reeves's attic

disclosed interesting photos of Sharon Reeves. The envelope had been taped closed with the written instructions, "Destroy unopened by fire." Reeves had signed the package on the sealed portion of the envelope, which had been found inside another envelope addressed to Reeves at a San Francisco address, and postmarked 1979. The packet had been mailed by his mother.

Evidently, Reeves's mother had no intentions of keeping the envelope for Jack. Wanting no part of whatever the package contained, she had mailed it back to him, unopened.

Enclosed in the envelope were several Polaroid snapshots of Sharon. The chronology of the photographs were determined by following the sequence of poses. Sharon systematically undressed, until she was totally nude. She had been positioned in the identical pose that her body was found in at the time of her death. It was obvious; the photos had been taken the day she died. Le Noir and Evans had learned that Sharon had had her hair cut short the day before her death. In the Polaroid shots, Sharon's hair was in the new neatly cropped style.

One picture depicted Sharon holding a can of beer; in another her eyes were glazed and unfocused. From the look in her eyes and the positions of her body, Le Noir and Evans thought Sharon must have been drugged. In one of the last photos to have been shot, Sharon's legs were spread open, exposing her vagina.

"Look at the vaginal wall," Le Noir pointed out. "It's relaxed. She's just had sex."

The detectives remembered what Reeves had told the police the night of Sharon's death. "We had sex. She went in to take a bath. I went to the kitchen."

There was no note and no explanation for the photos. Like the headboard in the storage shed, these must have been trophies of Jack Reeves's ultimate conquest.

Several items were taken into evidence in the case of Emelita Reeves, as well. Both fine and costume jewelry; photographs of Emelita wearing the jewelry; boxes of Emelita's clothing; Emelita's prayer book and her rosary beads and crucifix; a photo album of her family in the Philippines; makeup and fragrances;

and Emelita's record book, listing correspondence to and from her family in the Philippines. The entries began in January 1988 and ended September 27, 1994, two weeks prior to her disappearance. The entries ranged from one to two weeks apart. If Emelita's record-keeping was consistent, and it appeared to be, the next entry would have come within the first or second week of October—the time of Emelita's disappearance.

Emelita's diary was also taken into evidence, as well as her passport and luggage. More than forty guns were confiscated from the house, along with all the pornographic materials.

A contract for legal fees was discovered, paying the law firm of Ball, Haas, and Wisch nine hundred dollars in legal fees, and Holden Polygraph, $450. The contract indicated that between November 2 and November 12, 1994, Reeves had submitted to two separate polygraph examinations given by Mr. Holden.

Another document interested Le Noir even more. It was a petition filed by Jack Reeves to divorce Emelita Reeves, filed on October 28, 1994. The document clearly stated that Jack and Emelita had been married May 13, 1988, and ceased living together as husband and wife on October 11, 1994—the date of Emelita's disappearance. Reeves claimed abandonment.

"Well, first of all, they were married March twenty-seventh, 1987," Le Noir said to Evans, explaining the document. "Even more peculiar, they were legally divorced on May twelfth, 1988. They never remarried."

Le Noir read on. "Reeves actually admits that he traveled to Lake Whitney on October twelfth, 1994," Le Noir said. "Well, I'm gonna fight this. The court can't grant this guy a divorce on abandonment. It could cost us the case."

Near the divorce petition, were tickets to the Philippines for Jack Reeves and his son Theo. They were for a June travel date. *He must be planning on leaving the country,* Le Noir thought. *Well, he may have to change his plans.*

Also in the file cabinet of Reeves's makeshift home office the detectives discovered a "romance" file. The first page was a double-spaced personal ad with a header of hand-drawn stars and hearts.

Reeves described himself as single, wealthy, and good looking. He elaborated on his self-proclaimed wealth by adding that he had a six-figure income, a line sure to attract a lot of women. The interests he listed included fast cars and motorcycles and spending time with that someone special. "I like to give and receive lots of TLC," Reeves had written, claiming he was a hopeless romantic who enjoyed lots of hugs and kisses. His ad claimed he wanted a serious relationship and that he was not into "mind games." The woman he sought would be between thirty and forty years old, be emotionally secure, romantic, aggressive and want to be spoiled rotten. He encouraged any interested ladies to send a photo and phone number to his Arlington post office box.

The figure of $117 was scribbled in the center of the page. Tucked in the file with the personal ad were two letters of response. The first from "adventuresome, thoughtful, spontaneous" Stephanie. Evidently, Jack was impressed. On the outside of her envelope he had written, "Yes (underlined twice), Over 40, Beautiful Photo, Wants Photo returned." Her phone number was written with broad, heavy strokes.

The photo of Stephanie revealed she was a lovely blonde, medium height, with a good build. Not the "typical" Jack Reeves's love interest.

The second letter was from Anna, "a divorced white mother of one. D/D free & emotionally secure. . . . a 34 yr old, 5'4'' blond, blue eyed beauty with a smile That comes from within. . . . a happy-go-lucky positive thinker & maybe the girl of your dreams."

Anna was lucky; Jack Reeves never responded.

Apparently, Reeves found Asian women more to his liking. A second folder found in the desk drawer was entitled, *"Cherry Blossoms."* The publication provided a directory to its subscribers of women from all over the world seeking a romantic relationship. *Cherry Blossoms* was where Reeves had first seen

Emelita, and they discovered, most recently, a woman named Amy. It was obvious. Reeves was looking for another woman he could lure to America.

Reeves also kept a roster of pen pals, with dates of letters, cards, and gifts sent to various women. The list had been kept from January 31, 1995, to March 20, 1995—the day before his arrest.

In the file cabinet was another publication, *How To Meet Exciting Ladies From All Over the World*. The table of contents read like an instructional manual.

TABLE OF CONTENTS

CHOOSING YOUR CORRESPONDENTS
MAKING SURE YOUR LETTER GETS TO HER
MAKING YOUR LETTER STAND OUT
WHAT TO PUT IN YOUR LETTER
WHAT TO LEAVE OUT OF YOUR LETTER
SENDING GIFTS AND MONEY
MAKE IT EASY FOR HER TO ANSWER
WHAT IF SHE DOESN'T ANSWER?
WHAT ABOUT THE SECOND, THIRD, ETC.
   LETTERS?
WHAT IF YOU CHANGE YOUR MIND ABOUT
HER?

Appendix I covered such important items as religion, personal names, differences in word usage, educational differences, and salvaging stamps.

The remaining appendices addressed such issues as prenuptial agreements, international phone calls, and travel abroad.

It was evident that Jack Reeves had become familiar with the mechanics of how to meet ladies from all over the world. He had succeeded in marrying Emelita, and now he apparently had plans to marry Amy. Considering Reeves's past track record, only time would tell if Amy would be his next wife, as well as his next victim.

Dozens of boxes filled with evidence were taken from Reeves's house. Conspicuously missing were Emelita's cell phone and pager, the two things Le Noir needed most. Emelita's friends claimed she never left the house without them, and Jack had been claiming that Emelita had called him on her cell phone since she had been reported missing. The cell phone and pager were two important pieces of the puzzle.

Twelve

"Detective Le Noir, this is Gary Goodman. Randy Reeves just called me. He said his father called him from jail and instructed him to retrieve Emelita's cell phone from his leather motorcycle jacket in the closet. Randy also said his father told him not to tell the police."

"Thanks, Gary. I'll need to talk with Randy," Le Noir said.

"Randy turned the phone over to me," Gary stated.

Le Noir sat up straight in his chair, and in his most authoritative voice said, "You *will* give us that phone."

"I'll give it to you," Reeves's brother-in-law agreed.

Le Noir thanked Goodman for his help and hung up the phone. *Cell phone. Leather jacket. How did we miss it?* Le Noir wondered. *I didn't find it. Three other investigators and five crime scene techs didn't find it. I don't see how we missed it.* But Le Noir didn't really care at that point. The cell phone had been in the house, and now he was going to get it—thanks to Reeves's paranoia. With forty guns in the house, jewelry, and other valuables, the phone was the one thing Reeves was concerned about. The phone was just another piece of the puzzle. Another attempt by Reeves to manipulate the evidence.

Le Noir sat at his office desk and read letters written by Emelita to Jack Reeves while she was in the Philippines giving birth to their son. The letters from Emelita, found among the ones from other women, were heart-wrenching requests. For nearly two years, banished by Reeves to her home country, she desperately pleaded to go home. Home to a man she didn't love.

In her letter dated September 18, 1992, Emelita thanked Reeves for sending five hundred dollars to help her and the family. In broken English she wrote of her ailing mother. "Mama still can't speak, can't walk. Still under observation, but we still do massage to her, especially the dead side. We do it everyday. Her paralized is affected in right side, that's why she can't even eat by herself. We have to do it for her."

Her mother must have had a stroke, Le Noir thought as he read. *Emelita is desperate to go back to Jack to help her family, even though she knows he's dangerous. These people can't afford for Jack to stop sending them money.*

                                              October 22, 1992
Dearest Jack,
    . . . Dear, I didn't forget to write you, neither tired of writing you. I never miss responding your letter honey, I am the one who's willing and wanted us to get back together, so I'll do everything for it. . . . Well honey, I better go now, you take care yourself and be careful. I miss you hon, and I love you.

The only happy moments in Emelita's letters were when she spoke of Theo. How he danced to the music of the radio and how he was beginning to play by himself. Her letters were filled with hope, hope that Reeves would bring her back to the United States. In every letter she included photos of Theo. It was through those pictures that Reeves finally decided that the young Amerasian was indeed his child.

In her October 22, 1992, letter she wrote:

    I am so glad you thought about bring us back home as soon as can be dear. I hope it won't take long. I really miss you dear, and I miss our companionship. We gonna be together again. . . . when we get together again, I will be a lot different. I meant, we will be ok this time. I do everything to make sure we're not gonna be separated again.

She signed the letter, "I love you, Emelita."

In November 1992 Emelita told Reeves that Theo was walking, and that she was waiting for the papers he had promised to send her to bring her home. In January 1993 Emelita was still waiting. Still professing her love. Still willing to return to the man she didn't love, to help the family that she did love.

Finally a letter from Reeves, dated January 21, 1993, arrived for Emelita. He explained in great detail how and when to catch the plane to Los Angeles. It was almost as if he were giving a small child instructions before embarking on a trip alone.

The last line of Reeves's letter read:

I love you and will see you soon. We can make it this time if we both work at it and I hope that we will. I will close for now and get ready for bed. I love you, Jack.

Emelita would again leave her homeland for the promise of a better life. A life that would be ended in less than two years.

While reviewing the evidence seized from Reeves's residence Le Noir learned that the divorce petition filed by Jack Reeves had been granted. He went ballistic. He had talked to Dupont and urged her not to allow the divorce to go through.

"This man is suspected of killing his wife. Foul play is involved. I suspect that this divorce is a potential cover-up. That needs to be studied prior to allowing him to pursue this divorce," Le Noir had urged with his usual intensity.

Le Noir couldn't control his anger. He called Dupont. "How

did you grant this man a divorce?" Le Noir asked, without attempting to hide his anger.

"It was granted because she didn't show up," Dupont said.

"How do you expect a woman who is dead to show up?" Le Noir asked, with emphasis on "dead." "You granted this man a divorce by default. How do you do that?"

Le Noir was outraged. If a court of record recognized, acknowledged, and agreed with Jack Reeves that his wife abandoned him, then that could be used as a ploy for a criminal defense. It should never have happened. Le Noir felt a divorce should never be granted when there is an active criminal investigation against the primary party. Especially when that party is suspected of killing the other person listed in the petition. It was up to Emelita's attorney to fight against the divorce.

One day, I'll sit back and say, "You were wrong," Le Noir thought. *He did kill her.*

As Le Noir stewed over the divorce of Jack and Emelita, Evans was on special duty.

"Buddy, I have an assignment for you," Le Noir had said, trying hard to suppress a grin as Evans's eyes brightened with eagerness.

"What's that?" Evans asked.

"You have to go through these pornographic tapes and see if there are any of Jack and Emelita," Le Noir said, handing him a large cardboard box.

Evans's smile quickly melted. Buddy Evans was a church-going, Bible-carrying Baptist. He didn't want to look at the pornographic videos, but if that's what Tom Le Noir wanted him to do, he'd do it.

Evans slumped back in his chair. Relief swept over him when the last frame of the last graphically adult video rolled off the screen. But the reprieve was short-lived. Le Noir arrived, carrying another load. "Here's some more," he said, with a devilish grin.

"Oh, no," Evans muttered, putting his head on the desk. "Thanks. I appreciate it."

Le Noir's laughter drowned out Evans's muffled sounds.

There were dozens of videos, mostly Asian porno, with a few of Theo's Disney favorites mixed in. Although Evans fast-forwarded through most of the porno, he occasionally took in an entire Disney flick. Later he told Le Noir, "I watched Thumper, then I saw *Thump-her."*

None of the tapes, all commercially produced, featured Jack or Emelita Reeves.

March 23, 1995

"We found something interesting when we were booking Jack Reeves into the Copperas Cove city jail," Sergeant Berry told Le Noir. "He had three money-order receipts from NationsBank. Two of them were obtained on March 17, 1995. One money order was for two hundred fifty dollars, payable to Isidro Villa, Cebu City, Philippines. The other money order was for one hundred dollars, payable to Marisa Villa, also of Cebu City. Here's the kicker, the remitter on the money orders is listed as Emelita Villa."

Le Noir immediately figured that Jack Reeves was sending money to the Philippines in his missing wife's maiden name in an attempt to mislead Emelita's family, as well as authorities, into believing she was still alive. But Le Noir didn't buy it for a minute, and neither did Emelita's family.

Ramona, Emelita's older sister in the Philippines, provided a sworn statement to naval intelligence officers, who were assisting the Arlington detectives, expressing her suspicion that Reeves was trying to deceive them into believing that Emelita was alive. Ramona was convinced that Reeves had killed her sister.

Buddy Evans contacted NationsBank and obtained surveillance photographs for March 17, 1995. The photos clearly identified Reeves as the person purchasing the money orders. Reeves was caught in yet another lie.

"This clarifies a statement Reeves made during the early stages of the investigation," Evans told Le Noir. "Remember, he said that we should routinely contact Emelita's family to see if she had sent any money orders. He said that would prove she was alive somewhere."

"Yeah, and his sister told us that Reeves mentioned to her that Emelita was sending money orders to her family and that Emelita was most likely 'hooking' somewhere to get the money," Le Noir said.

Jack Reeves definitely had a flair for the dramatic. He was digging his own hole deeper and deeper.

March 27, 1995

Detective Le Noir received a phone call from Randall Reeves, Jack's son. He was with his uncle Gary Goodman, who was monitoring the conversation on the extension phone.

"I just want the truth about the allegations against my father," Randy told Le Noir, his voice cracking with emotion.

Randy was confused but objective in his assessment of his father. "My father has always been 'sick'," Randy said softly. "I think he's a psychopath. He has a trigger temper and would just go off over very minor, irrelevant matters. He's always been like that."

Randy told Le Noir that he had spoken with his father nightly since Jack's arrest. During one of their conversations, Reeves had instructed him to look inside the pocket of his leather coat hanging in the closet of the master bedroom, and get the cell phone.

"I did it. I got the phone. He told me not to give it to the police, so I gave it to Uncle Gary," Randy said.

Randy Reeves made it clear to Le Noir that he didn't want to be a part of an illegal act. He was frustrated by being placed in the awkward position of having to help his father with bail, and then finding out there was the suspicion that his father might be responsible for killing his mother. He began to cry as he spoke of his mother. The young man was going through a tornado of emotions. To some extent he was in denial about his father's potential to commit murder, yet his father had done so many unexplainable things in the past.

Randy recalled certain activities by his father on the day after the police first arrived to check on Emelita. He remembered his father crouched on the floor in the hallway next to Theo's room. Reeves had been cutting sections out of the carpet, including the padding.

"What are you doing?" Randy had asked his father.

"Bugs are coming through the foundation. The exterminators need to plug the holes," his father had explained.

Randy told Le Noir that he could see no evidence of bug infestation.

Randy Reeves was also suspicious about his father's purchase of a new sofa, when he believed the old one was perfectly good. The purchase of the new furniture was unexpected, but Randy's concern increased when he discovered that the fold-out sleeper from the old sofa was in the backyard. When Randy questioned his father about the frame, Reeves claimed that he had gutted and disassembled the sofa to make it lighter and easier to carry. But lighter for what reason? Randy or his uncle could have helped Reeves move the sofa. And why didn't his dad just have the new sofa delivered? "It's just not like my father to bust a gut like that," Randy told Le Noir.

It didn't make sense to Le Noir, either. If Reeves could get the new sofa in the house without dismantling it, why couldn't he have gotten the old one out? They were nearly the same dimensions. Randy also told Le Noir that Reeves told him and his wife, Debbie, that he removed the old sofa the morning of October 12—within hours of Emelita's disappearance.

"Dad kept the mattress to the dismantled sleeper," Randy said. "He put it on top of the mattress on the new sleeper for added padding. But that made the old sleeper completely worthless."

An empty, worthless sofa. Le Noir thought for a moment. Then, as if he could see into the past and watch as Jack Reeves hauled the sofa from the house, he envisioned a theory.

Could Jack Reeves have taken Emelita's body from his house in the hollow area of the dismantled sofa? She was petite. Surely she would have fit. No one would suspect a sofa being dragged from the house. If he was stopped by the police for any reason, he was just haulin' furniture. *Pretty slick, Jack,* Le Noir thought. *But not slick enough.*

Both Randy Reeves and Gary Goodman confirmed that Jack told them he and Theo had gone four-wheeling at Fort Hood the day following Emelita's disappearance. However, his divorce petition stated that he went to Lake Whitney. The petition established evidence that Jack Reeves drove to Lake Whitney in his Dodge four-by-four on October 12, 1994, returned to Arlington on the same date, then traveled back to Lake Whitney on October 13, 1994, pulling his camper trailer. But why? Le Noir considered the possibilities. He believed more than ever that Emelita was buried someplace at Lake Whitney. He now believed she was buried October 12, 1994.

Toward the end of his conversation with Le Noir, Randy asked, "Did you know my dad took two polygraph tests?"

"What do you know about it?" Le Noir asked, refraining from revealing any knowledge of the tests.

"Debbie and I took him to both tests. He failed the first one," Randy offered. "He took several Valium in an attempt to beat the second one, but he could not stay awake during the testing." Randy seemed puzzled and suspicious that his father had tried to cheat the polygraph test, even after his lawyer assured him that the police would not be provided with the results.

Both polygraphs had focused on the disappearance of Emelita.

March 30, 1995

On March 30, 1995, the Coryell County grand jury returned a true bill against Jack Wayne Reeves resulting in a felony indictment for murder in the 1978 death of Sharon Delane Reeves. The following day a bond-reduction hearing was held in the Coryell County district court in Gatesville, Texas, in protest of the initial bond set during arraignment.

Wes Ball, an Arlington defense attorney, was in Gatesville to represent Jack Reeves at the bond hearing. He'd replaced Scott Wisch as Reeves's attorney, when Wisch was elected district court judge in Tarrant County. Ball would plead Reeves's bond-reduction motion before Judge Phil Zeigler. Ironically, Zeigler was the court-appointed attorney who had represented Reeves in the 1978 divorce petition filed by Sharon Reeves. But Zeigler didn't remember Reeves; in fact, he had never spoken to him, since Reeves was in Korea at the time of Zeigler's appointment.

Detective Tom Le Noir took the stand for the state.

Wes Ball and Tom Le Noir were old schoolmates, attending high school together in Arlington. There was mutual respect for one another's ability, integrity, and passion for the law, but each viewed the other as an adversary.

Le Noir testified that during the search of Reeves's Iberis Drive address, plane tickets to Manila, the Philippines for both Reeves and his son, Theo, were discovered.

"He planned to leave the country," Le Noir testified. "Obviously, we're concerned that he would try to leave, and not come back."

But Ball rebuked the allegation, saying that his client was going to the Philippines in hopes of finding his missing wife. "He was free to travel, just like any other citizen," Ball said.

Ball, a medium-built man, was known for both his sharp dressing and his excellent courtroom demeanor. He was determined that Jack Reeves's bail would be reduced. Ball told the court that the intense media coverage of the arrest and of the police searches of Reeves's home had caused Reeves to lose his contracting job. Those who had read Reeves's bragging letters shook their heads at this contradiction to his purported financial status. Ball also said that because of the extensive media publication of Reeves's address, the home had been burglarized twice while Reeves had been in jail.

"Without his income from his contracting position, Reeves will have to live on his savings and his Army retirement," Ball said. He pointed out Reeves's financial responsibilities of payments on a 1995 Dodge pickup and a mortgage on his home. A home he would be unable to return to because of recent vandalism. Jack Reeves would now be living in an apartment.

"And he is the sole support of his youngest son, three-year-old Theo," Ball added.

Ball told Judge Zeigler that Reeves's defense would be expensive, requiring forensic experts to review the state's case. The articulate attorney was painting a picture of a man who, although he had sufficient funds, had enormous financial liabilities.

Ball called on both Randy Reeves and Gary Goodman to testify that Reeves owned his own home and had strong ties with the community. They added that Reeves had recently remodeled his home, at significant expense.

District Attorney Gately was quick to point out that Reeves had just as many ties to the Philippines, and reminded the court that he had round-trip tickets to visit there in June.

"Theo, his youngest son, has dual citizenship in the U.S. and in the Philippines," Gately said. "Reeves is planning to marry a Filipino woman, Amy Baltazar, and has sent her money."

Sandy Gately contended that the five hundred thousand dollar bond wasn't too high. "He just doesn't want to pay it," Gately said, a slight scowl on her face. Then she added that she further believed that Reeves was a flight risk because of the ongoing investigations into the deaths of two other former wives.

Judge Zeigler listened carefully to the arguments of both Ball and Gately. In the end, he lowered Reeves's bond from five hundred thousand dollars to three hundred thousand dollars. And, if Reeves posted bail, he would have to submit to electronic monitoring.

In addition, five original conditions of bond were retained: (1) That Reeves would be allowed to walk his dogs within his apartment complex on a regular basis for the needs of the pets. (2) That Reeves would be allowed to leave his apartment in order to accomplish household duties, not to exceed two hours per day. He would be required to notify the Community Supervision and Corrections Department in Tarrant County when leaving and when returning. (3) Reeves would be allowed to repair his former residence for sale, limited to four hours per day. Again, he would have to notify the Community Supervision and Corrections Department. (4) Reeves would be allowed to travel to the home of a family member in the Dallas-Fort Worth area for a meal, once a week. He would report before and after each visit. (5) Reeves would not be allowed time away from his apartment except during the regular office hours of the Community Supervision and Corrections Department in Fort Worth.

Within a week of the bond hearing, Jack Reeves was free. But for how long?

Thirteen

With Jack Reeves indicted and preparing for trial for the alleged murder of Sharon Reeves, Le Noir and Evans continued to build a case against Reeves for the murder of Emelita. Their number one problem remained—no body.

Le Noir and Evans had studied the photos of Emelita, found during their evidentiary search, carefully. In each photo she was wearing specific pieces of jewelry. They decided to call Emelita's friends to find out if it was Emelita's habit to always wear those particular pieces.

Lynn Combs provided a detailed description of the jewelry that Emelita was wearing the day they had met for lunch at the Lotus Restaurant, the day Emelita had disappeared. Among those items Combs described was a yellow gold band with diamonds surrounding a center-set emerald. The other, a gold, opal, and diamond ring.

Le Noir took a small box from his pocket. He opened it, placing the contents on the table.

"That's Emelita's jewelry," Combs said, instantly recognizing the familiar pieces her friend always wore.

Next, Le Noir and Evans met with Mona Pate who, like Combs, described the jewelry Emelita was wearing when Emelita dropped her off at the Jack in the Box, the night of her disappearance. The description matched that of Lynn Combs's, as well as the jewelry Le Noir was holding.

Pate stared at the familiar emerald ring. "Emelita is dead if that ring was found at Jack's house," Pate said with conviction.

That statement jarred Le Noir's memory. When talking with Dita Hayes, early in the investigation, Hayes had told Le Noir that Emelita wore a gold ring with a green stone. "She never took it off," Hayes had said.

The investigation was becoming typically tedious. Le Noir submitted a request for a subpoena from the Tarrant County grand jury to obtain the records for Emelita's phone pager to determine if it remained activated. He drafted a court order for the airtime records of the cell phones in police custody. Evans contacted immigration and confirmed that Emelita Reeves had not used nor applied for a passport to or from the United States. Evans also learned that Emelita had yet to pick up her green card, which had been available since her disappearance. Evans contacted Social Security and confirmed that Emelita had not applied for a Social Security card, either under the name of Reeves or her maiden name, Villa. Teletypes were sent throughout the United States with a complete description of Emelita in case she was residing in another state where she may have obtained a driver's license, or possibly be in custody somewhere. Le Noir asked that the disappearance of Emelita Reeves be incorporated into the periodical crime-analysis bulletin distributed throughout Texas by the Texas Department of Public Safety. He also asked the Texas Rangers to notify him if a human body or human remains were located anywhere in the state.

With all their efforts, there was still no trace of Emelita Reeves.

The cellular phone records for the three separate numbers maintained by Jack Reeves arrived for Le Noir's and Evans's evaluation.

"The use of Emelita's cell phone appears to have terminated on October eleventh, 1994. The last recorded call was to Reeves's residence at eight-thirty-one P.M.," Evans told Le Noir, reading from the phone record.

"But roamer calls were made from Hillsboro, Texas, on Emelita's cell phone on October fourteenth, 1994. That's within the same time period Reeves had camped at Lake Whitney," Le Noir said.

Randy Reeves later confirmed that his father had made calls to him on a cell phone on October 14. Again, Reeves was attempting to manipulate the facts of the case.

April 17, 1995

In a copyrighted story in the *Fort Worth Star-Telegram,* Robert McDonald, former chief of the Copperas Cove Police Department, stated that he and his officers may have made errors in the 1978 investigation of Sharon Reeves's death.

"I have dislocated my knee kicking myself in the butt several times about the case," McDonald said. "I am very sorry that maybe we made the wrong decision because I would have liked to see those other two ladies lead a long life."

McDonald cited several discounted or missed pieces of evidence that Coryell County prosecutors believe would convict Jack Reeves of murder.

The revocation of an order to have an autopsy performed on Sharon Reeves's body.

Not analyzing the handwriting on the sexually explicit suicide note, which Jack Reeves told police he discovered in a china cabinet, rather than in the bedroom with the body.

Not authenticating a handwritten will said to have been completed by the couple the night before the death.

Disregarding Reeves's reportedly nonchalant reaction to his wife's death and court records showing that Sharon Reeves divorced Jack Reeves the day before the shooting.

Not interviewing family and friends who now say they believed that Reeves killed his ex-wife.

Not discovering that Reeves stated his wife did not die violently and that the couple never divorced in an application for more than one hundred thousand dollars in Army death benefits.

"We boo-booed," McDonald said. "We based it on what we had, and I wish we'd been smarter than we were."

But Wes Ball, Reeves's attorney, attributed McDonald's mind change to Le Noir and Evans "loading (him) up with innuendo."

The case against Reeves was more than innuendo. The team effort by the Arlington detectives and the Coryell County officials was a case based on strong forensic evidence.

In mid-September 1995 Le Noir received a letter written by Jack Reeves to Monette, one of Emelita's sisters. In the letter Reeves mentioned how much he loved Theo and how much both he and Theo missed the boy's mother. He told Monette he had not heard anything from Emelita and asked if perhaps Emelita had contacted her. Reeves promised to send more photos of Theo in the future and gave Monette his new address, a post office box in Arlington. As always, Jack Reeves signed his name and that of his youngest son, Theo.

Le Noir read the letter a second time. Emelita Reeves had been gone for almost a year. Le Noir was sure Jack had killed her, but in order to cover his tracks he had sent this letter to her family. *Sick, Jack, real sick,* Le Noir thought.

September 13, 1995

Jack Reeves was a talker. He talked to anyone who would listen: his lawyers, family members, friends, work associates, police, and even the media. He continually repeated the same rhetoric; police had ignored his two alibi witnesses who would prove that Emelita was alive while he was camping at Lake Whitney on October 13, 1994.

"I guess we better check out Jack's alibi witnesses," Le Noir said with little enthusiasm. "He claims they saw Emelita driving her Pathfinder in the neighborhood on October thirteenth."

With Evans behind the wheel of the Big Blue Bomb, the name Le Noir and Evans had dubbed the old Chevy borrowed from the juvenile division, they returned to Iberis Drive to either establish or disprove Reeves's alibi.

Le Noir knocked on the door of Bette Earl, a neighbor of the Reeveses. In a short time he had explained Reeves's claim that she could serve as an alibi witness, verifying that Emelita had been seen driving her Pathfinder in the neighborhood during the afternoon of October 13, 1994.

"I clearly told Jack Reeves that I couldn't definitely say Emelita was in the neighborhood that day," Mrs. Earl said, a note of anger in her voice. "He came over here and said, 'Remember, if the police ask, tell them you saw Emelita's car on the thirteenth.' It seemed to me as if Jack Reeves was attempting to 'plant a seed' and convince me that I saw Emelita's car."

"Then you can't positively say Emelita was here that day?" Le Noir asked.

"He isn't going to use me," the thirty-something Mrs. Earl said.

Earl appeared to be a very candid and honest woman. She was becoming increasingly agitated. "I am not an alibi for Jack Reeves," she said, the emphasis on "not."

The detectives walked the short width of two front lawns to the house of Mrs. Earl's next-door neighbor, Dean Faber. They held a typed statement signed by Faber with his initials affixed in each of the four corners, a military-style procedure, but unusual in the civilian world. The statement had been found among the papers confiscated during the search of Reeves's home.

"Do you remember signing a statement for Jack Reeves?" Le Noir asked the young man.

"Yes," Faber said, nodding politely.

"Was the statement you signed truthful and accurate?" Le Noir and Evans watched Faber closely. He appeared relaxed. Co-operative.

"To tell you the truth, I didn't carefully read the statement. I trusted that Jack Reeves had typed it accurately," Faber said casually.

"Why did you do that?" Le Noir asked.

"I told Jack that I saw Emelita's car that afternoon. Sometime after three P.M., but that I didn't see who was driving. I agreed to sign a statement to that effect," Faber explained.

"But your written statement goes into much greater detail," Le Noir said. He read the December 21, 1994 statement to Faber.

Faber's written statement declared that on Friday, October 14, 1994, Jack Reeves had asked him if he had seen Emelita in a couple of days. Faber indicated that he had seen her driving towards their house the day before, but he was uncertain of the time. They waved at each other, as they had done in the past, and that Faber was certain, "without a doubt," that it was Emelita driving her Nissan Pathfinder. The statement also indicated that Jack Reeves had instructed Faber to remember the date because the police would be talking with him. Dean Faber signed the statement on December 21, 1994.

Faber's look of surprise told Le Noir and Evans that his statement had been altered. Faber emphatically denied any truth to saying "without a doubt" in regard to observing Emelita driving her Nissan on October 13, 1994.

"You know, Jack Reeves approached me almost daily, reminding me to tell the police, whenever they asked, that I saw Emelita's car on October thirteenth. I wouldn't even be able to identify Emelita on sight," Faber claimed.

"Jack Reeves is counting on your statement. He may possibly call you to testify in his behalf," Le Noir said.

"I'll testify. I'll testify that the statement typed by Jack Reeves is not accurate and does not reflect what I told him," Faber said.

It was a moot point. Le Noir and Evans knew that Emelita's

car had been recovered in the HyperMart parking lot on October 13, and that Randy Reeves hadn't moved it from that location until October 14. Jack Reeves also knew it. Once more, Reeves had clearly attempted to twist and manipulate the facts for his own benefit.

Reeves's second alibi didn't hold up any better. He had continually claimed to the police and the media that Emelita had been known to disappear for days at a time. This was Reeves's favorite excuse for why he failed to file a missing persons report.

"She's always going off. She'll leave for days at a time," Reeves would say.

"Well, give me some examples," Le Noir and Evans had prompted.

In eight years of marriage, Reeves could only come up with one example of an unexplained absence. And even that turned out to be false.

According to Reeves, Emelita had disappeared for several days on her last birthday.

Friends had thrown Emelita a party on May 27, 1994. They had been celebrating Emelita's twenty-sixth birthday. When Emelita had gotten home from the party Reeves had inspected the Pathfinder, as was his usual custom. He had become enraged when he had found crumbs on the seats and floorboard.

Emelita had tearfully telephoned her friend Cecil Zenk from her car phone. "Jack hit me," she had cried.

When Emelita had arrived at Zenk's home, she had a large knot on her forehead. "Jack hit me with his fist," she had sobbed. "He pushed me against the wall and hit my head real hard. I think my head's going to explode."

Emelita had claimed it hadn't been the first time.

Zenk urged her to leave Reeves, but Emelita, as always, had insisted that she had to stick it out.

"You better stay away from him," Zenk had urged.

But Emelita couldn't. She had known that if she had left Reeves, he wouldn't have continued to send money to her family. She had known she would have had to go back home.

Zenk convinced Emelita to spend the night.

While Emelita had sought refuge at her friend's, Reeves had gone to his sister's and brother's-in-law. When they had asked him how he had hurt his hand, and why his fingers were taped, Reeves had claimed that he and Emelita had had a fight and he had injured his hand attempting to block a punch thrown by Emelita.

The following morning Reeves and Emelita had talked by phone. He had begged her to come home. But before she would let Emelita go, Zenk talked to Jack herself, condemning him for hurting Emelita. As Emelita was leaving, Zenk had pleaded with Emelita to call her when she got home.

In less than an hour, Emelita had called. She was back home. Back with Reeves. Her "disappearance," as Reeves called it, had been less than twenty-four hours in length.

October 1, 1995

At 6:30 P.M. on a Sunday evening, Tom Le Noir's pager went off. He recognized the number. It was Fred Cummings of the Texas rangers.

"Tom, I may have some good news for you," Cummings's strong voice boomed over the phone line. "Skeletal remains have been found in a shallow grave at Lake Whitney. The forensic anthropologist tentatively identified them as belonging to an Asian female."

"It's Emelita," Le Noir said without hesitation. He just knew it.

Fourteen

Richard Shinpaugh and his two sons had been deer hunting in the Credron Creek area of Lake Whitney. Shinpaugh left his four-wheeler parked across Credron Creek, hidden from view in a stand of mesquite trees and cedar bushes. It was some twenty-five to thirty yards away from his deer platform.

Shinpaugh had been hunting in the desolate public hunting area of Lake Whitney for ten years. It was an area he was familiar with, but one few people, other than hunters and arrowhead collectors, knew about.

By midmorning the Shinpaughs' hunting day was drawing to a close. Shinpaugh and his sons hiked the short distance back to the truck. The heavy aroma of fresh cedar filled the air. Suddenly Shinpaugh stopped. He stared at the object resting in a clearing of bare earth and wild grasses. It was a skull. A human skull.

Shinpaugh knew that, more than likely, there were other bones nearby. He told his boys to go to the truck. He didn't want them finding a body.

Within minutes, Shinpaugh discovered a shallow grave, no more than fifteen inches deep, that appeared to have been unearthed by animals. An almost intact skeletal frame rested among the weeds. Several smaller bones were scattered about in a fifty-foot radius. Shinpaugh knew not to move a single bone. He returned to his truck, retrieved his cell phone, and called Bosque County authorities. Because of the remote

Emelita Reeves, 26, was killed by her husband Jack Reeves, 54, on October 11, 1994. (*Photo courtesy Bosque County, Texas District Court*)

A resident of Cebu City in the Philippines, Emelita met Reeves there in 1987. *(Photo courtesy Bosque County, Texas District Court)*

Emelita Reeves's Philippine passport. *(Photo courtesy Bosque County, Texas District Court)*

While investigating Emelita's unexplained disappearance, Arlington, Texas police uncovered enough evidence to arrest Jack Wayne Reeves on March 21, 1995 for the 1978 murder of his second wife, Sharon. (*Photo courtesy Arlington, Texas Police Department*)

The former Arlington, Texas residence of Jack and Emelita Reeves.

A year after her death, Emetita Reeves's grave was finally found by deer hunters near the Cedron Creek area of Lake Whitney. (*Photos courtesy Bosque County, Texas District Court*)

The grave was so shallow, it had already begun to cave in. (*Photos courtesy Bosque County, Texas District Court*)

Dragged from the grave by animals, a human skull and bones were found nearby.
(*Photos courtesy Bosque County, Texas District Court*)

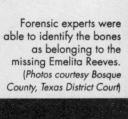

Forensic experts were able to identify the bones as belonging to the missing Emelita Reeves. (*Photos courtesy Bosque County, Texas District Court*)

CL 9507230

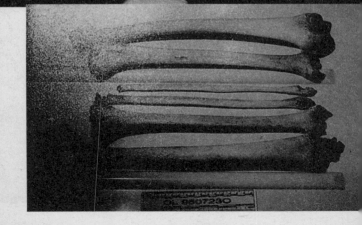

CL 9507230

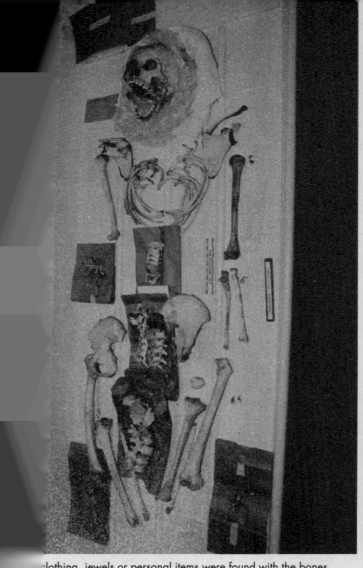

clothing, jewels or personal items were found with the bones
leading police to believe that the dead woman had not run
away as her husband had claimed.
(*Photo courtesy Bosque County, Texas District Court*)

Sharon Vaughn was Reeves's second wife with whom he had two children. Her death on July 20, 1978 by a shotgun blast to the heart was originally thought to be a suicide.

Reeves's third wife, Myong Hui Chong, drowned in only a few feet of water near the shores of Lake Whitney in North Central, Texas on July 28, 1986.
(*Photo courtesy Arlington, Texas Police Department*)

Larry Vaughn, Sharon's younger brother, testified against Jack Reeves during the October 1995 trial that ended with Reeves being sentenced to thirty-five years in prison for murdering Sharon.

Sharon Reeves's father, James Vaughn, leaving the Bosque County, Texas courthouse after hearing Jack Reeves convicted of murdering his fourth wife Emilita.

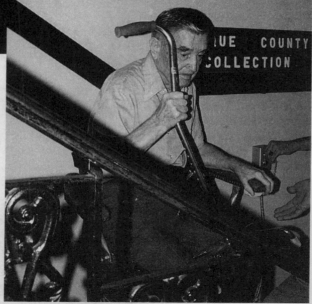

Police escort Reeves back to jail after his second conviction in August 1996.

Detective Tom Le Noir of the Criminal Investigations Division of the Arlington, Texas Police Department.

Detective Buddy Evans, of the Criminal Investigations Division of the Arlington, Texas Police Department

Sandy Gately, Coryelle County, Texas District Attorney successfully prosecuted Reeves for the murder of his wife Sharon.

Bosque County, Texas Judge James Morgan presided over Jack Reeve's trial for the murder of Emelita Reeves.

Bosque County Assistant District Attorney Ben Stoole.

Jack Reeves at the Gurney Unit, Texas Department of Criminal
Justice, Tennessee Colony, Texas in 1998.

area, Shinpaugh had difficulty getting a cell line. He had to drive to State Highway 56, about a half mile away, before his call would go through. Within twenty minutes a Bosque County sheriff's deputy was on the scene.

Shinpaugh led the deputy from the blacktopped highway, down the rutted grass and dirt road, to the location of the skeleton. About forty-five minutes later Shinpaugh and his sons were on their way back to their home in Ellis County, without a deer, but with a fascinating story.

Sheriff Tim Gage had arrived on the scene to direct his deputies. The short, dark-haired, quiet man took immediate control. He directed that every piece of bone found be measured, a picture taken of it, and a stake secured in the ground to denote its location.

The grave was shallow, so shallow that it had already begun to cave in, which allowed animals to have access to the skin and meaty parts of the body. The animals had dragged those parts of the skeleton from the grave. The legs and torso were still facing in the direction that they had been dragged, with a line of travel immediately obvious. It was hard to say if the grave had been ravaged by raccoons, coyotes, or wild dogs.

Sheriff Gage conferred with Christine Nix, the Texas Ranger assigned to Bosque County.

"My major concern is identification," Gage told Nix.

"Do you know who has missing bodies?" Nix asked.

After a bit of brainstorming, they remembered Arlington had a missing female.

Gage and Nix decided to call in Dr. Gill-King, director of the Laboratory For Human Identification, Physical Anthropology, at the University of North Texas, for more information. Was the skeleton male or female, Hispanic, Asian, black, or white? They needed to know.

Dr. Gill-King explained to Gage and Nix how to begin the excavation of the area. In the meantime, justice of the peace Bennet Morrow arrived, pronounced the body dead for legal purposes, and then directed that the remains be released to Dr. Gill-King for determining identity. It would then be taken to the Tarrant County Medical Examiner's Office. The justice of the peace would have a court order issued later.

Darkness was blanketing the grave site. Sheriff Gage posted a guard overnight, to insure the integrity of the crime scene. The excavation would continue the following morning after small rakes, picks, and shaking tools were brought from Waco.

When Dr. Gill-King arrived at the site at six-thirty the next morning, he personally searched the grave with gloved hands. On bended knee he gently scraped back thin layers of the dry soil. He dug the grave another seven or eight inches beyond the point it had silted back in. Each handful of dirt was carefully screened. Workers, who tediously sifted soil through quarter-inch wire mesh, discovered a large sample of scalp hair, pieces of bones, toes, fingers, fingernails, and teeth.

Recovery of the body had become an interagency effort with five people from the Bosque County Sheriff's Office, two from the Department of Public Safety lab, the Texas Rangers, and Dr. Gill-King. Personnel from the various agencies fanned out from the grave site to look around in the trees and under brush for anything of evidentiary significance. Everything was examined closely, even an old beer can found close to the nearby riverbed. The only thing discovered that was seemingly out of place was a gas receipt. No name. No license. No lead.

Le Noir and Evans arrived early that morning, anxious to take a look for themselves at the body they were convinced was Emelita Reeves.

"This is just super," Le Noir said to Evans, wearing a broad smile as he rubbed his hands together. With the discovery of Emelita's body, their case against Jack Reeves would intensify.

The two Arlington detectives walked to the shallow grave

and stared at the skeletal remains that had been dragged from its resting place. Their eyes carefully scanned the area.

"No sign of clothing," Le Noir said. He ordered metal detectors be implemented to search the immediate area for jewelry that may have fallen from the body, but the results were negative.

"No clothing. No jewelry. No personal belongings. I'd say she didn't voluntarily abandon her home, her child, and her worldly possessions. I think she was removed from her house, either dead or alive, and transported here, where she was buried," Le Noir speculated.

Sheriff Gage walked with Le Noir and Evans along the grassy dirt road that led from the highway to the grave site.

"The person responsible for burying the body could have easily driven directly to the grave site, or could have stopped along the roadway if concerned about scratching their vehicle on the mesquite brush," Gage said, removing his Western hat and wiping his brow on the sleeve of his long-sleeved Western shirt. He carefully smoothed his thick mustache. "He could have carried the body to the grave site."

The three men measured the distance from the roadway to the grave. It was forty-three feet. The grave site would have been accessible to either vehicle owned by Jack Reeves. No tire impressions were taken.

"How far is it from the paved highway to the grave?" Evans asked.

"It's about half a mile," Gage said.

"And how far to the lake?" Le Noir inquired.

"Oh, about three-quarters of a mile."

The body could easily have been trekked in from land or from the water.

The skeletal remains were collected and transported by Dr. Gill-King to his office at the University of North Texas in Denton. The doctor's initial opinion was that the bones found scattered in the underbrush adjacent to Lake Whitney were those of Emelita Reeves. With dental records provided by Le

Noir and Evans, Gill-King would be able to positively determine if the body was that of the missing Asian woman.

Detectives Le Noir and Evans accompanied Texas ranger Christine Nix in her vehicle in an attempt to measure the distance from the camp site where Reeves routinely stayed, to the grave site. By car, the distance was nearly fifteen miles. It would have been much shorter by boat.

It had been a long but productive day. Le Noir and Evans were positive Emelita had been found, that the most important piece of the investigative puzzle was in place. The two detectives were reenergized as they returned to Arlington.

The news media had gotten wind of the discovery of a body in a shallow grave at Lake Whitney. And, although the identification of the remains had yet to be positively determined, speculation was high that it was Emelita Reeves.

Gary Goodman called Detective Le Noir.

"Jack called. He heard the news reports. He claims the skeletal remains couldn't be Emelita because he didn't camp on that side of the lake," Goodman said. "He also told me that he had showered, shaved, and was waiting to be arrested."

Jack's preparing to be arrested? Le Noir thought. *An interesting reaction to hearing of human remains being found at Lake Whitney, when no identity had been established, and no location disclosed.*

October 9, 1995

Tom Le Noir walked to the front of the Coryell County courtroom and took his seat in the witness chair. The historic courthouse, situated in the center of the town of Gatesville, had been the setting for many an interesting trial since the cornerstone was laid in 1897. But the Jack Reeves trial was by far the most fascinating event in recent years.

District Attorney Sandy Gately wanted Jack Reeves in jail.

She didn't want to give him the opportunity to skip the country now that Emelita's body had been discovered, and Reeves was aware that a second murder charge was pending. She was determined to have Reeves's bond revoked.

"There are those who believe that there is no change in the status of the Sharon Reeves case just because the body of Emelita Reeves has been found. Detective Le Noir, could you tell the court whether or not there is any significance to the fact that the body was found in Bosque County, most particularly near Lake Whitney?" Gately asked.

"Yes, ma'am, there is significance," Le Noir said, leaning forward in the witness chair, clasping his hands together. "The location of the body itself, from an investigative point of view, is very incriminating against Jack Reeves."

"How is that?" Gately asked, walking toward Jack Reeves seated at the defense table.

"The body was found in the general location, which would be the Lake Whitney area, that the defendant was staying at during the time in question of her disappearance," Le Noir answered.

"And were you able to establish the fact that Mr. Reeves was at Lake Whitney shortly after Emelita's disappearance?"

"Yes, ma'am."

"And do you recall approximately how long after her disappearance he stayed at Lake Whitney?" Gately asked, looking from Le Noir to Reeves.

"Within twenty-four hours."

"Okay. Is there anything else significant about the particular location of the body in the course of your overall investigation?" Gately was setting up, moving in to expose a new twist to the already bizarre case of Jack Reeves.

"Yes, ma'am. The body is also in the vicinity, same lake, as the death of another woman, Myong Reeves. Another one of Reeves's past wives," Le Noir said, glancing at Judge Zeigler from the corner of his eye. If the judge had any reaction, he held it inside.

Sandy Gately had made her point. Not only had Reeves been charged with the murder of Sharon Reeves and was now under investigation for the murder of Emelita, but he also had a third wife who had mysteriously died. She passed the witness.

Wes Ball, his dark hair and dark beard sharply contrasted by his crisp white shirt, sat at the defense table beside his client.

"Detective Le Noir," Ball began, "did you secure or obtain records showing where specifically Jack Reeves had gone camping down at Lake Whitney on about the twelfth of October?"

"Exactly," Le Noir said, short and to the point.

"And how far, approximately, was this shallow grave site from the location where Jack went camping on October twelfth?" Ball asked.

"From the point where he was camping across the lake from where the body was found is approximately four, four and a half miles," Le Noir said, looking directly at Jack Reeves. "Four to four and a half miles looking from one point to the other across the lake." Le Noir expected a reaction from Reeves, and he wasn't disappointed.

Color rushed to the cheeks of the defendant. He grimaced as anger overtook him. His shoulders constricted as he turned to Wes Ball and murmured something angrily. He clenched his fists in an apparent attempt to control his temper.

Ball's cocounsel, Chris Thetford from Gatesville, placed a calming hand on Reeves's shoulder and began to massage his tightened muscles. Reeves had to be calmed.

"So the body was located on the complete other side of Lake Whitney from where Jack was camping?" Ball asked.

"That is correct."

"And to drive to that location, do you have any idea—from Jack Reeves's campsite, where it was believed to be, to where the body was found, how far that is?" Ball asked.

Le Noir allowed a slight smile at one corner of his mouth.

Ball was good. He knew where to go to get the answer he wanted.

"I drove it and measured it. Of course, there's two different routes that you can take. I measured the shortest route, which was approximately fourteen and a half miles, maybe fifteen miles," Le Noir said, smiling at Reeves.

Reeves sat back, his body relaxing. He nodded at Le Noir, as if in agreement.

"To get there across the lake, one would have to be a strong swimmer, or have some kind of boat, is that right?" Ball asked.

"That's correct," Le Noir said, knowing Ball was doing his best to maximize the distance between the campsite and the grave site. But his tactics wouldn't work—it wouldn't have taken Reeves much longer to drive the fifteen miles from his camping spot to the grave than it would have taken him to go to town for a hamburger.

At the end of the bond-restriction hearing, Judge Zeigler ordered that Jack Reeves could only leave his house for two hours at a time, two days a week. He would have to notify his bail bondsman when he left, carry a cellular phone, and be accompanied by someone from his attorney's office. Reeves was effectively under house arrest.

After the hearing Le Noir spoke with Wes Ball and confirmed that neither Ball, nor any member of his office, had measured the distance from the grave site to where Reeves had camped. Ball also stated that Reeves had not been to the grave site since the discovery of Emelita's remains. Since the movement of Reeves had been electronically monitored by the Tarrant County Probation Department, Evans was able to confirm that Reeves had not been to the Lake Whitney area at all since Emelita's disappearance.

Le Noir called Randy Reeves.

"Randy, this is Le Noir," the detective said. "Can you tell me if you've been to Emelita's grave site, or have you taken your father?"

"No, I haven't been there, and Dad hasn't been to Lake Whitney at all since Emelita's disappearance," Randy said.

Le Noir and Evans pondered the significance of Reeves's statement that the body couldn't be Emelita's when he hadn't camped on that side of the lake. First, the media had no confirmation that the body was indeed Emelita Reeves, and second, only general geography of the area had been released, no specific location. The correlation between the grave site and where Reeves camped should be known only to law enforcement personnel—and the person responsible for disposing of Emelita's body.

Le Noir and Evans were certain that person was Jack Reeves.

October 13, 1995

One year and two days after Emelita Reeves vanished from her Arlington home, Dr. Gill-King issued his official report on the human skeletal remains found near the shores of Lake Whitney.

The doctor's report read:

General—These are the remains of a skeletally and dentally mature human female. The bones show differential bleaching and express an aroma of active decay/decomposition upon wetting. Shreds of dry connective tissue adhere to the lower extremity and spinal column. Some long bones have begun to lose periosteum (dense membrane) which can be seen actively flaking. There is considerable canid scavenging. No insects were present in the shallow grave from which the remains were removed nor with the exhumed, scattered components. . . . One small freshwater snail was removed from the cranium and several were noted on the ground near the remains. No clothing was recovered with the remains.

The remains were initially buried in a shallow pit. . . . The majority of the skeleton was removed by canid scavengers during advanced wet decomposition and distributed over an area. . . . The grave was excavated by technicians from the Texas Department of Public Safety laboratory. Metal sweeps and screening of grave contents were performed.

The Arlington Police Department has supplied one missing person report on Emelita Reeves and two pre-mortem dental x-rays of Emelita Reeves taken 3-23-94.

Sex—The sex of the remains is female based upon morphological, (pelvic and cranial criteria) and metric, (cranial discriminate function and diameters of femoral and humeral heads) criteria.

Population Affinity—Based upon (1) dental incisal shoveling, (2) Giles-Elliot discriminate function, and (3) mid-face anatomy the subject is Angloeuropean-Asian hybrid.

Skeletal Age of Death—Based upon (1) rib phase analysis, (2) sacroiliac joint phase, (3) root closure, and (4) cranial suture status we estimate an age range of 22-30 years.

Stature Physique—Stature is . . . 59.6 to 63 inches. . . . The decedent was a small but well-developed individual at some point in life. The skeleton gives the appearance of sustained physical labor.

Parity—The subject was pregnant at least once in life.

Postmortem Interval—The postmortem interval is six months to one and one-half years. This

estimate takes into account: (1) the condition and
quantity of remains, (2) the absence of insecta,
(3) the presence of the slight odor of decomposition, (4) the presence of adipocere, (5) the fact
of initial burial, (6) the condition of the head hair
recovered, (7) the quantity and condition of connective tissues present, (8) the likelihood of burial
without clothing, and (9) known climatologic information for the area of discovery.

   Individual Identity

	Individual #95100820	Emelita Reeves
Sex	F	F
Skel Age	22-30 y (as of 10-2-95)	DOB 5-27-68
Race	Anglo-Asian mix	Philippina Nat.
State	61.3" + 1.7" (Miss.Person report)	61"
Weight	small frame (MP report)	105 lbs.
Missing	PMI 0.5 to 1.5 yrs.	356 days
Dental	(see below)	

   Pre-mortem bitewing dental radiographs for
Emelita Reeves were compared to the maxillary
and mandibular detition with six points of comparison (extractions and crown) and no inconsistencies.

   Based upon the foregoing we conclude that the
remains known as #95100820 and Emelita Reeves
are one and the same individual.

   Cause and Manner of Death—Because of the

condition of the remains cause of death cannot be determined. Based upon (1) the age of the decedent and (2) the circumstances of discovery the manner of death is homicidal violence.

The report was signed by H. Gill-King, Ph.D.

Once Dr. Gill-King had completed his report, the remains of Emelita Reeves were transported to the offices of Dr. Mark Krouse at the Anatomic and Forensic Pathology Consultants of Fort Worth.

Dr. Krouse laid out the human remains of the victim in a fiberglass tray, roughly in anatomic order. The skull, lower jaw, shoulder blades, long bones of the left arm, the right upper arm, pelvis, most of the spine, legs, several ribs, both kneecaps and a few small bones from the hands and feet lay in the tray. It was all that remained of the once vibrant Emelita Reeves.

There were several bones missing, as well as a number of teeth. The most relevant absence was the hyoid bone from the neck. Although it is a small bone, anywhere from a quarter of an inch or less and about an eighth of an inch thick, it is a stabilizing structure for the muscles and ligaments that hold the larynx in place. If it had been found intact it would have meant a lot. If fractured, it would have indicated that Emelita had been strangled, without it, no determination could be made in a case for strangulation.

The sternum was completely missing, as well as a number of ribs. The remaining ribs were extensively damaged from canids. Again, Dr. Krouse was unable to determine a cause of death based on the examination of that portion of the body.

The skull had been exposed to the sun and weather for at least six to eight months.

A visual and radiographic inspection of the remains revealed no evidence of bone trauma. No bullet holes. No knife wounds. It was impossible to determine if Emelita had been asphyxiated, either by suffocation or drowning.

Although Dr. Krouse didn't know how Emelita Reeves had died, in his official report he ruled the manner of death homicide. "The circumstances of the discovery of the remains, indicating an illicit burial to dispose of the body, provide the evidence for determination of a homicidal manner of death, by means as yet unknown."

Detective Le Noir met with Randy and Debbie Reeves at their Arlington apartment the week following the discovery of Emelita's body.

"I want to give you the opportunity to provide anything that would direct the focus of suspicion away from your father as the responsible party for the death of Emelita," Le Noir said. He was ready to pursue an indictment but wanted to be certain he hadn't overlooked anything.

Randy Reeves began to cry. He shook his bowed head.

"Nothing," Randy said quietly. "I'm afraid my father is responsible for Emelita's death."

Fifteen

Emelita Reeves had desperately wanted to go home. Her friends and family scraped together what money they could, seven hundred dollars, but it wasn't enough to grant Emelita's final wish. The Texas State Attorney General's Office heard about the funding problem and offered the Texas Crime Victims Compensation Fund to fill in the gap. Emelita's wish would be granted in death.

Emelita's family of three brothers, five sisters, and her mother and father awaited her return. It would not be a happy reunion, but one filled with tears of sadness. Emelita was coming home to be buried.

Through the tears of anguish, the Villa family recalled the beautiful, graceful child they named Emelita. She was pretty, prettier than most in the small poverty-stricken town of Cebu City. She had been a beauty queen in nearby Basak. Her beauty had given the family hope. Hope she would marry well and help them out of poverty.

Emelita's parents had placed an ad in *Cherry Blossoms Magazine*. Emelita's picture had appeared along with 261 other black-and-white photo ads. Jack Reeves had been immediately drawn to the picture of Emelita with her shoulder-length dark hair, her delicate features, and her radiant eyes and smile. The description of Emelita under her photo told Reeves she was young, only eighteen years old, had a petite frame of five-foot-three inches and one hundred five pounds, and that she liked magazines, movies, and television. But most of all Jack Reeves liked that she was looking for a sincere gentleman over thirty years of age.

Emelita had turned down three marriage offers before Jack Reeves arrived on her doorstep. One, a musician from New York; another a doctor from Los Angeles; and the third a "bald guy," as her sisters described him. Reeves had sent pictures of his house, his cars, and of himself. Most importantly, he had sent money and a promise to move the entire Villa family to his "estate" in Texas.

As the Villas lamented their unwise decision to marry Emelita off to the "wealthy" American, they recalled the first time they had met the sour-faced, forty-six-year-old, twice-widowed suitor. Emelita had been shocked to find that the man she considered handsome from the photos he had sent, photos she soon realized must have been at least ten years old, was an aging old man. Reeves never smiled. He would only answer questions asked of him, he wasn't interested in becoming close to the family, and Emelita's siblings were curious as to why the man who wrote such passionate letters was utterly disengaging in person. But Jack Reeves had been determined to make Emelita his wife at any costs.

Reeves's victory hadn't taken long. He had courted Emelita, had made the final financial arrangements with her family, and then the wedding had taken place.

Sitting in their tiny shanty waiting for the body of their daughter to arrive in the Philippines, the Villas held a wedding photo of Emelita and Jack. She was a picture in white, her black shiny hair framing her face as a veil of white encircled her head. She smiled pleasantly, but her husband's visage bore no smiles. In all the pictures taken on what was supposed to be a happy day, Jack Reeves frowned, almost scowled, at the camera. He would later give two excuses; first, that he never smiled in photos because he didn't like his picture being taken; and second, because he was angry at Emelita for being fifteen minutes late for their nuptials.

After the Catholic wedding ceremony was over and the newlyweds were in their luxurious Cebu Plaza Hotel room, Jack Reeves and eighteen-year-old Emelita had sex for the first time. An act that she would later describe as feeling like rape.

From that first night with Jack Reeves, Emelita wanted to go home. When Reeves sent her back to Cebu City in 1990 to give birth to her son, she begged her family to let her stay. But they needed Emelita to return to her husband because of the financial support he provided. Emelita asked Reeves to take her back. The family recalled finding a prayer scribbled on a piece of paper after Emelita had flown back to Texas. "Dear Father in heaven, forgive us our sins and the sins of my husband. Amen."

Now, finally, Emelita would be home for good. After the customary three-day vigil and funeral service, Emelita rested in the Pardo Roman Catholic Cemetery, a hillside churchyard cluttered with large rocks and unkempt graves. It was a safe site, one that would not be ravaged by wild animals. A simple marker placed at her grave read: "Emelita V. Reeves, May 28, 1968-October 11, 1994. In memory of her loving parents, sisters & brothers, in-laws, relatives & friends."

As the Villa family mourned the loss of Emelita, they asked for justice for the man they believed killed her—Jack Reeves.

Le Noir and Evans wanted justice for Jack Reeves, as well. They continued their investigation, pressing for an indictment.

October 27, 1995

Jack Reeves, dressed in a conservative dark suit, white shirt, multicolored tie, and electronic monitoring device around his ankle, climbed the steps to the Bosque County courthouse. His attorney, Wes Ball, was by his side.

Reeves was at the two-story, 1875 rock courthouse, built in the center of the Meridian town square, for a grand-jury hearing concerning the death of Reeves's twenty-six-year-old wife, Emelita. For more than seven hours the jury met without returning an indictment. They reconvened on Monday, October 30, to hear further testimony.

District Attorney Andy McMullen presented the evidence of an extensive year-long investigation by the Arlington Police Department, and in particular, Tom Le Noir and Buddy Evans. The case contained a mass of information, intelligence that only Le Noir and Evans had been able to make sense of, at first. Although the officers felt very strongly that Emelita had been killed in Arlington and her body transported to Bosque County, it was decided the case would be tried in Bosque, rather than Tarrant County.

The tactical move paid off with a murder indictment.

The October 31, 1995, headline of the Waco *Tribune-Herald* read: "Reeves held for another wife's death."

The Bosque County grand jury indicted Reeves after the second day of deliberations, with Judge Morgan setting bond at three hundred thousand dollars.

Wes Ball faced the press on the courthouse steps. The media was anxious to hear the attorney's reaction to the second murder indictment. Ball stretched his neck and straightened his tie before speaking. "His [Reeves's] behavior, I guess, was suspicious to some, and her [Emelita's] body has been found, obviously a victim of foul play," Ball said, making an effort to give reason behind the second murder charge.

Within hours a despondent Jack Reeves was again behind bars.

Ron Barr and his wife, Cristi, Emelita's cousin, awaited the news of the grand jury's decision at their Wichita Falls home. They wondered if justice would finally be done. When word finally reached them of Jack Reeves's indictment, Cristi let out a yell. A grin crossed her slender face. "It sure makes me happy that he's in jail," Cristi said, her eyes dancing with excitement.

"I've been sitting here on pins and needles all day," Ron said, hugging his toddler son, who had grown up playing with his cousin Theo Reeves.

Ron and Cristi hoped that Jack Reeves, after posting bond in the case of Sharon Reeves, wouldn't have enough money to bond

out of the Bosque County jail. They wanted Jack Reeves to stay
behind bars.

Jack Reeves's troubles were not over by a long shot. While he
awaited his January 22, 1996, trial date for the murder of Sharon
in the cramped, dingy Bosque County jail, Hill County lawmen
were investigating the suspicious drowning incident of Myong
Reeves. Unlike Sharon, Myong's body had been cremated, but
Hill County investigators believed that, under the circumstances,
the case was worth reviewing.

Hill County authorities analyzed the evidence of a modus operandi and pattern of behavior displayed by Jack Reeves for several years, prepared by Detective Le Noir.

1. The deaths of Sharon, Myong, and Emelita
a. occurred within 8 years of each other
Sharon 7/20/78
Myong 7/28/86
Emelita 10/11/94
2. The common denominator in the relationships
a. possessive/controlling
b. sexual deviance
3. The common denominator in their deaths
a. each woman died during the immediate stage of
        terminating their relationship with Reeves
4. The manipulation of each crime scene
a. Sharon . . . staged to appear a suicide
b. Myong . . . staged to appear an accidental drowning
c. Emelita . . . staged to appear as missing person
        abduction
5. Fabrication of alibis
a. Sharon . . . reconciled divorce
b. Myong . . . filed insurance benefits

    c. Emelita . . . filed for divorce, claimed abandonment

    6. Packaging and storing their property, allowing each preceding wife to have access to said property, clothing, jewelry, etc.

    7. The manipulation of all principals involved in the investigations of each death

    a. the police and witnesses

    b. friends and family

    c. the media

    d. his attorneys and the legal system

    e. the facts and evidence

While Hill County officials were reviewing the chilling similarities between the deaths of Sharon, Myong, and Emelita, Arlington detectives Le Noir and Evans continued to search for Natalie, the Ukrainian woman who'd mysteriously disappeared from Jack Reeves's home in 1992. Could she have been another victim of Jack Reeves's controlling character and vicious temper? The detectives didn't know; they were just exhaustively exploring every reasonable possibility.

Reeves claimed to have information that would lead to the whereabouts of Natalie; however, he and his attorney, Wes Ball, refused to provide that information to Le Noir.

"Jack claims Natalie is alive and well and living up north somewhere," Le Noir told Evans. "He claims she is now married and that her husband is not aware that she once lived with Jack. He doesn't want to embarrass her. Isn't that sweet, Buddy? He would kill her, but he wouldn't want to embarrass her. What a wonderful man."

Evans chuckled at Le Noir's sarcasm. He knew that it was just Le Noir's way of releasing tension as Reeves's body count seemed to grow higher.

But Le Noir gave Reeves the benefit of the doubt. What if it were true? What if Natalie was married and living a happy life up north? Exposure of her involvement with Reeves could ruin her life. Le Noir dismissed his original idea of putting Natalie's photo on the television program *Unsolved Mysteries*.

Wes Ball appeared irritated at the insinuations leveled by Le Noir and Evans regarding Natalie. He lashed out in the media.

"The police want to infer that he's done something to her because . . . [they] can't find her," Ball said. "I'm sure there are other people like Jimmy Hoffa that you don't know where they are, but Jack Reeves isn't responsible."

Le Noir laughed when he read the Ball quote.

At three o'clock on the afternoon of Tuesday, November 7, 1995, Jack Reeves walked out of the Bosque County jail. Reeves's son, Randy, had posted the $45,000 required on the three-hundred-thousand dollar bond for Reeves's second murder charge.

Randy and his father walked to his waiting truck, their heads lowered. Both men were tired. Jack, tired of jail. Randy, tired of the responsibility of handling his father's finances. Jack and Randy returned to Fort Worth, where Jack Reeves would wait for the first of two impending murder trials to begin. One of many hearings requested by both the prosecution and defense was scheduled for one o'clock that afternoon. The order of business: to determine the ground rules for hypnotizing Ricky Reeves, the oldest son of Sharon and Jack Reeves.

Sandy Gately, Coryell County district attorney, planned to hypnotize Ricky Reeves in Austin, Texas, at the Department of Public Safety, to determine if he actually knew more than he remembered about the death of his mother. Although Ricky was away from the house at the time of the shooting, Gately hoped he could shed some light on the incident.

"It's a technique used to help people recall details they can't recall now—there are certain details this might help him remember better," Gately explained.

But even though Texas law allows the use of testimony from

witnesses under hypnosis under limited circumstances, Wes Ball
had reservations about the process.

"We thought we'd bring our tarot cards and wear turbans and
have a seance with candles and stuff," Ball said, belittling the
impact of the hypnosis process.

But Ball was serious when he requested that the defense be
allowed to be present during the hypnosis session, that the session
be videotaped, and that the defense be allowed to take a deposi-
tion from Ricky Reeves prior to being hypnotized to find out
what he remembered.

"If this is a fishing expedition by prosecutors, rather than a
demonstrated need, we don't think it should be allowed," Ball
argued.

A former Tarrant County prosecutor, Ball had seen hypnosis
used once in fifteen years. He argued that hypnosis is normally
used during the investigative process, not after an indictment has
been returned.

J.C. Rappe, an investigator for the McLennan County District
Attorney's Office, disagreed. "You don't always get everything
you want, but you always get more than you had. So in that
regard, every session is successful because you always develop
new information," Rappe told the court.

Ricky Reeves was hypnotized, with no new evidence discovered during the session.

November 9, 1995

Attorneys for Jack Reeves requested a change of venue in the
Sharon Reeves murder trial. "Our request is based solely on the
blanket of media coverage from Gatesville to the Red River,"
Chris Thetford argued. Indeed, the bizarre murder of Sharon
Reeves seventeen years earlier, the exhumation of her body, and
a second charge of murder filed against Jack Reeves had brought
media attention not only from nearby Waco, Texas, but from

Dallas, Fort Worth, and Houston. There was even a film crew from *Inside Edition,* based in New York.

"It's unusual that you have a case that continuously generates so much scrutiny," Thetford said. "Usually there's a down time. We're about two months from trial—there's still intense media coverage and scrutiny."

But Judge Zeigler didn't buy the argument. He knew the people of Coryell County. He knew they would give Jack Reeves a fair trial. The trial would be held in Gatesville, the county seat of Coryell County.

Thetford and Ball filed a number of motions, in anticipation of the January 22 court date:

A motion to dismiss the murder indictment against Reeves. His attorneys alleged that evidence taken during the 1978 police investigation into Sharon Reeves's death no longer existed.

A motion that the judge, rather than the jury, access punishment in the case.

A motion to suppress evidence in the other death in which Reeves had been charged, or any other death in which he might be a suspect.

A motion to suppress evidence seized during the second of two searches of Reeves's home. The lawyers contended that both warrants were issued by municipal court judges in Arlington. The Texas Code of Criminal Procedures allowed a municipal court judge to issue only one search warrant; subsequent warrants must be issued by a higher court of record.

A motion to suppress evidence from what defense attorneys called the "improper exhumation" of Sharon Reeves's body. Attorneys claimed that an exhumation could only be performed when an inquest had not been conducted. A Coryell County justice of the peace had conducted an inquest into the death in 1978.

All five of the motions filed by Ball and Thetford were denied.

District Attorney Sandy Gately had a motion of her own. She wanted the trial delayed until after the Bosque County trial for the murder of Emelita Reeves. "If Reeves is acquitted in Coryell County, it could damage the Bosque County trial," Gately argued.

Wes Ball reacted swiftly by filing a request of a speedy trial. Judge Zeigler rejected the motion to delay. Jack Reeves would stand trial for killing Sharon Reeves, as scheduled.

"It made my day," Wes Ball told reporters outside the Gatesville courthouse. "We want to get this case going. We were concerned about any further delays. But I'm going to have to get real busy."

The stage was set. The trial would begin in less than a week, on January 22, 1996, in Gatesville.

Jack Reeves sat alone in his Fort Worth apartment. Tears filled his sad brown eyes as he thought of Sharon. In two months he would be on trial for murdering the only woman he had ever really loved.

Sixteen

Ninety potential jurors from a pool of two hundred climbed the steps of the Coryell County courthouse. One of the finest Romanesque Renaissance Revival architectural structures in Texas, the courthouse featured a colorful Texas star-patterned interior stained-glass dome. On the second floor, ranchers, housewives, teachers, and businessmen and businesswomen took their seats in the old wooden theater-style folding chairs that faced the judge's bench. From the ninety, twelve would be selected to hear the details of the death of Sharon Reeves.

These were good people. Working people from a rural county where the chief employer, Fort Hood, was the largest military base in the free world. They carried to the courtroom the frontier spirit of their forefathers, who settled on the banks of the Leon River. And who built the double-wall log jail in 1855 dedicated to preserving law and order on the frontier. The size of four phone booths, the jail had been large enough for only the guard. The prisoner had been kept underground and fed through a trapdoor in the floor.

Just as the founders of Gatesville showed courage when threatened by fierce Comanches, the six men and six women who were chosen on the second day of jury selection to hear the evidence in the death of Sharon Reeves, accepted the challenge of determining truth from lies, guilt or innocence.

The players were in place.

"All right. Ladies and gentlemen, we're ready to begin at this time," Judge Zeigler said.

Sandy Gately rose from her chair at the prosecutor's table and approached the jury. A trim, well-groomed professional, Gately appeared confident. She was ready to push forward. Le Noir, Evans, and Berry had given her the ammunition; it was up to her to pull the trigger on Jack Reeves. Just as, she believed, he had done to Sharon.

"May it please the court," Gately began. "Good morning, ladies and gentlemen. My statement's going to be very brief because I think it's important that we get to the testimony and get into the evidence that you came here to hear."

"I am not giving evidence at this time. The evidence that you hear will come from this witness stand," Gately said, touching the railing that enclosed the witness chair.

"So please keep that in mind when either myself, Mr. Ball, or Mr. Thetford are speaking.

"What I anticipate you will see in this case, what the evidence is going to show you in this case, is that in 1978 Sharon Reeves was found dead. She and the defendant, Jack Reeves, had been married, had been divorced. That subsequent to that divorce Mr. Reeves was still in the home. That on July twentieth, of 1978, the police were called to her home in Copperas Cove and found her dead. She had died from a shotgun blast to her chest.

"At that time, the evidence is going to show, although an autopsy was ordered, none was ever performed. That the justice of the peace at that time, without an autopsy, ruled Sharon Reeves's death a suicide.

"But I think the evidence is also going to show that in 1994 an investigation was reopened into the death of Sharon Reeves.

"You're going to hear evidence that an autopsy was done. You're going to hear evidence of new scientific capabilities, which were put into play in order to reinvestigate this case and to make a determination as to what the real cause of death was in Sharon Reeves's case."

Sandy Gately confidently paced in front of the jury. She was sure of her ability to make the jury understand the scientific evidence. Sandy Gately was at home in a courtroom. Comfortable in front of a jury. She was in her element.

"Ladies and gentlemen," Gately said, looking from one jury member to another, "through the testimony, through the evidence that you will hear about blood-spatter analysis, through other scientific tests done, I believe when it's all said and done that you will find beyond a reasonable doubt that Sharon Reeves's death on July twentieth of 1978 was not suicide.

"I believe that you will find beyond a reasonable doubt that the cause of Sharon Reeves's death was murder, and that the person responsible for the murder of Sharon Reeves was that man right there," Gately said, pointing to Jack Reeves, "Jack Wayne Reeves. Thank you."

Gately returned to her seat. Jack Reeves scowled at the competent female prosecutor. He didn't like Sandy Gately. But was it because she wanted to convict him, or because she was a woman he couldn't intimidate?

It was Wes Ball's turn to face the jury. He was a formidable adversary for Sandy Gately. He approached the jury with the same confident air.

"May it please the court, Mrs. Gately, Mr. Huckabee, ladies and gentlemen, I apologize for my notes, my memory's not as good as it used to be," Ball began, perhaps hoping the jury would relate to his pretext of memory loss. "An opening statement is kind of like a road map, kind of tells you a little bit about where we might be going. It's an opportunity for us again to kind of put our point of view across.

"I expect the evidence and testimony that you'll hear in this case is that in 1978 Jack Wayne Reeves was ordered to go to Korea to serve his country in the United States Army; he was in the Army." Ball knew in a military community there would be those on the jury sympathetic to anyone serving their country.

"Sometime, either slightly before or just after that, Sharon Reeves struck up an affair with a colonel, Colonel John Behneman at Fort Hood. After Jack went to Korea this came out in the open and it was known by Jack's children." Ball hoped he had made Sharon Reeves a less sympathetic victim.

"Subsequently Sharon filed a petition in this court, District Court of Coryell County, for divorce. And as the law provides, people who are away from the United States serving their country are entitled to notice, and Jack got notice.

"And I expect you'll hear evidence that Jack returned to Coryell County, Texas, on emergency leave to try to save his marriage. And he came back to the home. And ultimately you'll see divorce documents, I anticipate, from the clerk of this court in Coryell County, that kind of track through what happened in that divorce case. And on July thirteenth, 1978, Jack Wayne Reeves and Sharon Reeves came into this courtroom, and ultimately a divorce was granted on that day by agreement. They signed agreements as to how to divide property and provide for the custody and care of their children.

"I anticipate from the evidence that you will also hear that Jack and Sharon still stayed there in the home after this divorce was granted. The documents were prepared; the judge of the court at the time signed the divorce decree, granting the divorce, several days later.

"On July twentieth, 1978, as Mrs. Gately indicated, I anticipate you'll hear that Sharon Reeves met her untimely death. I anticipate you'll hear Sharon Reeves ended her life because of this affair and the conflicting emotions between her husband of some seventeen years and this Colonel Behneman. And she took her life, and the police were called.

"And what happened next is very important," Ball said, leaning toward the jurors, "and I want you to pay attention to what happened next and the police officers that came to the scene and what they did and how they conducted this investigation.

"In spite of earmarkings of suicide, a suicide note, and other information, they went ahead and processed this case as a homicide. It's a standard procedure to do that. And they did a crime scene search, so to speak, which means they looked for items of evidence. They collected evidence. They collected the shotgun, they collected a suicide note, they collected some other documents and some other weapons from the home, and took them to the police property room." Ball was into the meat of his argument. The Copperas Cove police had investigated the incident, had ruled it suicide, and he was going to make sure the jury knew it.

"Sharon Reeves's body was taken to Darnall Army Hospital at Fort Hood where a pathologist, whose identity may still not be known, examined the body. There was no autopsy performed, but a pathologist examined the body. The justice of the peace conducted an inquest under the law at the time, and ruled that this death, after thorough investigation by Detective Hunter of the Copperas Cove Police Department, and based on the pathologist's opinion at Darnall Army Hospital, that this was a suicide.

"Unfortunately, on August second, 1978, I think, you'll hear evidence that the suicide note was destroyed by the police department and is no longer available. In fact, I think you may hear evidence that reports of the original investigation and officers were destroyed and are no longer available." Ball was slowly moving down the jury box, stopping to emphasize these points.

"You'll see also the divorce documents, some documents signed by attorneys representing both Sharon Reeves and Jack Reeves. Each had their own attorneys in the divorce, documents filed—a document called a 'Motion for New Trial' stating that they had reconciled, and a new trial was actually granted by the judge of this district court."

Jury members' faces remained expressionless. If Ball was giving them cause to ponder, they were giving no indication.

"You'll hear some expert testimony. There are really three components that you'll hear about. Blood-spatter or blood-splatter interpretation evidence. There's a single photograph that exists from 1978. I anticipate the evidence will show that a crime scene officer took a roll of twenty-four photographs, but there's only one in existence, and this is what the interpretations are going to be based on, this single black-and-white photograph. And that definition of beyond a reasonable doubt and the words common sense. You can look at that photograph and you can make some interpretations about it.

"You'll hear some testimony from the medical examiner of Dallas County, Dr. Barnard, he'll give you his opinion."

Ball was winding down. There was only one major point to make before closing.

"Finally, you will also hear that the police department investigators did a reconstruction of this event. They took a shotgun, in fact, they found a shotgun of the same supposed model, brand and so forth, and they took an individual they believed to be the size approximately of Sharon Reeves, and they had this individual sit and go through various motions to see, could a person do this, could a person kill themselves with this shotgun of this stature and size. And not only would it be possible, you'll see from this reconstruction a person could do this. This model was able to do this time and time again, pull the trigger. The same angles and so forth."

Ball had made his point. He had cast doubt on the state's best evidence before it was even presented.

"And we believe from all of the evidence that you'll hear in this case, both from the state and from the defense, at the end of this case you will conclude that they got it right in 1978, and that this defendant," Ball said, pointing at Reeves, "Jack Wayne Reeves, is not guilty of the murder of Sharon Reeves. Thank you."

Ball returned to the defense table where Jack Reeves sat a little taller than he had during Gately's opening statements. Ball had matched Gately's articulate opening.

District Attorney Sandy Gately began the prosecution of Jack Reeves by calling a string of witnesses that portrayed Reeves as an abusive husband.

Larry Vaughn, the short, stocky brother of Sharon Reeves, slowly walked to the witness chair with his head bowed and his eyes fixed on his destination. Vaughn feared Jack Reeves. He avoided eye contact with the man he considered evil, as he told jury members about the night he heard Reeves and Sharon quarreling.

"During the height of the argument, I heard Jack load a gun," Vaughn said, looking at Gately as he spoke, deliberately avoiding Reeves. "I heard my sister say, 'Put that thing away.' "

Shaking his head slightly, Reeves stared at Sharon's younger brother as he left the stand. He had explained to others that it was not a gun Sharon asked him to put away, but his penis.

Ricky Reeves, Jack's and Sharon's oldest son, reluctantly took the stand for the state. Ricky was having a very difficult time handling his father's current situation. He just couldn't believe that his father would kill his mother—it just wasn't possible.

Buddy Evans had first contacted Ricky at his home in Austin, concerning his father's possible involvement in the death of his mother. Ricky had immediately shot Buddy down.

"My dad didn't do that," Ricky had snapped angrily over the phone. "Y'all are barking up the wrong tree."

Sitting in the Coryell County courtroom as a state witness, Ricky was face-to-face with his father. He was ill at ease in the awkward position of state witness. He wanted to be anywhere but Coryell County.

Defense attorney Wes Ball immediately objected to Ricky Reeves's testimony. The jury was escorted from the courtroom to the adjoining jury room to wait for the court's ruling on admissibility.

Ricky Reeves, sixteen at the time of his mother's death, explained to the court that he was working a forty-hour week at a summer job while living with his mother and brother in their house in Copperas Cove.

"Where was your father on July twentieth of 1978?" Gately asked.

"I was told he was at home," Ricky said.

"Okay. When did he get back from Korea?"

"Roughly about two weeks prior to that date."

"Was he expected back?"

"No."

"How did your parents seem to get along after he got back?" Gately prodded.

"I think there was a lot of tension; there were some arguments; they seemed to be having a lot of just talking sometimes; sometimes it was arguing, but there was definitely a lot of tension," Ricky said, shifting uneasily in his chair.

"Were you aware at that time that there was another man in your mother's life?" Gately asked gently.

"Yes, I was."

"Did you become aware at any point that your mother was seeking a divorce from your father?" Gately asked pointedly.

"Yes."

Ricky painfully told the jury that a neighbor had come into the store where he worked and told him his mother had been in an accident. The neighbor took Ricky to the hospital. He'd been unaware that his mother was dead.

"Do you recall anything specifically that happened the night before her death?" Gately asked.

"I was awakened by an argument—sounds of an argument coming from their bedroom. Loud enough to wake me up," Ricky said.

"Were you ever aware of your father being violent toward your mother?" With Ricky's testimony, Gately was emphasizing the abusive behavior of his father, just as his uncle, Larry Vaughn, had done.

"Yes," Ricky said softly.

"Could you specify that situation for the jury?"

"The one that stands out as a definite memory is, I was awakened one night by the sound of him beating her with a belt in the bedroom, and listening to her scream."

Gately passed the witness to the defense, leaving courtroom spectators with the image of six-foot Jack Reeves hovering over five-foot-one Sharon Reeves with a belt and beating her while her children listened to her screams of pain, and her fear.

Wes Ball stood, then walked to the witness-box, where a distressed Ricky Reeves waited for questions.

"I just want to ask you brief questions about this," Ball began. "When to the best of your recollection was that event? I have a note that maybe it was a year before. . . ."

"That's about as best as I could say it was." Ricky stammered slightly.

"It was not during that two-week time frame?" Ball pressed.

"No, it was prior to that, it was prior to him going to Korea," Ricky said.

"And what you heard, was what sounded like somebody being struck and—"

Ricky quickly interrupted Ball. "It wasn't—sounded like it—it was someone being struck," Ricky said sharply.

Judge Zeigler upheld the motion of the defense to disallow the testimony of Ricky Reeves regarding the violent incident between his mother and father one year before his mother's death. The jury returned to the courtroom and heard Ricky explain only the argument he overheard the night before his mother died.

"What was your mother's tone of voice?" Gately asked.

"It wasn't raised, I mean, I barely heard her speak, her voice was not raised."

"What was your father's tone of voice?"

"His voice was raised and loud, shouting at times," Ricky said, before being passed to Wes Ball for cross-examination.

"The night before the argument that you heard, did your mom and dad go out for dinner that evening? You remember that?" Ball asked.

"Yes, they did," Ricky said.

"And back—I think the times have changed, was that back at a time when sometimes folks dressed for dinner, got dressed up, and didn't go just in whatever they happened to be wearing?" Ball asked.

The question seemed to make Ricky irate. "Well, they did, they did wear nicer clothes than you would mow the lawn in, if you want to say that," he said curtly.

"Was it fair to say that during that two-week time frame [when Jack returned from Korea,] your mom was her normal, talkative, happy self?"

"Yes."

Ricky Reeves gratefully left the witness stand.

Randall Reeves, Ricky's younger brother, followed his brother in the successive line of prosecution witnesses. His right hand trembled slightly as he swore to tell the truth regarding his mother's unexpected death.

Sandy Gately knew that Randall Reeves was having an emotionally trying time with the prosecution of his father. She asked her questions, then quickly turned him over to the defense.

Wes Ball approached Randall Reeves with a smile and a few frivolous questions about Randy's ten-month-old daughter. Randy was obviously nervous. Ball hoped to calm him before getting into the meat of his cross-examination.

"If you need to take a break or anything—you need water or anything?" Ball asked, noticing tears welling in the eyes of the witness.

"I'm okay," Randy said.

Ball took Randy back to the night his father unexpectedly returned home from Korea.

"My father came home without letting us know, and we thought there was a burglar trying to get into the door. My mom or my brother, I can't remember, was calling the police. My mother had a thirty-eight that she had—that my father had bought for her protection, and she was telling the person at the door—at this time we didn't know it was my father, to go away or she'd shoot, and my father said, 'Don't shoot, it's Jack.' And I said, 'It's my daddy,' and I opened up the door."

Jack Reeves stared at his son, obviously recalling the night of his arrival in Copperas Cove. Both Jack Reeves and his son broke into tears.

Then Ball took Randy back to the night of his mother's brutal death.

"Now, that particular day in 1978, you were outside, is that right?" Ball asked.

"I was outside playing, I don't remember if I was by myself or with a neighbor," Randy said, his voice beginning to quiver. "I had wanted to come inside, and my mom and dad were talking. My mom told me to wait outside, and I laid down between the two cars. I believe my head was on a skateboard. I fell asleep. And then I heard a noise, heard my father on the phone, and then my father came outside . . . grabbed me and took me next door to the neighbors. Somehow we got to the hospital, I'm not sure when or how we got there."

"Your dad's demeanor at the hospital, was he upset?" Ball asked.

"Yes, sir."

"Did he cry?"

"Yes, sir." Randy Reeves's efforts to hold back his tears failed; they tumbled down his cheeks.

Then Ball led Randy Reeves back to an event that occurred just days prior to his mother's death. An event Ball hoped would show the jury Sharon Reeves was in the state of mind to commit suicide.

"I told my mom I wanted to ride with her, I was afraid that she was going to commit suicide," Randy told the jury. Murmurs were heard from the gallery, but not a sound was uttered from the jury box.

"What happened after you expressed those feelings to your mother?" Ball asked.

"She was happy that I wanted to ride with her until I added the last sentence, that I was afraid she was going to kill herself, and she got upset and got in her car and drove off without me," Randy explained, his voice noticeably shaky.

Sandy Gately approached Randy Reeves in the witness-box for a second time. "When was this occasion that you remember?" she asked.

"It was during that week when my father had come back from Korea, but I can't tell you exactly what day."

"And you say she seemed happy when you asked to ride with her?" Gately wanted to reemphasize the point that Sharon Reeves had not been unhappy or suicidal prior to July 20.

"Yes, ma'am," Randy Reeves's voice broke.

Relief swallowed Randy when Gately passed him to Ball, and the defense had no further questions. The ordeal was over. He had survived.

Judge Zeigler prevented the jury from hearing Sybil Frueh, a friend of Sharon Reeves's, say that a distraught Sharon Reeves told her within two weeks of her death, that Jack Reeves had tied or handcuffed her to a tree against her will.

"She had mentioned that she had been handcuffed to a tree . . . I can't recall whether she said handcuffed or roped to a tree," Frueh, who had worked with Sharon as a Fort Hood secretary, said. Frueh added that she had been horrified when told of the incident.

On the day Sharon Reeves died, Frueh said the two had talked again. "I asked her if she wanted to go home with me, or if I could go home with her," Frueh said.

Although the judge disallowed the statement as hearsay, jurors were allowed to hear that in the days prior to her death, Sharon Reeves changed from the outgoing, real bubbly, real fun-loving person Frueh knew, to someone who was very troubled, worried, and fearful.

Connie Sanders, a former coworker of Sharon Reeves, told the court that on the night of Sharon's death she was sitting on the porch of a friend's house and noticed Sharon drive into her driveway, get out of her car, and go into her house.

"She appeared to be happy, certainly not sad," Sanders said.

Jack Reeves stiffened as Sandy Gately called her next witness. As Colonel John Behneman walked to the front of the courtroom, Jack Reeves glared at his former adversary through narrowed eyes.

"Colonel, I'll show you what's been entered as state's exhibit number three and ask, do you recognize—is this the Sharon

Reeves that you knew?" Gately asked, handing the colonel a photo.

John Behneman choked back a sob as he stared at Sharon's smiling photo. "Yes," he whispered.

Gately asked how his relationship with Sharon Reeves had developed from one of casual acquaintance at work to an intimate affair.

"I was divorced and then I was going to college at night. I met her outside one night. My car was there and her car was next to it, and we got to talking. From then on, it went sort of more familiarity as it went along for the next year, I guess. In 1978 we had decided to try to get married, but of course she had to get divorced first. And at the same time I got—received orders for Thailand and she was to get her divorce. Then we would see what we could do after that," Behneman said, having gained emotional control.

"How did y'all communicate?" Gately asked.

"By letters primarily. Very seldom phone calls. It gets very expensive and difficult to get through," Behneman said.

"What was her state of mind during your communications with her?"

"She was looking forward very much to getting divorced and coming over to Thailand with me," Behneman said with sadness in his voice.

Behneman discussed their plans to marry, his search for wedding rings, and his displeasure at Jack Reeves returning to the house where Sharon and the boys were living.

"What was Sharon Reeves's state of mind the last time that you talked to her?" Gately asked, referring to a phone call the night of Sharon's death.

"She was upset."

During cross-examination, Wes Ball had Behneman admit that his affair with Sharon had begun prior to Jack Reeves leaving for duty in Korea. Sharon had obtained a post office box where he wrote to her, and they stole private moments at his room on base. Their affair had to remain secret. After all, a colonel sleeping with a sergeant's wife would be frowned upon, could even cause career problems.

Ball read aloud a letter written by Behneman:

"Sharon, I was never so glad to hear your voice and message as I was on Friday morning, to hear that your divorce is final. Got me so excited I didn't really know what to say. When you asked about Jack staying in the house until the twenty-sixth of July, I didn't even think about it at the time because I was so excited about the good news of your divorce being final. Of course I don't like the idea of him staying there, but I guess for the kids' sake it might be okay. But I still don't like the idea if he still thinks he can make you feel sorry for him and the kids to the point that you will call the divorce off, maybe that's part of his plan."

"Do you recall writing those words to Sharon?" Ball asked.

"Yes," Behneman said solemnly, as Jack Reeves stared at him with a scowl.

Under redirect examination, Behneman said that Sharon had called him distraught three times in the days before she died.

"I can say she was very frightened," Behneman said, looking toward Reeves.

Sandy Gately had introduced evidence to the jury as to the state of mind of Sharon Reeves on the fateful night of her premature death. Sharon was happy, excited about her marriage to John Behneman, and looking to the future. Why, then, would she commit suicide? With the forensic evidence yet to be presented, Gately would prove that it wasn't suicide.

It was murder.

Seventeen

Detective Tom Le Noir felt pent up. He was used to being on the move, looking for clues, and tracking down leads. Sitting in the small room adjacent to the Coryell County courtroom cramped his style. He wanted to be where the action was. He wanted to see the expression on Jack Reeves's face as Sandy Gately unfolded her case.

Le Noir had been relegated to the fringes of the trial because Wes Ball had convinced the judge that his mere presence in the courtroom would be prejudicial because of the Emelita Reeves trial. Le Noir wasn't fond of his unfamiliar position. After all, he'd been an intricate part of the investigation that led Reeves to trial in the first place.

Inside the courtroom things were heating up. Sandy Gately was ready to attack the suicide claim made seventeen years before.

Michael Galiana, a reserve officer with the Copperas Cove Police Department on July 20, 1978, told jurors he and Officer Rick Carson were riding together when the call came in to go to Pleasant Lane, the scene of a death. Galiana was assigned to the front door of the residence, to insure that no one disturbed the crime scene.

"Did you talk to Mr. Reeves at that time?" Gately asked.

As he had with Le Noir and Evans, Galiana told the court that he and Reeves had begun talking about Korea, maybe because

Reeves had just returned from duty there, and Galiana was part Korean.

"Basically he told me that in Korea you can have sex real easy, that females would come up to you while on duty and give the GIs blowjobs," Galiana said.

Jurors showed little reaction, except for a few widened eyes.

"What was his demeanor as he spoke to you that day?" Gately asked.

"Cool and calm, nonconcerned."

"With regard to the note that was found at the scene, do you know whether or not the signature or the handwriting on that note was ever verified as being Sharon Reeves's?" Gately asked.

"No, I do not."

Wes Ball approached the witness.

"Likewise, you don't know if it was verified that it was not Sharon Reeves's?" Ball questioned.

"That's correct."

"And since the note was destroyed by the police department, no determination could be made now, correct?"

"That's correct."

Richard Carson, who had been with Officer Galiana the night of the shooting, took the witness stand. Gately asked him what his duties were the night of the shooting.

"I remember checking with some neighbors, and I don't think anyone assigned that to me. Just as a precaution, just checking to see if anyone heard or saw anything throughout the night," Carson replied.

"Did you remain outside of the house for most of the time?" Gately asked.

"The majority of the time, yes."

Carson stated that, while posted on the front porch of the Reeves's small frame house, he began talking to Jack Reeves and Officer Johnny Smith.

"What did his [Jack Reeves's] demeanor seem like to you?" Gately asked, glancing toward the defendant.

"He was not upset; a grieving husband, no feelings or anything. It was just like normal everyday conversation that he was having with Officer Smith," Carson explained.

"Was Mr. Reeves's behavior consistent with that of a bereaved husband?"

"No."

"Could you describe the death scene for the jury?" Gately asked, looking toward the six men and six women intent on Carson's testimony.

"The best I can recall, the master bedroom set off from the living room. The victim was lying on the bed at the foot of the bed or around the side of the foot of the bed. She was lying on her back. She had her feet on the floor, and a shotgun was between her legs," Carson said, keeping his attention on Gately.

Although a couple of the jury members shuddered slightly as Carson described how Sharon Reeves's lifeless body had been found, most of them remained expressionless.

The witness was passed to Wes Ball, who asked about the suicide note.

"What I recall about the note was that the note was a—an apology-type note, referring, like, to her husband as, 'Sorry, Big Dick, things couldn't work out.' She may have been referring to another lover, a boyfriend or something. Kind of like she was torn between two lovers," Carson said.

Sandy Gately asked one quick follow-up question to reiterate Reeves's unusual behavior, considering his wife had just been killed. But Ball wasn't going to let Carson's opinion be entered into record without trying to smooth the tainted image.

"Would it be fair to say that there really isn't any normal re-action to someone being informed or learning that their loved one has killed themselves? Do people react differently?" Ball asked, attempting to give the jury a wider range of acceptable emotions.

"I disagree," Carson said emphatically.

Ball had been unable to shake the mental image Carson had painted of Jack Reeves as an unemotional husband.

Officer Johnny Smith testified that the 1978 incident had been investigated as a homicide.

"Even though there were some earmarkings of suicide, such as a suicide note and Mr. Reeves's description of the events, y'all went ahead as a standard procedure and processed it as a homicide, correct?" Ball asked.

"Yes, sir," Smith answered.

Under redirect, Sandy Gately attempted to negate Smith's testimony under cross-examination.

"Mr. Smith, based on your experience as a peace officer and an officer for the City of Copperas Cove at that time, were you comfortable with the ruling of Sharon Reeves's death as a suicide?" Gately asked.

"No, ma'am," Smith said emphatically.

Wes Ball quickly objected. "I object to that on the same basis, not relevant, what his comfort level was," Ball told the judge.

"Sustain the objection. The jury will disregard the response to that question for all purposes," Judge Zeigler instructed. But the jury had heard the officer's response. No one would know how the admission would affect their consideration of the case.

Jack Reeves appeared to be growing increasingly irritated with Sandy Gately. He often stared at her, his jaw rigid, his lips pressed tightly together. Only Jack Reeves knew the thoughts that raced through his mind as the clever prosecutor built her case against him.

The unsuspecting jury sat calmly in their seats as John Davis took the stand. Within minutes they were shifting uneasily in their chairs as a large photo of Sharon Reeves's nude, blood-stained body was passed among them. They noted the blood, the rumpled sheets, the gun between her legs.

Davis told jurors that he had taken approximately ten to twelve photos at the Reeveses's home on the night of July 20, 1978, but that the lone photo presented was the only one he had retained. He explained that he had chosen that particular shot to keep because it more or less covered the entire scene.

Jurors now had a visual idea of how Sharon Reeves looked

minutes after her death. It was up to Gately to explain how Sharon Reeves's body came to rest on the crumpled, bloody sheets.

Dr. Jeffery Barnard briskly walked to the witness stand. The Texas A&M graduate adjusted his eyeglasses and prepared to explain his autopsy report of Sharon Reeves. The entire report, including the condition of the mummified body when he first observed it in late 1994, was covered in detail by Sandy Gately. In Barnard's opinion, Sharon Reeves died of injuries sustained from a shotgun wound to the chest. And, based on the blood-spatter examination, reconstruction of the shooting event, historical information, and scene investigation information, the event was suggestive of a homicide.

Wes Ball asked the Dallas County medical examiner if he was operating on an assumption in reaching his conclusion that the trigger had been pulled with the victim's left toe.

"Well, the part that played a role in that, is the fact that there is a wound on the bottom of the toe, and I find that to be an extremely unusual sort of finding to start out with, and whether it can be done or not and maintain that same trajectory, all of which did play a part," the doctor answered.

"Did anyone ever inform you that the trigger was pulled with the right toe?" Ball asked.

"I think the information was historically that it was triggered by the left toe. Now, I looked at the right toe. There certainly was nothing that I saw there, and there definitely was something that was on the left toe. The historical information provided at the time I did it, was that there was reportedly something on the left toe at the time. So certainly triggering it from—say taking out the left foot, switching to the right foot, would change a little bit of the dynamics, but again, I'm not sure that it would change the overall impression at all," Dr. Barnard said.

Jack Reeves turned uneasily in his chair. It was Reeves himself who had initially pointed out the cut left toe to officers the night of Sharon's death. They had clearly remembered him saying, "She must have pulled the trigger with her toe; it's cut."

To establish him as an expert witness, Sandy Gately asked Dr.

Barnard to explain his credentials to the court. Barnard had graduated from Texas A&M University, interned at Scott and White Hospital in Temple, Texas, served a four-year combined anatomic and clinical pathology residency at Scott and White, then served a one-year fellowship in forensic pathology on Long Island in New York. He stated that he was board certified in anatomic pathology, clinical pathology, and forensic pathology. As chief medical examiner he would oversee some three thousand autopsies a year. Dr. Barnard's credentials were impressive.

Dr. Barnard explained the condition of Sharon Reeves's mummified body when he first observed it at the SWIFS laboratory in Dallas.

"What kind of steps did you take with respect to examination of the wound?" Gately asked.

"After making some measurements of the defect [wound], then measuring from the top of the head and from the center of the body, the wound was then examined for any type of particles or residue around the wound, and then the internal examination was performed. That would include a Y-shaped incision, which is begun from the shoulder area, meets somewhere in the midline, and then the incision is carried down to the pubic area. The skin is then reflected outward to allow visualization into the abdominal cavity, as well as to be able to see the chest wall.

"The chest wall, or chest plate, is then removed to allow visualization of the heart sack, as well as where both lungs are."

"And what were you able to determine from this investigation? What did you see?" Gately asked.

"Well, there was a slightly oval-type shotgun wound of entrance, and there was no visible residue that we could see around the wound surface. The charge, after going through the skin surface and the left chest—and in so doing went through the left side of the heart—went through the lower portion of the left lung, and into the left lateral chest wall," Dr. Barnard explained.

"And from that, were you able to decide or see what the trajectory of the shotgun wound was within the body?"

"Yes," Dr. Barnard said, "because what you do is, you look

at where the defect is and where the main charge ends up, and then you're able to determine which way it's going. The internal examination also showed that the charge went into the left lateral chest wall and created a defect that involved the chest wall itself."

Gately suggested that Dr. Barnard use a plastic model to visually show jurors the trajectory of the gunshot. Dr. Barnard stepped down from the witness-box and held the model in his left hand as he pointed with his right.

"We count down from the top to the bottom, rather than bottom to top, so it would be one, two, three, four, five, six, seven, eight. So it's involving these ribs, and the charge was going from front to back. It's going from right to left, and it's going almost horizontally to make it very slightly downward, that being to the center of the defect," Dr. Barnard explained as he indicated the angle of the wound entry.

"So we're looking at a trajectory that basically is from the front to her side?" Gately questioned.

"Correct, to the lateral chest."

"You stated that the event is suggestive of a homicide. Could you explain to the jury what you mean by suggestive of a homicide?" Gately asked.

"When you take into account the wound having an unusual trajectory, and I did not see any residue on the skin surface, which doesn't mean it wasn't there. But at a point years later I can't tell if that was something that could have been cleaned off by the funeral home or was never there—period, which would say whether that was a contact wound or not a contact wound, meaning that the barrel tip is away from the body. That, in account with the investigative information, I thought there were—these findings were suggestive of a homicide," Dr. Barnard explained.

The jury listened attentively as Dr. Barnard spoke. He explained in layman terms so that they all understood—in his opinion Sharon Reeves had been murdered.

"What about the trajectory was unusual to you?" Gately questioned.

"Well, it's a very sharp direction from right to left going in the lateral chest wall. To fire that yourself you've got to somehow get this weapon in a position that has a horizontal to minimally downward trajectory. Being a long-arm, a shotgun, that is a fairly unwieldy weapon.

"You have to do some manipulation of the body to be able to get that weapon in that trajectory and then get in a position to trigger it to allow for that—and maintain that same trajectory, and that's a difficult thing to do," Dr. Barnard concluded.

"Why couldn't you come out and say simply it was a suicide?" Gately questioned.

"Well, the features surrounding it were not consistent with a straightforward suicide," Dr. Barnard said.

Gately questioned Dr. Barnard as to the overall length of Sharon's body. Sharon was five feet, one and one-half inches tall. From the undersurface of the toes to the groin area was thirty-two and one-half inches. Her right arm, from the armpit to the tip of the right thumb, was nineteen and three-quarters long, and the left arm nineteen and one-half inches long. Dr. Barnard told the court that in his opinion it would have been extremely difficult for Sharon Reeves to have pulled the trigger on the Winchester shotgun. Dr. Barnard's testimony set the stage for the prosecution's most damning evidence, yet to come.

Under cross-examination, Dr. Barnard explained that the fatal wound had shown some kind of serration or tearing, indicating that the bird-shot pattern had started to open up. It looked like the shot had been fired at a distance from the victim's skin—perhaps inches, maybe as much as two to three feet away. Nor had he seen any soot or stippling where the gunpowder had struck the skin surface, again indicating the shot came from several inches to three feet away.

A shotgun essentially has a shell and a cup or something that holds the pellets of the shot, and when it's propelled down the end of the barrel of the gun, that passage begins to open up at some point and the shot spreads out. The resistance of air pressure as the shot goes through the air, causes it to open up more.

A shell has petals and starts to open up. If those petals are open at the time they strike the skin surface, petal marks are visible. If, however, they are already folded back at the time of impact, they are not.

"As a rule of thumb," Dr. Barnard testified, "if you see a pattern of pellets that have struck the skin surface, you know that indicates at least some distance, because it takes awhile for the shot to spread out and make a pattern. For every one inch of pattern, you may have up to around three feet of distance."

Dr. Barnard explained that when a weapon is discharged you have ignition of primer components, creating a kind of explosive effect to cause ignition or burning of the powder. That powder builds up gases and helps propel the projectiles out the barrel tip. And in so doing, some of the powder will escape with the projectile, as well as some of the burnt gaseous material. The soot, the blackened material that comes out, falls on the skin. It can blow into the wound or onto the surface of the wound. The powder itself can also travel. It can travel a little farther than the black material, the soot, but in general somewhere around two feet. Even if it hits the skin, it may not mark the skin.

Wes Ball asked if Dr. Barnard was able to determine whether that material was ever present on the body of Sharon Reeves.

"I didn't see any," Dr. Barnard said, explaining again that it may have been removed by the funeral home, or may never have been present.

The doctor confirmed that the wad of bird-shot had failed to exit the body and was lodged in the back of the victim. The wadding in the back had helped the doctor in determining the trajectory of the shot.

Outside the courtroom, Buddy Evans was readying himself for testimony. He nervously paced the hallway. Although the veteran officer had testified in court on numerous occasions, the Jack Reeves case was by far the biggest case he had ever had a part in. He walked to the door of the courtroom. It was show time. Evans, Officer Scarborough, and Dana Para would be reconstructing the shooting, just as they had done on videotape at the APD.

Evans took the stand and began explaining how the reconstruction would be performed. "By using a carpenter's level, we're able to keep the shotgun level and not downward, which would be inconsistent with the medical examiner's report. We gave the benefit of the doubt by making it level instead of leveling it a little bit up because we don't know how far exactly it was," Evans said as he looked directly at Jack Reeves.

Reeves looked down at the defense table, then at his attorney. He avoided direct eye contact with the detective.

"Would you proceed to allow Ms. Para to see if she can pull the trigger with her left toe?" Gately asked.

But as Dana Para was placing her left toe into the trigger mechanism, Judge Zeigler stopped her.

"Just a second," the judge said abruptly. "Counsel, I think this probably has already been done, but I would appreciate it if somebody in front of me and in front of the jury will check the weapon to see that there's nothing in it."

Smiles crossed the faces of many of the courtroom spectators. Better safe than sorry, they concurred.

"Ms. Para, attempt to pull the trigger with your left toe," Gately instructed.

The dark-haired police receptionist placed her bare left toe into the trigger and pushed.

"Are you able to do it?" Gately asked.

"No."

The gun was rotated clockwise to the left, lined up with the marks consistent with where the wound was on the body of Sharon Reeves, and then Para tried once again to pull the trigger. Again, she could not fire the gun.

The third gun angle failed, just as the first two had done. But to Sandy Gately's shock, when Para turned the gun to the side, with the trigger guard on the outside, to the left, she successfully pulled the trigger.

"What does that position feel like to you?" Gately asked, still overcome with surprise.

"It's awkward," Para said.

The demonstration continued, showing a variety of other positions in which the gun could have been held. Only when the butt of the gun rested on the floor, was Para able to again pull the trigger.

The trigger click silenced the courtroom.

A brief recess was called and Sandy Gately hit the door to the room where Tom Le Noir waited. "Why did the trigger go off?" Gately shouted. Her voice was loud and higher than usual. Her face was flushed.

"What trigger?" Le Noir asked.

"The trigger went off!" Gately said excitedly, waving her right hand in the air.

"Well, Sandy, what are you telling me?" Le Noir asked calmly. He didn't understand Gately's excitement, nor the obvious distress she was under.

Taking a deep breath, Gately said, "Well, the trigger went off."

"Did it go off at the right angle?" Le Noir asked.

"Well, no," Gately admitted.

"So what's the problem?"

"It just caught me off guard," Gately admitted, less ruffled by then.

"Well, she can pull the trigger all day, she just can't pull it at the angle the shot went into the body," Le Noir said.

Sandy Gately took another deep breath. Composed and ready to convince the jury that Sharon Reeves had not pulled the trigger and caused her own death, she reentered the courtroom with renewed determination. She guided Evans, Scarborough, and Para through the remainder of their demonstration, explaining with the aid of a yardstick and the angle of the shot that the trigger on the shotgun could not have been pulled by Sharon Reeves to enter her body at the precise angle explained by Dr. Barnard. Utilizing the measurements made by Dr. Barnard, Gately emphasized that Para's arms and legs were longer, thus actually making it easier for her to discharge the gun.

Gately had succeeded. She had defused the impact of the trigger click heard by everyone in the courtroom. The silence was forgotten and only the optical image of Para awkwardly holding the gun remained in the minds of jurors.

Sandy Gately had one final witness. Tom Bevel, an Oklahoma City police captain with twenty-seven years' experience, was internationally recognized as an authority on bloodstains and crime scene reconstruction. Gately asked Bevel how he formed his opinion on the position Sharon Reeves was in at the time of the shotgun blast.

"Well, the four basic positions that I looked at were with her in the prone position, on the bed, for example, as she was found; possibly sitting on the edge of the bed; upright on her knees, with her knees on the floor; and upright with her feet on the floor, basically standing straight up.

"And in looking at the physical evidence, my ultimate conclusion, based upon the physical evidence, was that the victim was in a standing position with her feet or foot on the floor at the time of the firearm discharge," Bevel explained.

"And with respect to the blood pattern that's found in this photograph, what leads you to make that conclusion?" Gately asked.

"The blood flows on the front of the upper thighs where the blood is going in a downward direction again. What is occurring is that gravity is pulling the blood down. In order for the blood to go along that line of the leg, the leg has to be upright with the blood flow going downward.

"And then the blood flow changes direction. It almost looks like an L laying on its side, again because of gravity continually pulling on that blood as it flows. If a position changes, then the blood flow is also going to be changed. You can observe that in that photograph," Bevel said as he pointed to areas of the crime-scene photograph.

"Could she have been sitting?" Gately asked.

"In my opinion, no. And the reason for that, is that if you are sitting—as I'm sitting up here, and if you can envision the blood coming from the wound down to the thigh area—what you end up having is stains that are approximately seventy to ninety degrees, depending on how much of a gravity arc there is. That would not produce the downward flow.

"In this instance, if there was a downward flow, if there's sufficient blood, instead of running the length of the long axis of the leg in an upright position, it's going to run on the short axis, or to the sides, either the inside or outside of the leg."

Next, Bevel explained how he determined if the wound had been self-inflicted, or if someone else inflicted it.

"Using the information, for example, from the medical examiner's autopsy as to the length of her arms from the auxiliary to the end of the fingers—both of them end up being slightly under twenty inches. Next, looking at the length of the weapon that was reported to have been used, approximately thirty inches to the beginning of the trigger of the mechanism. Then to basically role-play with a similar weapon to try and include or exclude any positions, if possible, again based upon the physical evidence.

"I am depending upon experience from past cases that I have worked, and the training from conferences I've attended. So it's a process of really trying to identify which is the most probable. If you are able to eliminate certain positions, then certainly that is the goal."

"What were you able to determine was the most likely way that Sharon Reeves died?" Gately asked.

"Based upon the trajectory, which is very sharply from right to left and slightly downward, and based upon the physical anatomy, for example, measurements of the victim, the measurements of the gun, it is much more consistent with another person holding the weapon to be consistent with that trajectory, and also where she ended up, than the opposing, which is self-inflicted," Bevel stated.

Bevel held the jurors' undivided attention. They seemed to concentrate on every word he spoke. Jack Reeves, on the other hand, rolled his eyes and tossed his head back slightly as Bevel remarked that in his opinion someone other than Sharon Reeves caused her death.

"Captain, let's assume that Mrs. Reeves was able to sit on the edge of the bed," Gately said as she picked up the shotgun.

"Counsel," the judge interrupted.

"I'm not going to pull the trigger," Gately assured Judge Zeigler.

"I prefer you check it anyway," Judge Zeigler instructed.

After a few moments, Gately continued. "Assume Mrs. Reeves was able to position herself on the bed and get the gun here," as she pointed the gun to her chest, "and assume she was able to pull the trigger, wouldn't that be a possibility in this scenario?"

"Well, it would be a possibility, however, it does not fit the physical evidence of the blood flows that are there," Bevel explained.

"Captain Bevel, we have in evidence the official death certificate of Sharon Reeves, which states that she died by pulling the trigger of the shotgun with her left toe. What is the likelihood that she could stand, put her toe in the trigger guard, and pull the trigger?" Gately asked pointedly.

"Well, I'll state that if she's able to reach the trigger, that is not an impossibility. It is certainly highly improbable, for again a number of reasons.

"Where the shotgun is reported to have ended up, that is not consistent at all. If you end up with a wound to the toe, and frequently you do not, but if you do, it is a common wound that is either a bruise or an abrasion that is to the top of the toe or side of the toe, as opposed to the underside of the toe. The reason for that is, as the discharge is coming forward—and anybody who's ever shot a shotgun can appreciate this—it has a pretty good kickback against your shoulder. The same thing is occurring with the weapon resting, for example, against the floor, the equal and opposite reaction. The shotgun is going backward, and as it does, the toe being in place, the area that is affected is either the top of the toe or side of the toe, and not the bottom of the toe.

"If she was sitting on the edge of the bed, leaning forward, I would expect for her to actually fall forward and maybe even to the extent that her head was actually touching the floor, because the buttocks are on the bed. The gun would be on the floor a short distance away from the edge of the bed.

"If she had been sitting on the bed and pulled the trigger with her finger, she would have fallen back. The gun would have been on the floor a short distance from the end of the bed.

"If she was standing and leaning over to pull the trigger, she would be forward on the floor. The gun would be either under her or some distance out from her on the floor."

"In your expert opinion as a bloodstain analyst and crime scene reconstructionist, based on the bloodstains, the autopsy, involving the trajectory, and any other information which you've used, what is your opinion with regard to how Sharon Reeves was shot?" The courtroom was quiet, waiting for Bevel to answer Gately's direct question.

"That she was in a standing position. After receiving the shot, she fell back onto the bed. In my opinion, it is highly improbable that she was the person who triggered the firing mechanism," Bevel said.

"Can you explain the location of the gun in the photograph, if you assume Sharon Reeves shot herself?" Gately asked as her final question.

"Well, whether it was this picture or some other scene, if I saw it in this position, I would automatically consider that it has been placed there by somebody else."

After the damning testimony of Captain Bevel, Wes Ball needed to make points. He attacked the allegation made by police that Sharon Reeves's panties had been removed from the body after death.

"Did you consider as one of the segments or parts of your analysis the question of panties on or panties off? Was the individual wearing clothing in the panty-line area at the time of her death or not?" Ball asked.

Bevel stated that he had considered the panty issue and had determined that she had not been wearing underwear at the time of the gunshot. He explained that blood spatter was found in the panty-line area and that the blood flow along the top edge of the tan line was simply flowing with gravity in a downward position toward the bed. The panties had nothing whatsoever to do with the blood-flow line.

Regardless of the concession that Sharon Reeves's panties had not been removed from her body after death, the prosecution had produced explosive expert evidence.

Jack Reeves sat next to his defense attorneys, his shoulders stooped, his jaw drooping, a pronounced reversal of the Jack Reeves who had laughed and joked with reporters outside the Coryell County courthouse earlier that morning.

"I've never had this much publicity in my whole life," Reeves had said with a broad smile to reporters. He'd added that he would like to talk with them after the verdict was reached.

But Reeves wasn't smiling now. Bevel's testimony, along with the reenactment, had dealt the defense a severe blow.

After two days of testimony, Sandy Gately rested the state's case.

Wes Ball approached the bench and offered defendant's exhibit number 2 into evidence.

"This is from defendant's exhibit number two, certified copy of Inquest Proceedings, JP Court, number twelve-D-seventy-eight, inquest held by C. W. Storm, JP, Precinct Number one, on the twentieth day of July, 1978, in Copperas Cove, Texas, on the body of Sharon Delane Reeves."

Ball proceeded to read the document to the jury:

"Nature of Information given Justice of the Peace and by
    whom given: Jack Reeves, Husband.
I was called by the Copperas Cove police about seven P.M. and told there was a death at *** Pleasant Lane. The Cove Police picked me up at 7:14 P.M. We arrived at *** Pleasant Lane at 7:16 P.M. There I found several policemen, Chief McDonald, and others. Sharon Reeves was on the bed with legs off bed and there was no life left in her

body and she had a wound in her left chest which appeared to be caused by a gunshot which appeared to be a twenty gauge. I pronounced the said Sharon Reeves dead at 7:19 P.M., July 20, 1978, and ordered an autopsy performed.

DATE OF INQUEST: July 20, 1978 7:19 P.M.

WHERE INQUEST WAS HELD: *** Pleasant Lane

WHERE DIED, OR WHERE BODY WAS FOUND: In bedroom at *** Pleasant Lane, Copperas Cove, Texas

NAME OF DECEASED: Sharon Delane Reeves

DESCRIPTION OF DECEASED: white female, thirty-four years old

FINDING OF THE JUSTICE: The Chief of Police and the detectives made a very thorough investigation. I talked with Detective Hunter and they determined the death was suicide caused by a gunshot wound which appeared to be self-inflicted.
I revoked the Order of Autopsy as the chief pathologist at Fort Hood said the gunshot wound appeared to be self-inflicted triggered by the toe.

STATE OF TEXAS
COUNTY OF CORYELL

I the undersigned do hereby certify that this document is a true and correct copy of page thirty-four of the inquest records of the justice court, precinct one, Coryell County, Texas.

Signed: John B. Guinn, Justice of the Peace, Precinct One, Coryell County, Texas."

Ball passed the document to the jury for each of them to review. After reading the copy of the report ruling the 1978 death of Sharon Reeves a suicide, the jury was excused for the weekend. The judge exempted the usual rule of no television to allow the jury to watch the Super Bowl on Sunday.

The jury may have been impressed with the strong evidence presented by the prosecution, but the last thing they would remember of the trial was a document stating Sharon Reeves committed suicide.

The trial had moved ahead more quickly than either side expected. Wes Ball would use the two-day break to finalize Reeves's defense. He had a bloodstain expert of his own who would partially refute assertions by Tom Bevel. And Ball planned to introduce the reenactment video produced by the Arlington Police Department. Sandy Gately would prepare for rebuttal.

"Basically, we're comfortable with where we are right now," Gately told reporters on the steps of the courthouse. "If I feel like it's necessary after the defense finishes their case, I will try to introduce the additional evidence."

She was referring to the fate of Reeves's other wives.

Eighteen

The buzz around the Coryell County courthouse as Jack Reeves's murder trial reconvened wasn't blood spatters or inquest reports, but the victory of the Dallas Cowboys in the Super Bowl. Spectators settled in their seats and hushed their Monday-morning quarterbacking as Judge Zeigler called court to order.

The defense called as their first witness Max Courtney, of Forensic Consultant Services in Fort Worth. During questioning Ball asked about contact wounds caused by the barrel of the gun pressed against the chest.

"If we assume for a moment that this was a contact wound, the twenty-gauge shotgun, single gunshot wound, what, if anything, does that tell you concerning whether this is self-inflicted or not self-inflicted?" Ball asked.

"Well, I would say it would be an unusual observance based on my own experience and observations that a single gunshot wound at contact range was the result of a homicide," Courtney said.

"Why is that, sir?" Ball asked.

"Well, unless you sneak up on somebody, there's going to be a certain amount of resistance or struggling or trying to get away from the weapon, so unless they just stand there and let somebody shoot them, it's not going to occur," Courtney offered.

Le Noir and Evans had discussed that very point during their investigation. Why would Sharon Reeves let Jack Reeves pull a gun on her, point it at her chest, and pull the trigger? She wouldn't; unless she was used to Jack pointing a gun at her. They had determined that more than likely Sharon was not unfamiliar with the situation, recalling the story Larry Vaughn had told them when he had overheard Sharon say, "Put that thing away," after hearing a clip slipped into the chamber of a gun.

"Let me talk a moment about something called back spatter," Ball continued his questioning. "If a person either self-inflicted or is shot with a shotgun, what if anything—is there something called back spatter that might occur?"

"Just as the blood would go to the gun, it is possible—does occur on many instances, particularly with a high pressure wound like a shotgun wound, where the blood will actually go backward, up range whence the shot came, out to a distance of several feet," Courtney explained.

Wes Ball asked Courtney if there were an assailant present, would he or she have blocked any blood spatter from the floor?

Courtney answered yes, and further stated that had other photographs of the Sharon Reeves crime scene been available, he may have been able to detect if blood were on the floor in front of the victim, or if the blood spatter had been blocked by someone or something. But there were no other photos. Like Tom Bevel, Max Courtney was forced to make his assessments based on the lone photo provided.

"Did you notice in examining the photograph anything about any areas that appeared to be void, that is, there was no blood apparent on those areas of Mrs. Reeves's body?" Ball asked, handing the photograph to Courtney.

To demonstrate the point, Courtney stepped down from the witness stand and stood before the jury.

"One considers the pattern, let's say going down the right leg. There's a pattern where there's almost no blood going down from the front of the left thigh, all the way down the outside of the left thigh, until we get down to, oh, an area just above the knee. And since the knees again don't show, I can't say exactly how far, there is an area where there's not nearly as much blood. But this could be a bloodstain here, resolution. I'm not sure, I can't say for sure. But there certainly isn't much blood, any blood in this area on the front and outer left thigh, upper part," Courtney said, indicating on the photo with his finger the area of the body he was discussing.

"What, if anything, does this tell you concerning the position of Sharon Reeves at the time of the gunshot?"

"That the position was different from that in the photo."

"What about blood flow?" Ball asked.

"There are a number of examples showing where the blood travels down the abdomen. If a person were standing upright, that would be in accordance with gravity. Similarly, you should see some on the legs, also," Courtney responded.

"Do you have an opinion as to how this void of blood in the left, I guess, hip and thigh area, could have occurred?" Ball asked.

"The left leg was cocked up at the time, not allowing the blood to flow down on it," Courtney said.

Ball produced a yardstick. Courtney lifted his right leg and placed it on the stick, as though he were putting it to the trigger mechanism of the gun.

"If the person were leaning over, pushing around a little bit with the leg up like this, then the blood is flowing down at this point and not necessarily dripping, or really not dripping over onto the left leg from the open wound at this point," Courtney demonstrated.

"All right. Based on your training, experience, education, and examination, do you have an opinion as to whether this individual, Sharon Reeves, could have shot herself in that leg-cocked position that you've shown the jury?" Ball asked.

"I'd say it's a possibility that I cannot exclude."

"Can you exclude suicide as a cause of death?"

"No, sir."

Ball then led Courtney into the realm of possibilities of where the shotgun could have landed after it had been discharged.

"How it was held to start with, which way it was leaning to start with. Any actions by any person, let's say, while the victim's falling. Any subsequent rearrangement of it after the victim was lying there dead," Courtney explained.

"Basically, where it lands depends on the forces that are acting upon it," Ball stated.

"Sure," Courtney agreed.

During her cross-examination Sandy Gately concentrated on Courtney's assumption that the gunshot wound could possibly be a contact wound, and thus an unusual occurrence for a homicide.

"Are you aware of whether or not this was, in fact, a contact wound?" Gately asked.

"It is listed as a possibility."

"So," Gately prodded, "you don't know whether or not it was, in fact, a contact wound?"

"I don't know," Courtney admitted.

Murmurs of surprise filtered through the courtroom gallery as the defense called their next witness, Officer E. G. Scarborough of the Arlington Police Department. Ball was introducing the videotape reconstruction of the crime. Scarborough had played a significant role in that reconstruction.

Wes Ball began playing the videotape for the jury. After a few minutes, Ball interrupted the tape.

"Let me stop right there. This discussion about if Ms. Para can get her toe into the trigger guard, can't she?" Ball asked.

"At certain times she can get her toe in there, but it's difficult," Scarborough answered.

"Well, there's nothing about the dimension of her toe and dimension of the trigger guard that prevents her from getting her toe in there, is there?" Ball asked.

"No."

"And when we turn the trigger guard to the side, there is no difficulty at all in Ms. Para getting her big toe under that trigger guard?" Ball prompted.

"She has to stretch at times to get to it, but she can get her toe in it," Scarborough responded.

The tape continued to roll and Ball continued to ask questions concerning the procedures used during the reconstruction.

"Stop right there," Ball said loudly. "You asked her if that was an awkward position?"

"Yes, sir," Scarborough said matter-of-factly.

"Is there any particular rule in committing suicide that says it's supposed to be comfortable and not awkward?" Ball quipped.

"Are you asking for my opinion?" Scarborough responded dryly.

"I'm asking, is there some rule in suicide," Ball shot back.

"There's not any rule in suicide."

"In a few seconds it won't make any difference how uncomfortable it is, correct?" Ball said sarcastically.

"Correct."

The tape continued to play.

Ball again stopped the tape, this time to discuss the trigger pull.

"Some weapons might be described as having what's called a hair trigger? Have you heard that term, sir?" Ball asked.

"Yes."

"And that means the weapon can be discharged with very little finger or—using toes or what have you—with very little pressure, correct?"

"That's correct," Scarborough said.

But without the weapon used to kill Sharon Reeves, the pressure needed to discharge the weapon was a moot point.

Sandy Gately asked that Dana Para enter the courtroom for a live demonstration of the videotaped reenactment.

Officer Scarborough stepped down from the witness stand and pointed out markings made on the clothing of Ms. Para that indicated both the entrance wound and the position on the back where the bird-shot wadding stopped.

Scarborough then handed Para the gun and asked that she place it so that it would approximate the trajectory of the shot.

"Detective, her arms are a little over an inch longer than Sharon Reeves's, is that correct?" Gately asked.

"That's correct."

"And yet at this angle, showing the path through the body, she's not able to pull that trigger?"

"She's also moving her torso as she moves her shoulder to reach—turning her torso. If I might hold her torso to keep her from moving and keep these dots lined up and have her try it again," Scarborough said, placing his hands on Para's torso.

"So when she moves, as she stretches, she's not just stretching, she's moving her body and therefore the angle?" Gately pointed out.

"Exactly."

"Allow her to move the weapon so she can actually reach the trigger," Gately requested. "Detective Scarborough, where does that put the angle of entry?"

"In my opinion, it would probably shoot through the breast and probably enter the arm and miss the majority of the chest area," Scarborough said. "So that's a severe change in the angle where she is able to pull the trigger, is that correct?" Gately asked, reemphasizing the point.

"That's correct."

"Was there any other position where she was able to pull the trigger with her toe, at the same time maintaining the appropriate trajectory?" Gately asked.

"No."

The jury had seen both a live demonstration and the videotaped reenactment of Dana Para attempting to fire the shotgun at the exact angle that the shot had entered Sharon's body. Neither live nor on tape was the young police employee able to fire the gun at the accurate trajectory.

Wes Ball had one last witness on his list—Dale Just. Just was an officer assigned to the legal office at Fort Hood during the time Reeves served as a legal clerk. Although the men worked together, they were not close friends.

"On the night of July twentieth, I received a call from Mr.

Reeves at my house to the effect that his wife had shot herself, and he wanted to know if I could come over to his house at Copperas Cove.

"When I got there I moseyed around, and the police asked me what I was doing, and I told them that Sergeant Reeves had called me. At that time, Sergeant Reeves appeared and he took me in the house and he talked. He took me in the bedroom and showed me to the effect something about where a gun had been on the wall above the bed. I might add, when he did call me at my house, he was very distraught. I got the impression by the way he talked that he was on the verge of crying. And I told him I would come right over, and I did," Just told the jury.

"Did you have occasion later to be at the hospital?" Ball asked.

"Best I remember, sir, I rode with Sergeant Reeves in a military ambulance to the hospital. He put his head on my shoulder and he was sobbing something to the effect, 'What am I going to do,' or 'What can I do,' " Just answered.

The defense was finished. Ball spoke briefly with Judge Zeigler at the bench, then Zeigler announced a recess. Outside of the presence of the jury, Ball spoke before the court.

"The defense has presented—the last witness was Mr. Dale Just. And before we decide to rest, the issue always comes up as to whether my client is going to testify. I just want to put something in the record briefly.

"It's my intention to rest the defense case, and depending on what the state does, if they rest, that will be the conclusion of the evidence. I've explained to Mr. Reeves he has a right to testify, but he also has a constitutional privilege not to, and we've discussed that, and he's decided to elect to invoke his privilege and not testify. Is that correct, sir?" Ball asked, looking toward Reeves.

"Yes, sir," Reeves responded solemnly.

The jury filed back into their seats in the jury box. Judge Zeigler asked, "Who will be your next witness, Mr. Ball?"

Wes Ball stood up behind the defense table and spoke with authority, "Your Honor, ladies and gentlemen, the defense rests."

Sandy Gately had no further state's witnesses, therefore the evidence portion of the trial was officially over. It was now up to each of the attorneys, Gately for the state, and Ball and Thetford for the defense, to summarize their cases to the jury. Sandy Gately would go first.

The next morning Sandy Gately dressed carefully for her day in court. She was a powerful orator, in command of her case, and she wanted to project that confidence to the jury. She chose a bright red dress. Red for power. Red for confidence.

Sitting in the front row of the courtroom were Detectives Tom Le Noir and Buddy Evans, along with Sergeant Dave Berry—the three men Gately considered the heroes of the case. Without their undying bulldoggedness, she would not be standing before the court presenting her final arguments. She glanced at them momentarily, saying a silent thank-you, before beginning her remarks.

"May it please the court," Gately began, "Mr. Ball, Mr. Thetford. Good morning, ladies and gentlemen. I bet y'all thought we'd never get to this point, but we did. I want to thank you all for the service that you've rendered up to this point. I think Mr. Ball and Mr. Thetford would probably agree with me, it's been very obvious that y'all have paid very close attention to the witnesses in this case and to the evidence in this case. And, frankly, that's all that can be expected from a jury, because if you have paid close attention and you do know all the evidence, then you are the ones that are capable of making a decision, and you sit here ready to do so."

Gately explained procedural matters to the jury, then began recapping her witnesses' testimony.

"The first witness that took the stand was Johnny Smith. What did he tell you? First on the scene. He talked to the defendant to find out what happened. He also reviewed what's been described as a suicide note from the deceased. Where did he find the suicide note? The defendant told Officer Smith he found the suicide note in the china cabinet.

"Lieutenant Mike Galiana. What did he tell you? The defendant's demeanor at the time. He wasn't upset. What was he talking about? He started talking to him about how easy it was to have sex in Korea.

"Rick Carson. He told you the same thing. Said the defendant's demeanor was not that of a man who was grieving, it was everyday service, matter-of-fact. He said Jack's demeanor was not consistent with someone who was bereaved.

"Sybil Frueh. She talked about Sharon's state of mind. Described Sharon generally as a happy-go-lucky person. But when Jack came back from Korea, that changed. She talked about her concern for Sharon.

"Connie Sanders, she was the lady across the street from the Reeveses' home that evening. She said she saw Sharon drive up. Approximately forty-five minutes later she looked out the window, a hearse was there. Gives a very small frame of time.

"Randall Reeves. What did he tell us that was important? What could a ten-year-old at that time tell us that's really important? What he told us was, he, the defendant, and Sharon were the only three people in the house that day at the time that this happened. And that the defendant sent him outside and said that he and his mother had to talk. That leaves us with two people in the house. Only two people. One of those two people pulled the trigger.

"Ricky Reeves. Ricky told you that at some point he became aware that his mother was having an affair with another man. That she seemed happy until his father came home. He said that she became tense and they argued. After the defendant came home, his mother was not happy.

"He told you something else very important. That on the night before Sharon Reeves died, he was awakened by an argument loud enough to wake him through the walls of that house. Said his father had his voice raised and was yelling.

"Larry Vaughn. What did he have to tell us that was important? He told you he went to his parents' home in Wichita Falls, that unexpectedly Sharon and the defendant showed up that night. As he was preparing to go to bed he heard a loud argument. But he heard something else, too. He heard the sound of a clip sliding into the butt of a pistol and heard Sharon say, 'Put that thing away.'

"Colonel John Behneman, the man who planned to marry Sharon. He spoke of a phone call that he had with Sharon shortly before her death. What was her mind-set at that time? She was scared. She was upset. I think we know why.

"Now, the defense counsel is going to explain to you, hey, you know, yeah, she was upset, that's why she took her own life. But, ladies and gentlemen, think about what was going on in that house. Who was it that was pulling guns on whom? What were the dynamics in that household at the time of Sharon's death? Sharon had a future to look forward to, a marriage plan, and a way to get away from the defendant."

Sandy Gately sat at the prosecutor's table while the defense took their turn at final summation. She would be back before the jury. The burden of proof fell to her. She would have the last word.

Defense Attorney Thetford stood and approached the jury.

"May it please the court, Mrs. Gately. Ladies and gentlemen of the jury, how many experts is the state going to have to hire in an attempt to convince you that my client, Jack Reeves, murdered his wife, Sharon? And still after all that hiring, only get answers like, suggestive; cause of death, undetermined. How many times is the state going to attempt to re-create the events of 1978 in an attempt to show you that it was impossible for Sharon Reeves to pull the trigger on the gun that night and take her own life, and still get results that show each and every one of you that it was indeed possible for Sharon Reeves to pull the trigger on that gun and take her own life back in 1978?"

Thetford touched on bits and pieces of the evidence but concentrated his efforts on reasonable doubt.

"My client is a human being, just like I'm a human being, and just like you're human beings, and he deserves that day of justice a court of justice provides him. Make the state prove its case to you beyond a reasonable doubt so that he can have that day of justice in this courtroom of justice.

"I want to leave you with one last thought. I was thinking on Sunday night as I was watching the Super Bowl, like each of you were, that a criminal trial such as this one is really not that different from a football game," Thetford said.

Sandy Gately looked at the defense attorney with her brow wrinkled. Football game? She didn't get the analogy.

Tom Le Noir glanced at his partner, Buddy Evans, and mouthed the words ringing in Gately's head, "Football game?" Evans gave a slight shrug, and the duo returned their attention to Thetford's closing arguments.

"If you take the presumption of innocence, which we've talked about at length, and imagine that being the football on one end of the field at one goal line, that's where the game starts. And as the game progresses through the days of trial, through the evidence that comes on the witness stand, the state is under an obligation to pick that ball up at that goal line, and with each piece of evidence move that ball down the field.

"And the only way that ball can be moved down the field by the state is by proving facts to you beyond a reasonable doubt that cause you to believe, yeah, we can move that ball down the field a little bit. And by the time the state rests its case, the state needs to score a touchdown. Because without a touchdown, you can't reach a guilty verdict."

By this time, Le Noir and Evans were suppressing smiles as they pictured Sandy Gately in her red dress running down an open field carrying a pigskin. They didn't get the correlation between a football game and a murder trial—and from the expressions on the jurors' faces they were certain the jury shared their confusion.

"So you have the two ends of the field. And I challenge you to consider the evidence in this case. Hold it up to the test of beyond a reasonable doubt and ask yourself these questions," Thetford continued.

"Is the word 'suggestive' a touchdown word that would allow me to move that ball all the way from one goal line to the other? Is the word 'possibly' the sort of word that would allow me to believe, yeah, the state picked that ball up and moved it all the way down the field and scored a touchdown? Or is the word 'probably' the sort of word that would allow you to believe after hearing all of the evidence, that, yeah, the state scored a touchdown in this case.

"The evidence has shown you that those aren't the sort of words that do cause a touchdown, and since Mrs. Gately has not scored a touchdown in this case, the only verdict that you can enter is a not guilty verdict. Thank you."

Thetford had completed his summation and turned the floor over to lead counsel, Wes Ball. Ball avoided the game analogy and presented a comparison of his own.

"Ladies and gentlemen, y'all remember the story that we had read to us or read as children, 'The Emperor's New Clothes.' That's the story about the emperor who had a suit of clothes made, but there weren't any clothes at all. And he walked down the street amongst the townspeople, with no clothes on at all. No one had the courage to tell the emperor, 'You have no clothes on. That's not a suit of finery.' The emperor had no new clothes."

Ball quickly abandoned the fairy tale in favor of addressing the evidence. He told jurors that everything they heard in the courtroom had been available to police investigators in 1978, and yet a determination of suicide was made. He told them that he'd like to have the suicide note written by Sharon Reeves and be able to bring in a handwriting analyst to say it was written by Sharon, but that the note had been destroyed. He would like to have presented the gun into evidence, but it, too, was missing.

Ball asked the jury, "What led to their decision in 1978? We don't know. Things were destroyed. Police reports were destroyed. Ask yourself this when you go back in the jury room. Do you want to second-guess the people in 1978 in the absence of the information that they had? Is that fair? Is that just? I submit to you, it is not."

The defense attorney then challenged the credibility of the state's witnesses, claiming the Copperas Cove policemen were inexperienced officers at the time of the shooting. Ball challenged Galiana's statements by asking why the state presented testimony concerning sexual conversations by Jack Reeves only minutes after his wife's death.

"Now, there's this talk about this sex business in Korea or something," Ball said. "Why did they bring that to you? To get you mad at him or go, 'That's goofy, you bad person. We're going to make this leap and find you guilty of murder because you had that discussion.' If you decided, 'Hey, I'm going to kill my wife, and I'm going to fake a suicide so that I can get away with it,' what would you do? You'd have crocodile tears, wouldn't you? You'd have faked concern and cried. So I submit to you that's a point for the defense, not for the prosecution."

Ball asked jurors to consider that John Davis took ten to twelve photos of the crime scene in 1978—all of them available for the 1978 investigation. But the 1994 investigation considered only one of those photos.

"Sybil Frueh talked about the trouble; the worried, fearful Sharon. That fits. People who commit suicide are not joyful people.

"Connie Sanders said Sharon wasn't distraught or troubled when she walked into the house. I don't know what that means.

"Randy Reeves tells you his father came home from Korea and he said, 'Mommy, it's Daddy, let him in.' You know the kind of pressure that could put on Sharon Reeves, who is considering leaving her family and going off to Thailand with this colonel?

"Randy also said his dad was upset at the hospital. Now, we've had this cool, calm, collected demeanor at the scene and this upset or crying later. It may be that Jack Reeves is the sort of person that doesn't cry in front of people he doesn't know. But when he's around people that care about him and he cares about, he shows emotion.

"Randy also told you that he was afraid his mother was going to hurt herself, that she was going to commit suicide, and even through the eyes of a ten-year-old boy, he knew there was something wrong.

"Ricky Reeves tells you about tension, arguments in the home.

But what he also told you is that they went out to dinner, his mom and dad got dressed and went out to dinner. What does that tell you? Look at the reconciliation documents and divorce file. It was all available in 1978.

"Colonel Behneman—an officer that's sleeping with the sergeant's wife. She is torn between two lovers.

"Dr. Barnard told you the manner of death was undetermined. He can't come right out and say it's a homicide, can't totally exclude suicide.

"The reconstruction. Well, we've got video one, we've got video two, we've got video three. We've got live one, we've got live two. After you reach your verdict, we'll still be tinkering with this thing, I guess. The case is being investigated during the middle of the trial.

"Was this a search for the truth? Or was this an effort to try to make this a homicide, to pound that square peg in that round hole? That's what it was. And they want you to jump on that same train and help them pound that square peg in that round hole. You shouldn't do it. You can't do it.

"If you find from the evidence Sharon Reeves committed suicide by shooting herself, or if from the evidence you have a reasonable doubt that Jack Reeves caused the death of Sharon Reeves as alleged in the indictment, you will acquit the defendant and say by your verdict not guilty.

"Someday when you get up in the morning and you look yourself in the mirror, do so with the knowledge that you have followed and applied the law in this case, and that you haven't rushed to judgment. That you've applied these rules, and there's a reasonable doubt. And the proper verdict is not guilty. Because the emperor has no clothes. Thank you."

Wes Ball had done all he could for Jack Reeves. He had presented the best defense he could. It was up to the jury to decide if they believed that there was reasonable doubt of Jack Reeves's guilt. But the trial wasn't over. Sandy Gately had the last shot. The last chance to fire her arguments at the jury.

"Ladies and gentlemen," Gately began, "I love the Dallas

Cowboys, but this is not a game. This is not a game for the Vaughn family. This is not a game for Sharon Reeves. This is a murder trial."

Smiles of pleasure mixed with respect crossed the faces of Le Noir and Evans. Sandy Gately was dynamite in the courtroom. In one sentence she had wiped out fifteen minutes of defense rebuttal by Thetford.

"What did Dr. Barnard tell you about why he said suggestive of homicide?" Gately asked the jury. "You've got a small woman, got a big gun. You've got a trajectory that is extremely sharp through the body. You've got somebody committing suicide with a gun at an acute angle. Dr. Barnard found that to be suggestive of homicide because that is not what you expect in this situation if it's a suicide.

"Mr. Ball commented on the fact they continued their investigation during the trial. Wouldn't you expect a good police officer to use all the information that he can possibly get? Would you expect him to shut down because the jury's been sworn?

"We've got this theory out, too. Couldn't have been a homicide, because if he had pulled this gun and pointed it at her, she would have moved or struggled. Not if she was used to him pulling guns on her. Happened in Wichita Falls a week before this. Sharon Reeves's mistake was not believing him this time. And this time it happened.

"Mr. Ball talks about the divorce file. Sharon Reeves's signature is nowhere on here," Gately said while holding up a copy of the "Motion for a New Trial." "Sharon Reeves did not say anywhere in here that she, by her signature, wanted to get back with the defendant. And you'll read, it says, filed herein on the twentieth day of July of 1978. Attorney's signature. This isn't even signed by David Bragg, who was the attorney of record for Sharon Reeves, it says David Bragg, by W.B. Phillips. So not only did Sharon not sign this, her attorney didn't sign it.

"And I submit to you from the relationship that you have seen what was going on in the immediate days before her death, the testimony of Ricky, the very night before her death, her friends and other people talking about her state of mind. Her state of mind was not getting back with Jack Reeves, it was getting away from Jack Reeves.

"Use your common sense. Someone wants to commit suicide, they're going to take the most expedient route available to them. Kind of makes sense, doesn't it?

"But what did you find out? That gun is not the most expedient route, because you found out she had a gun, she had a pistol. She got it out the night that Jack came back from Korea and surprised them. Her instinct was not to go get the shotgun off the wall. It was to get the pistol.

"And don't you think, if she wanted to kill herself, that pistol would be nine hundred times easier to pull than that thing?" Gately said, pointing to the shotgun used in the reenactment. "Common sense. That's all I ask for you to do, is apply your common sense.

"Thank you for your service. I know this is going to be tough on you. I know you'll do the right thing. Thank you."

Sandy Gately had given a powerful closing argument. It was up to the jury to decide if she had proven murder.

After the jury had left the courtroom to deliberate, Le Noir stood and stretched. He had been sitting for hours.

As Wes Ball and Sandy Gately conferred at the prosecutor's table, Jack Reeves stood up and walked out a side door. He held a pack of cigarettes in his hand.

"Where does that door go?" Le Noir asked Fred Cummings, who was standing nearby. Cummings had grown up in the Coryell County courthouse while his father served as sheriff.

"It goes to the stairs, then down and out," Cummings said.

"Well, Jack just walked through that door to smoke a cigarette," Le Noir said with some concern.

Le Noir crossed the courtroom and exited the same door Reeves had gone through only minutes before. As Le Noir swung open the wooden door he came face-to-face with Jack Reeves.

"What are you doing, Jack?" Le Noir asked.

"Don't worry about me," Jack said, taking a deep draw on his cigarette. "I'm not going anywhere. I'm just smoking a cigarette."

"Trust me, Jack," Le Noir said with an air of confidence, "you're going somewhere, and it's not out this courtroom door."

Nineteen

January 30, 1996

It took seven days to try Jack Reeves for the murder of his second wife. The jury had retired to the jury room to deliberate. No one could guess how long it would take them to reach a verdict.

At 5:18 P.M. a note was sent to the judge that read, "We have reached a decision."

Court reconvened and Jack Reeves stood before the court to be presented the verdict. The courtroom was silent until the foreman of the jury uttered the word that rang throughout the courthouse: guilty.

Jack Reeves appeared stunned. Sandy Gately relieved. Le Noir and Evans thankful. The Vaughns wept in gratitude.

But the trial was not over. Punishment had to be assessed.

Collecting himself from the news of the guilty verdict, Wes Ball called his client to the stand.

Ball asked Reeves about his bond restrictions, including electronic monitoring and community supervision. Reeves was asking the court for the same probation with the same provisions.

"You have a granddaughter?" Ball asked the stone-faced Reeves.

"Yes, I do."

"What's her name?"

"Skyler."

"Is that Randy's child?"

"Yes."

"Are you asking the jury to consider your application for probation?" Ball asked.

"Yes, I am," Reeves said without looking at the jury.

"On July twentieth, 1978, did you murder your wife, Sharon Reeves?"

"No, I did not," Reeves said strongly.

"You understand the jury has found to the contrary by their verdict?"

"Yes, sir."

"Are you quarreling with these people or arguing with them?" Ball asked.

"No, sir, they voted like they believed," Reeves said.

Sandy Gately approached Reeves for questioning. Reeves's eyes disclosed his resentment of the authoritative female prosecutor.

"Mr. Reeves, how old would Sharon be right now?" Gately asked.

"She'd be fifty-one. She's four years younger than I was[sic]."

"And your two sons grew up without a mother; is that correct?"

"Yes, ma'am," Reeves said, his jaw rigid.

"And your grandchild is going to grow up without a grandmother; is that correct?" Gately asked, speaking of Skyler.

"Yes."

"And yet you've been able to go on with your life for the last eighteen years; is that right?" Gately said, making her final point.

"Yes." Reeves said without expression.

Gately turned and walked away.

Wes Ball spoke to the jury for the last time. It was his final opportunity to help Jack Reeves.

"You know from the testimony of Mr. Reeves that he's already been on some supervision for approximately almost a year at the probation office. He's complied with all their rules and terms, and if that's not correct, you know Mrs. Gately would have brought you information that wasn't so, so you know he can do it.

"Jack Reeves is fifty-five-and-a-half-years old. Any time in the penitentiary, and the minimum here is five under the law, is a significant portion of the rest of his life. He's not a young man. So he has only so many years left, and I would ask you to give him some years to be with his granddaughter, watch her grow, Skyler, in the community in which he was living."

Wes Ball's job was done. Reeves's fate rested in the hands of the jury, but not until Sandy Gately had her final argument.

"Sharon Reeves was a young woman," Gately told jurors. "She was thirty-four. And it certainly made a significant impact on her life. It ended it. He wants time to be able to be with his grandchild. Sharon Reeves never had the opportunity to be with her grandchild. Sharon Reeves never had the opportunity to watch her children grow up. She hasn't had the past eighteen years that this defendant has had as a free man. She hasn't had the ability or the opportunity to enjoy life that he's gotten away with. And maybe I'm wrong, but I don't think the defendant ought to be given credit for killing somebody close to him, and whom he had pledged to love, honor, and obey, to protect, instead of killing a stranger. I don't think he ought to be given credit for killing somebody that trusted him.

"Your choice, five to ninety-nine, to life. I ask you, make your decision in that range. But make it justice. I know you'll do that."

Two hours after Sandy Gately completed her closing arguments in the penalty phase of the Jack Reeves trial, the jury was back in the courtroom with another verdict.

Jack Reeves would spend the next thirty-five years of his life in a Texas prison.

After sentence was imposed, an ailing James Vaughn weakly hugged Arlington police detective Tom Le Noir. Both men wept.

"It's a good deal," Sharon's father said, leaning on his cane. Vaughn, who suffered from cancer, added, "She never would have killed herself."

Le Noir was blanketed in warmth. He was filled with renewed

life, renewed determination to see Emelita's case through to the same end. *Now we're rocking,* Le Noir thought. *If we can beat this one, we can beat them all.* Months of bottled-up emotions came spilling forth.

"We're satisfied, definitely happy with the judgment," a jovial Le Noir told reporters of the verdict.

But the realization that there was a lot more work to be done, hit Le Noir on the way back to the motel. Le Noir and Evans returned to the room that they had called home during the days of the trial. They were tired of the trial, tired of the press. They wanted to be by themselves.

As they sat quietly talking about the events of the prior seven days, Tom Le Noir's chest tightened. He gasped for air. His heart was racing and he felt like he was on a treadmill doing sixty miles an hour. He was having an anxiety attack.

"We gotta go through it all again," he told Evans as he gulped a glass of water. "We have another battle."

Evans knew Le Noir was referring to the Emelita Reeves trial. They had to present a good case. Reeves had gotten thirty-five years for the murder of Sharon, he could be out in seven.

He could kill again.

Twenty

February 16, 1996

Four-year-old Theo Reeves peered out the window of his uncle's car, his huge brown eyes fixed on the spot where his mother's body had been criminally buried sixteen months earlier.

Detective Le Noir had arranged for Theo, accompanied by his aunt and uncle, Pat and Gary Goodman, Detective Evans, and child psychologist, Dr. Barbara Howard, to be taken to Emelita's grave site. The field trip could be tricky. Le Noir and Evans were concerned about Theo's emotional well-being. But Dr. Howard had approved the experiment—even encouraged it.

Dr. Howard, an experienced professional, had been seeing Theo for several months. The child's social skills had steadily improved and he was beginning to adjust to life with the Goodmans.

According to Dr. Howard, during play therapy, Theo had acted out scenes of hostility and violence between male and female dolls. Theo had labeled the dolls "Mommy" and "Daddy."

"In my opinion," Dr. Howard had told Le Noir, "Theo witnessed an act of violence between his parents involving the daddy doll as the aggressor toward the mommy doll."

Dr. Howard further explained that during play Theo had the daddy doll undress the mommy doll and hold her head under water.

Le Noir had considered all the possibilities from the information obtained from Dr. Howard. It was beginning to add up. The cause of Emelita's death was undetermined. But because there was no trauma to the skull or skeletal remains, odds were, it was some type of suffocation. Emelita's body was nude. No jewelry. No clothing of any kind. *When does a woman take off all her clothes, as well as all her jewelry?* Le Noir asked himself. The answer was simple: when she takes a bath.

Emelita Reeves had made plans for later in the evening of October 11, 1994, the night of her disappearance. She probably went in to take a bath, removing not only her clothing, but her jewelry, as well. While relaxing in the tub, the warm water soothing her petite frame, Jack Reeves violently pushed her under the water until the last breath of life bubbled to the surface.

Now it was obvious; Theo had watched his mother drown.

While at the grave site, Detective Evans held back, allowing Dr. Howard to walk with Theo and observe his reactions.

With familiarity Theo wandered the area surrounding the shallow grave. As he approached the grave site he pointed to the location where his mother's remains had been found.

"Hole," he said.

"What do you know about the hole?" Dr. Howard asked, stooping to meet Theo's eye level.

"Bad man dug hole. Used a green shovel that broke. And a white rake," Theo said in broken sentences.

The young boy repeated the phrases several times, but had no further elaboration.

A green broken shovel? Evans thought as he watched Theo cautiously encircle the grave site, his short legs lifting to step over broken cedar branches. *Military. It could have been a military shovel. They break down for packing. I bet Jack Reeves has just such a shovel.*

The expedition continued with Dr. Howard and Theo walking a wide perimeter of the area. The Goodmans and Evans were not far behind.

Theo indicated to Dr. Howard that there was water nearby. Taking her tender hand in his small one, he led her to a nearby creek.

"Watch out for hole," Theo warned as they crossed a makeshift ramp.

Evans scanned the horizon for the hole Theo was referring to, but saw nothing. Not until he crossed over the ramp, could he observe a significant hole in their path. Theo was definitely familiar with the geographic surroundings.

February 22, 1996

Detectives Le Noir and Evans met with Dr. Howard in her Fort Worth office on Hulen Street to discuss Theo's progress and the possibility of Theo testifying in court. Dr. Howard, highly articulate, explained that after the field trip to Bosque County, specifically the area near Lake Whitney where Emelita's body had been found, she had decided to take the direct approach with Theo and ask him what happened to his mother.

"What happened to your mommy?" Dr. Howard had asked Theo.

"Mommy fell. Hit her head in the tub," Theo said, his bright eyes saddened.

"Who hurt mommy?" Dr. Howard had asked sympathetically.

"Daddy."

Dr. Howard was a good-hearted person. The sympathy and concern she felt for Theo were obvious in her eyes as she related the details of her session with the small, fragile boy.

"In my professional opinion," Dr. Howard said, "I believe Theo observed his mother killed and buried by his father, Jack Reeves."

Le Noir and Evans were filled with a mixture of sadness and rage. Not only had Jack Reeves killed Theo's mother; the boy had watched.

Following the interview with Dr. Howard, Detective Le Noir researched the law that governs children's testimony, and then arranged a meeting between Dr. Howard and Bosque County district attorney, Andy McMullen. Le Noir hoped he was building a strong enough case without relying on Theo's testimony in court. He hated the idea of putting the four-year-old child on the stand to face his father, but he was leaving nothing to chance. He wanted the killer of Theo's mother brought to justice.

Jack Reeves's second murder trial was six months away. As he sat in a prison cell for the murder of Sharon Reeves, Le Noir and Evans continued to reinforce their case against him for the murder of Emelita.

Le Noir again interviewed Dita Hayes, Carolina Mansor, and Maria Langston, all close friends of Emelita. All three Asian women reiterated their previous statements that Emelita was planning on leaving the abusive Jack Reeves, that she never went anywhere without her cell phone and pager, and that she was never seen without both the opal ring and the emerald ring.

In addition, Le Noir spoke with Liza Matthews, another of Emelita's closet friends.

"Jack sent Emelita back to the Philippines when she became pregnant with Theo," Matthews recalled. "Jack was angry with Emelita for becoming pregnant and blamed her for not taking her birth control pills."

During the two years Emelita remained in the Philippines, she wrote Matthews regularly. Her letters were filled with her love of Theo and, at the same time, her fear of Reeves.

"I was troubled by Jack," the pretty Asian-born woman told Le Noir. "The first time he called me after Emelita disappeared he said that he had not hurt Emelita. I didn't say he had.

"Another thing that bothers me is that Jack didn't go to work on the night Emelita disappeared, as scheduled," Matthews said.

"Are you assuming that, or do you know that for a fact?" Le Noir asked.

Matthews assured him that she knew that as fact. Her husband, Tommy, also worked at the Vandorvort Dairy. Concerned about Emelita's sudden disappearance, Tommy Matthews had spoken to the second-shift personnel. They had confirmed that Reeves wasn't at work on October 11, 1994.

Jack Reeves, a contract painter for the dairy and not a regular employee, was responsible for completing his own time card and billing Vandervort. His presence at the dairy on the night of October 11, 1994, could not be confirmed by a time clock or time log.

Liza Matthews had known Emelita Reeves for eight years, longer than anyone Le Noir had spoken with. Like the others, Matthews told the detective stories of Reeves's abuse of his wife. "She would call me crying, saying Jack had hit her in the head," the longtime friend said. "She said she couldn't take it anymore and wanted her independence."

Matthews called the Reeveses's house often, but on October 13, 1994, her conversation with Reeves was markedly different.

"Usually when Jack answered the phone and Emelita wasn't there, he would simply say to page her. But on October thirteenth he started telling me bad things about Emelita," Matthews said.

"What kinds of bad things?" Le Noir urged.

"He called Emelita a lesbian and said she was having lesbian affairs with Mona, Cecilia, Lynn, and Dita. He never talked to me much before that day," she recalled.

Like all of Emelita's friends, Liza Matthews described Emelita as a very sweet person who would do anything for anybody if they needed her.

"Did Emelita have any enemies?" Le Noir asked.

"None," Matthews quickly responded. "The only person Emelita feared was Jack Reeves."

The statement had a familiar ring. That was exactly the response Le Noir had gotten from all of Emelita's friends. Could they all be wrong? Not likely. Emelita Reeves had feared her husband. With just cause.

March 9, 1996

"Tony, you may very well be targeted by the defense as the person they claim is responsible for Emelita's disappearance and death," Le Noir told Tony Dayrit during an interview at the APD.

"I understand, but I didn't have anything to do with Emelita's death," Dayrit said emphatically, shaking his head, his jet-black hair falling across his forehead.

"Will you take a polygraph?" Evans asked, giving the Asian man the same questions provided Jack Reeves before he refused the same procedure.

Without hesitation, Tony Dayrit agreed to take the lie detector test.

Dayrit was a serious young man, quiet and soft-spoken. Obviously a hard worker, maintaining a job at National Semiconductor during the week and working at the Lotus Restaurant on weekends, Tony was planning for his future. A future that didn't include a physical relationship with Emelita Reeves, but marriage to his Filipino fiancée back in Cebu City. He had nothing to hide. No reason not to cooperate with the police. Over the course of the investigation Dayrit had learned to trust Le Noir and Evans.

"Tony, we need for you to account for your whereabouts during October eleventh, 1994 and October twelfth, 1994," Le Noir said. As Dayrit began his account, Le Noir and Evans noted that he never invoked his constitutional right to counsel, but cooperated fully.

"I worked at the Lotus Restaurant on October eleventh. Emelita and I had made plans to meet at the Baja Beach Club in Arlington between 11:00 P.M. and midnight. She had said she couldn't leave until after Jack got home at eleven. I paged her several times that night but never got a response. I also called the house and left a message on the answering machine. I didn't go out. Not able to reach Emelita, I finally went to bed. I had to be at work at National Semiconductor the next morning at nine A. M. for a twelve-hour shift." Dayrit was calm and appeared to be truthful in his account. Le Noir and Evans had no reason to doubt him, but would verify his story nonetheless.

"About two weeks after Emelita disappeared," he continued, "I received a phone call at work from a man I didn't know. He spoke to me in my native Filipino. He claimed that he had come to Texas from New York and was looking for Emelita because Theo was his child and that he was going to get an attorney to bring him back to the Philippines. The man didn't tell me how he got my phone number. He asked me if I knew where Mona worked. He said he wanted to get the camcorder that Mona and Emelita had borrowed from him. He also said he wanted to meet me, but refused to give me his name, address, or any way to reach him."

"Did you know that Jack may not have been Theo's father?" Le Noir asked.

"Emelita never mentioned it," Dayrit said, a hint of confusion in his voice.

The telephone conversation Dayrit described made no sense to Le Noir and Evans for several reasons. First, the caller refused to reveal how he had gotten Dayrit's work number, yet cellular phone records showed that Emelita called Dayrit at work often. Jack Reeves had access to those records. Second, if there had been any truth to the allegation that Jack Reeves was not Theo's father, Reeves would have used it against Emelita in her character assassination to them, to her friends, to the media, and to his divorce attorney. Although Reeves didn't speak Filipino, he certainly had connections with the Asian community and could easily have coerced or hired someone to make the call.

The detectives had reason to believe he might have had the call made in an attempt to find Mona Pate and set up a meeting with Tony Dayrit. Le Noir and Evans believed that, once again, Jack Reeves probably was attempting to manipulate the investigation in another direction.

Reeves's manipulation appeared incessant. He had produced a "log" in an attempt to convince Le Noir and Evans that, indeed, Emelita had been running around on him. However, the "log" was filled with obvious inaccuracies.

An entry made by Reeves on October 11, 1994, the night Emelita apparently disappeared, showed that Emelita left the Reeves's residence at 12:45 A.M. to spend the night with Cecil, but returned at 2:30 P.M. The log indicated that Emelita then left again at 2:45 and returned at 5:20 P.M. The last entry on October 11th showed that Emelita left the house at 11:30 P.M. to spend the night with Dita, one of Emelita's closest friends.

Lynn Combs and Cecilia Zenk had already established that they lunched and shopped with Emelita from 2:05 P.M. until five o'clock. Emelita's cell phone records showed she called the house at 8:45 P.M. on her way home from dropping Pate off at work. Reeves's log was bogus—yet another attempt to jockey the suspicion away from him. In his endeavor to divert the investigation, Reeves unknowingly continued to provide incriminating evidence against himself.

"Jack Reeves is the best partner I've ever had," Le Noir told Evans with a degree of sincerity as they reviewed their investigative report. "He's provided me with more evidence than any other partner I've ever had."

It had been an exhausting seventeen months. Le Noir and Evans had run down every lead, talked to everyone who had known Emelita or Jack Reeves, and had maintained a realistic approach by inviting any exculpatory evidence that would focus the investigation away from Jack Reeves.

But nothing had changed. An analytical approach to the evidence and chronology of events from the time of Emelita's disappearance to the discovery of her remains identified Jack Wayne Reeves, and no other person, as possessing the motive, means, and opportunity to have committed the murder of Emelita Villa Reeves.

Jack Reeves would stand trial for murder—for the second time in less than a year.

Twenty-one

Andy McMullen was a stoic, cunning lawyer. Opponents easily mistook his natural shyness for inability. They were wrong. Often dead wrong. He had prepared a strong circumstantial case based on no forensic evidence. The case was like a book that had to be read chapter by chapter to be understood. If any of those chapters were missing, the jury would miss the whole plot, and he could lose the case. He couldn't let that happen.

McMullen knew that in order to get all his chapters read, he had to make certain that Wes Ball was denied a series of pretrial motions for discovery—he couldn't let Ball rip out pages of his book.

"Man, the judge is getting mad at me. Wes Ball is getting mad at me," McMullen told Le Noir during a break in one of the pretrial hearings. "But this is my last term in office. I'm not out to impress anybody. And I'm not going to let them prepare for this trial. If they read this case, they can prepare. I won't let that happen."

McMullen was true to his word. He stood firm against Wes Ball.

"If we were in Tarrant County . . . ," Ball began complaining to Le Noir later that day.

"But we're in Bosque County," Le Noir reminded Ball. "We all have to play by their rules."

Andy McMullen refused to bend. And he won. The judge ruled

that the defense could not have access to the prosecution's case files.

August 7, 1996

Just as prospective jurors had filed into the Coryell County courthouse seven months earlier to hear the murder trial of Jack Reeves, the Bosque County jury pool arrived at the 1886 courthouse in Meridian for yet another Jack Reeves murder trial. It was the biggest trial the town of 1,390 had ever held. But, even if convicted, Jack Reeves would not suffer the same justice as convicted Bosque County criminals had experienced one hundred years before him.

In the late 1800s it had been legal to hang a man if he had been tried by a jury in Bosque County. Justice was swift, with scaffolding erected right on the courthouse lawn. But the murder of Emelita Reeves was not considered a capital offense. Even if found guilty, Jack Reeves wouldn't die at the hands of the Texas justice system.

Reeves's attorney, Wes Ball, remained optimistic, continuing to de-emphasize the number of victims believed to have fallen at the hands of his client. "I think there are lots of situations where people have lost multiple spouses," Ball told reporters.

But even if that were true, the events surrounding the deaths of Sharon, Myong, and Emelita Reeves had drawn much attention.

On the eve of Jack Reeves's second trial *The Dallas Morning News* ran an article by Chris Payne quoting Arlington chief of police David Kunkle.

"I think the perception among a lot of people is that our crime rate is much higher than it really is because of the media attention," Chief Kunkle said. "We tend not to have high numbers, but we get ones that have such a very high profile."

In 1995 *U.S. News and World Report* ranked Arlington as the lowest in the nation for homicides among cities with populations over 250,000. But the Jack Reeves case, among others, had brought negative attention to the city. Stories of Jack Reeves, sometimes dubbed "the black widower," were seen in newspapers across the country, on the Internet, and on the television news magazine *Hard Copy*.

The notoriety Jack Reeves had received was not over. His second murder trial was about to begin.

August 9, 1996

"Wes, since Thetford isn't sitting in on this trial, who's going to sit by Jack and keep him under control?" Le Noir asked Ball before the trial began.

"I'll be by myself," Ball said.

"You can't do it," Le Noir said, smiling. "There is no way you'll be able to control him. This is going to be hilarious." Le Noir knew that during the Coryell County trial Ball's cocounsel had been able to keep Reeves's volatile emotions under control. But he was certain there was no way Wes Ball could present a defense and keep Reeves in his seat at the same time. Le Noir couldn't wait to take the stand.

Fourteen jurors, twelve regulars and two alternates, were seated from a jury pool of 133 to hear the evidence concerning the death of Emelita Reeves. Judge James Morgan, who served a three-county area, presided.

Wes Ball paced the hardwood floor of the courtroom presenting his opening arguments with silver-tongued elegance to the Bosque County jurors. Ball's demeanor was that of the slick-city-lawyer-come-to-the-little-country-town.

Le Noir and Evans watched the judge, the prosecutor, the jury with interest. Ball's expensive suit and expressive rhetoric didn't seem to be playing any better in Bosque County than they had in Coryell County. Jurors' expressions reflected disapproval. *They think he's talking down to them,* Le Noir thought. *These may be country people, but they're smart.*

With the first state witness called to the stand, Andy McMullen set the tone for the basis of the prosecution's case: Jack Reeves was a lying manipulator.

Rene Lee, a reporter for the *Fort Worth Star Telegram,* was the first to be called. Ms. Lee testified that she had conducted a telephone interview with Jack Reeves shortly after the disappearance of his wife and asked him why he had not filed a missing person's report.

"He said it wasn't unusual for Emelita to leave home for days at a time. He thought that maybe that was the case in this incident, that maybe she just left for a couple of days," Lee said.

Lee also told the court that Jack Reeves had told her that he loved his wife and would like to see Emelita return. However, Lee stated that Reeves failed to indicate that he had already initiated divorce proceedings.

McMullen abandoned the character portrayal of Jack Reeves for the time being, and diverted his attention to the forensic evidence by calling Dr. Mark Krouse, a forensic pathologist with the Tarrant County Medical Examiner's Office. Krouse explained that he had received the bones of Emelita Reeves from the office of Dr. Gill-King, anthropologist. He described how he had laid the bones out in physical order for identification.

Krouse told jurors that from his personal inspection of each and every one of the bones he agreed with Dr. Gill-King that the body was indeed that of Emelita Reeves.

"The bones failed to reveal any evidence of any physical trauma that might have broken any bones," Krouse told the court. "And there was extensive damage, obvious postmortem damage, well after the woman had died, by scavengers. We found enough tooth marks to assume that the body had been partially scattered, exhumed, and consumed by canines of some kind, either dogs or coyotes in this area."

A few of the jury members grimaced at the image of Emelita's body being dragged from the earth to be eaten by wild animals. Their level of discomfort increased as Dr. Krouse explained that the hyoid bone, which goes upward from the base of the skull, and is linked by a ligament to the thyroid and holds the larynx in place, was most probably eaten by animals.

"Scavengers go for the soft tissue very quickly when they find an injured body," Krouse explained. "It's probably in a heap of coyote dung somewhere."

Dr. Krouse explained that it was because of the absence of the hyoid that he was unable to determine if Emelita had been strangled. After lengthy testimony Dr. Krouse was asked for his conclusion.

"In my opinion, the manner of death would be homicide," Dr. Krouse said.

"What do you base that opinion upon?" McMullen asked.

"Several factors. The circumstances under which the remains have been found. The concealment in a—actually, I say concealment rather than burial, because it's obviously such a shallow burial that the remains were easily exhumed by scavengers. The area in which the burial occurred, being very concealed and remote. The lack of any clothing remnants just means the body was most probably nude or clad in extremely flimsy clothing. And the relative age of the decedent. Through my examination of the bony remains, I uncovered absolutely no evidence of any significant natural disease that might have affected bones, which rules out a number of disease states that might have caused death at a young age. Additionally, we performed multiple drug screens on hair that was recovered from the scene, and those screens uniformly came up negative. That indicated that there was no possible role of any drug or medication in the decedent. Based upon all of that, and given the limitations of examination of scattered, fragmentary, animal-modified human remains, it remains my opinion that the death involves foul play."

During Wes Ball's cross-examination, Krouse stated that from the skeletal remains it was not possible to determine if the victim had been submerged in water or drowned. Nor could he say for certain that it was murder. It was simply, in generic terms, one person causing the death of another. Without knowing the mental state of the person causing the death, nor the cause of death itself,

Krouse could only say that in his opinion it was homicide. It was impossible to determine if the act had been intentional.

McMullen had a follow-up question.

"Given the fact that a person is buried naked or in very flimsy garments, in the location where it occurred, does that tell you something about the cause of death?" McMullen asked.

"Not in any great detail, except in my opinion, evidence of foul play," Krouse said.

"Does it indicate a desire to cover something up?" McMullen pushed his point.

"Yes, sir, it certainly does."

"Does it indicate a desire to hide the occurrence of a crime?"

"Yes, it certainly does."

Krouse was finished. Although he admitted that he could not say with certainty that Emelita Reeves had been murdered, courtroom spectators theorized that was exactly what had happened to the ebony-haired beauty.

Dr. Terry Teague took the stand to verify, through his dental records of Emelita Reeves, that the skeletal remains found near Lake Whitney where indeed those of his patient.

"Every patient, no matter who they are, has a unique fingerprint of their teeth. While they may look just like teeth on Xrays—fingers and toes to a . . . to a dentist it's very characteristic. Every patient in my practice, some several thousand patients, could be identified by an Xray of their teeth, virtually one hundred percent of the time," Dr. Teague explained before he was excused.

Jack Reeves glared at the pretty young woman who walked from the side door of the courtroom to the witness stand. She avoided Reeves's steely scowl as she nervously stated her name. "Liza Matthews," the Asian-born woman said softly.

Matthews was the first of Emelita's friends to testify. The first to address the volatile relationship of Jack and Emelita Reeves. Matthews nervously shifted in her seat. Although she and the rest of Emelita's friends scheduled to testify had been encouraged by Detectives Le Noir and Evans to look Reeves in the eye,

Matthews deliberately avoided eye contact. Reeves frightened her.

Liza Matthews told jurors of Emelita's becoming pregnant, of Jack banishing her to the Philippines to have Theo, and of Emelita's return to the United States.

"Are you telling us that when Emelita returned, it was not good from the beginning? Or are you telling us it was good and it deteriorated and got bad?" McMullen asked.

"It was not good," Matthews said, staring at her hands she twisted nervously in her lap, "because of that Russian girl he had. Emelita could not forget about it."

Through Matthews, McMullen established Emelita's habit of carrying a pager and cell phone and always responding to her friends' calls. He also established in the minds of the jurors that Jack Reeves was an abusive bully, by introducing testimony concerning Emelita's last birthday.

"Emelita called me from outside her house in her car," Matthews explained. "She was crying. She was upset. She said that Jack hit her in the head."

McMullen closed his examination of Liza Matthews by asking her to explain the phone call she made to Jack Reeves soon after Emelita's disappearance.

"He told me that he did not hurt Emelita," Matthews said. "I did not accuse him. I just told him that I just hope and prayed to God Emelita was out there okay."

Liza Matthews's prayers for her best friend, a woman she loved like a sister, had not been answered. It was too late. Emelita was already dead.

Wes Ball approached Liza Matthews, apparently with the intention of defaming the character of Emelita Reeves. This was a tactic used by many defense attorneys—attack the people who are not there to defend themselves.

Ball asked Matthews if she knew that Emelita was involved in a relationship with Mona Pate and Tony Dayrit. Matthews denied having knowledge of any relationship Emelita had with either Filipino, other than friendship. Ball then asked her if she was aware that Emelita socialized with her friends, going to discotheques and "things of that sort" without her husband.

The jury listened intently, giving no indication of how the testimony was being weighed.

Judge Morgan recessed Court for lunch, stepping down from the wooden bench at the front of the courtroom. The short, silver-haired, distinguished-looking judge wore a dark blue suit, white shirt, and multicolored tie rather than the typical black judge's robe.

Detective Le Noir roamed the halls of the Bosque County courthouse, anxious for Reeves's trial to reconvene. He strolled in the courtroom before going back to the area where he waited for his call to testify.

Jack Reeves sat alone at the defense table, his back to Le Noir. The detective stood for a few minutes, staring at the defendant. Jack Reeves's hair was turning grayer by the day and he was beginning to show a bit of a bald spot in the back. Le Noir walked to the front of the courtroom, past the wooden railing that separated the judge, prosecution and defense tables from courtroom spectators. There, Le Noir stood face-to-face with Jack Reeves.

Reeves raised his weary head to see Le Noir in front of him. Instantly he rose and walked to the northwest corner of the courtroom. There he stood, his face turned to the wall, like a child taking a forced time-out. Le Noir shook his head, smiled slightly, and quietly left the courtroom.

Judge Morgan returned to the bench and took his seat in front of a large set of windows flanked by American and Texan flags. Moments later the jury took their places in the blue-green upholstered swivel chairs that faced the railed-in area of the courtroom.

The Bosque County courtroom was sparsely decorated, only two pictures adorned the walls behind the jury box. Spectators were relegated to positions on one of the forty long wooden slatted benches. It was a stark setting for ominous proceedings.

Dr. Gill-King was called to the stand by the prosecution to establish an approximate time of death.

"The most significant factor is temperature," Dr. Gill-King said in describing how he derived his opinion. "That is to say, the time required for a body to become skeletonized is really a result of chemistry, and the speed with which that chemistry takes place is temperature dependent. That's why you put things that you don't want to decompose in a refrigerator. The second most important factor in this kind of case is whether or not the remains are buried; so we would expect some slowing of decomposition owing to the fact that the body was initially buried. Then the decomposition speeds up again when the remains are removed from a shallow grave or any kind of grave. It picks back up a bit."

Based on Dr. Gill-King's findings, Emelita Reeves died sometime between April 1994 and April 1995. But the noted anthropologist was unable to determine when the shallow grave had been unearthed by animals.

"Based on my experience, that's going to be sometime within the early part of that time table. When a human dies, the bacteria in the large intestine begin to go to work and they produce a number of different decomposition gases. This is why people bloat when they die. That aroma attracts a wide variety of scavengers, from birds to carnivores. Ordinarily, it's during that period that these scavengers are attracted and haul off components of the body, so it would be very early on," Dr. Gill-King explained.

So far Andy McMullen had established, through testimony, that Emelita's death was a homicide and that her death occurred sometime between when she disappeared in October 1994 and April 1995.

After a brief afternoon recess, McMullen called Lynn Combs, who had been waiting in an outer office for her turn to testify. Detective Le Noir had given her last-minute advice, last-minute encouragement. "Lynn, look Jack right in the eye," Le Noir had told Combs before she entered the courtroom. "Remember, he can't hurt you. Look him in the eye."

Combs took a deep breath and walked to the witness-box, her

head held high, her long, shiny black hair resting on her squared shoulders. She was ready to take on Jack Reeves.

Lynn Combs testified that she and Emelita were close friends and that Emelita had confided in her that she was afraid of her husband. Combs knew that Jack and Emelita went camping regularly at Lake Whitney. Emelita often encouraged her to go along.

"I'm scared of Jack. I don't want to go," Combs said. "Emelita tried to get me to go because she's scared. I'm scared. I don't want to go."

The seven-man, seven-woman jury panel heard more evidence of Reeves's behavior. Combs told how, on October 11, 1994, Emelita Reeves had sobbed at an Arlington restaurant as she told Combs and other friends that Jack Reeves had choked her and pulled her hair during a violent confrontation earlier in the day.

"She said that the next day she was going to see a lawyer and divorce Jack Reeves," Combs reported.

She explained, that during their shopping trip to the Parks Mall, Reeves had called, demanding that Emelita go home.

"Emelita told me, 'when you page me and I don't return your call, call the police.' " Combs lifted her large-rimmed glasses to wipe her brown eyes.

Like Liza Matthews, Lynn Combs explained that Emelita constantly carried both a pager and cell phone. There had never been a time that her friends had been unable to reach her—not until the late hours of October 11, 1994.

Under cross-examination, Wes Ball questioned Emelita's relationship to her husband.

"Now, in regards to Emelita and Jack, would it be fair to say that Emelita Reeves never really loved Jack Reeves?" Ball asked.

"That's what she said," Lynn Combs answered.

"In fact, Emelita married Jack, primarily at the request of her family, and for financial or money reasons. Is that true?" Ball questioned.

"Correct."

"She misled Jack by entering into such a marriage, didn't she?"

"I think Jack did the same thing to her, too," Combs said sharply.

"She called Jack 'grandpa' and 'old man' when she was around her friends, didn't she?"

"Correct."

"And that wasn't a term of endearment. He's old, that's kind of what she was getting at, right?" Ball pushed.

"He looks old to me, too," Combs said, glaring at Jack Reeves, their eyes locking momentarily. She felt a sense of empowerment. She was telling the jury about the mean, abusive, old Jack Reeves that she knew, the Jack Reeves she believed killed her friend.

Jack Reeves quickly turned his gaze away from Lynn Combs. Perhaps because he didn't like hearing himself characterized as "old," or perhaps because Lynn Combs's eyes were no longer filled with fear of him.

Ball continued Combs's examination by asking about Emelita's alleged affairs with both Mona Pate and Tony Dayrit. Combs admitted that Emelita had told her about these liaisons, but that she had no firsthand knowledge of the affairs.

With each question Combs answered, she grew in strength and determination. She looked Jack Reeves in the eyes as she spoke, and each time he turned his gaze away from her. Le Noir was right. When faced directly, Jack Reeves, the bully, was a coward.

As Lynn Combs exited the witness-box and strode across the courtroom floor, she sneered at Jack Reeves. "Burn in hell," she told him.

Outside the courtroom Lynn Combs was exuberant. "He wouldn't look at me, he wouldn't look at me," she told Le Noir excitedly. Her own personal victory had been won.

Court was recessed for the weekend. The state had presented seventeen witnesses in the first chapters of the prosecution's book, a book that told the story of the Reeveses' troubled marriage.

Wes Ball smiled broadly as he faced a number of reporters on the first floor of the Bosque County courthouse. He hinted that the defense's strategy would continue to focus on possible motives of other persons for killing Emelita Reeves.

"Testimony concerning Emelita Reeves's alleged extramarital affairs is not for the purpose of shaming anyone," Ball said. "It's for the purpose of showing certain lifestyles, where they were going, and who they were running around with. What the jury does with it, is up to them."

Clearly, Ball hoped the jury would think Emelita's lifestyle had led to her murder.

August 12, 1996

The trial of Jack Reeves was all the buzz around the scenic town of Meridian. The proceedings were unprecedented in the town that touted itself as the "Top of the Hill Country." Some residents saw the circus atmosphere of TV crews and news reporters as an invasion of their sleepy little town.

Indeed, it was an unusual event. The city, only a few miles from Lake Whitney, one of the state's top recreational areas, usually played host to deer, dove, and quail hunters—not alleged killers.

On the second day of trial, Cecil Zenk, like Liza Matthews and Lynn Combs, stepped into the witness-box and faced Jack Reeves.

Zenk told jurors about Emelita calling her the night of Emelita's birthday in May 1994. She remembered Emelita being very upset.

"She said that Reeves been hitting her on the head," Zenk said in a thick Asian accent. "She was just crying. I meet her in Arlington. I told her to come over to HyperMart, because that's where Lynn Combs work. I told her to come over there, to wait for me, and when she come over there, Lynn already off from work. I meet her over there. She just crying, scared.

"I asked her if she want to go home. She said she don't want to go home that night, was scared. I said if you want, you can stay in my place tonight. And she say okay."

"How did her head look?" McMullen asked.

"She has a bump like a bruise on her head and I give her some ice cube to put on it," Zenk said, pointing to her forehead.

Zenk indicated that Emelita refused to see a doctor or to call the police and report the incident.

"She said her head hurts like it's going to explode," she said. "He kept hitting her."

The next morning Emelita received a page from Reeves. He wanted her to return home. He needed to go to work and there was no one to watch Theo. Emelita left Zenk's house and returned to her own house on Iberis Drive.

To Cecilia Zenk's knowledge, the night of the birthday party was the only time Emelita ever failed to return to her own house at night. "Every time we would go out she always go home afterwards," she declared. "Even like four o'clock, three o'clock in the morning, she always go home the same day."

Zenk also confirmed, as did Lynn Combs, that there were two rings that Emelita Reeves always wore. To their knowledge, she never took them off. Zenk identified both pieces of the jewelry obtained in the search of the Reeveses' home.

Murmurs rippled through the courtroom spectators as the name of Monalisa Pate was called. The gallery anxiously awaited the testimony of the last known person to have seen Emelita Reeves alive, someone the defense had portrayed as Emelita's lover.

Mona, as her friends called her, admitted to jurors that she and Emelita had been having a sexual relationship for the four months prior to Emelita's death. She indicated that they planned to run away together with the thirty thousand dollars Emelita had been promised by Jack Reeves as a divorce settlement.

"Y'all fell in love; is that right?" Wes Ball asked.

"Yes," Pate responded softly in English that was less than perfect.

Pate admitted to Ball that once she learned that Emelita was trying to have a relationship with the Asian male she was concerned that Emelita might like the attention of Tony [Dayrit] rather than her. But Pate fell short of admitting any jealousy.

"I do not have any jealousy," she told jurors, indicating that Emelita's marriage never gave her cause to feel jealous.

Wes Ball was true to his plan. He was attempting to put doubt in the minds of jurors by presenting other people who might have had motives to kill Emelita—including Monalisa Pate.

Other state witnesses that appeared included Dita Hayes, who testified that she was very upset when she learned that Jack Reeves was telling friends and police that she was lesbian and involved romantically with Emelita.

"It just make me mad that somebody tell that I am lesbian. I am the mother of two children. I don't want that because I'm a Christian," Hayes explained. She, too, had a heavy Asian accent. "That why I called him Jack. I don't want nobody to tell me I am lesbian. My husband going to get mad at me."

Oxedine and Hirschman, the two officers who first investigated the welfare check, also testified. A few minor witnesses followed. Court adjourned at 5:35 P.M.

Twenty-two

August 13, 1996

Pat Goodman climbed the steps of the white stone Bosque County courthouse, her husband Gary by her side. The clock at the top of the two-story structure read 8:30 A.M. Pat was scheduled to testify sometime during the third day of her half brother's murder trial. She wasn't sure exactly what time.

Shortly before the midmorning recess, Pat was called. Her hostility toward Reeves was evident from the beginning of her testimony.

"Just for the record, would you point out your half brother?" McMullen asked.

"The man with the fake glasses on right there," Pat Goodman said, pointing to Reeves.

"Did you say fake glasses?" McMullen asked, not sure he understood his witness.

"He's never needed glasses before, as far as I know," Goodman replied sarcastically.

McMullen shook his head. He didn't need an antagonistic witness. No one in the courtroom understood why the animosity existed between Pat and Jack. Maybe it was jealousy that Jack apparently lived larger than the Goodmans, especially since Gary Goodman had given one of his paint contracts to Reeves to help him out when he first left the military; perhaps it was childhood events known only to the siblings; or possibly, Pat just disliked the attitude Reeves took toward women in general, and his wives in particular.

"We would ask the record reflect the witness has identified the accused," the prosecutor said, moving on in his questioning.

"Mrs. Goodman, are you presently the managing conservator of the son of Jack Reeves, Theo Reeves?"

"Yes, we are."

"How long have you been responsible for Theo Reeves?"

"Since one week after he [Reeves] was arrested in the murder of Sharon," Pat said.

Wes Ball was on his feet. "Objection, Your Honor. May we approach the bench?"

Wes Ball was livid. He had filed a motion to squelch any reference to other murders the defendant was convicted of or suspected of committing. He knew that if the jury heard about the conviction of his client for the murder of Sharon Reeves, it would be overwhelmingly prejudicial. Although the remark was stricken from the record, the jury had heard what Pat Goodman wanted them to hear.

McMullen continued his questioning.

"Was Theo able to talk?" The prosecutor asked.

"He said basically two words. Meemee meant anything liquid, especially milk. Dada referred to any male," Pat Goodman answered.

"Would you classify his development as normal or abnormal for a child his age?"

"It was abnormal. We had him tested in the Arlington Independent School District. He was two and a half years behind his age level," Goodman said, sadness momentarily replacing her anger.

"Since coming to live with you, has he improved?" McMullen asked.

"He is now within six months of his age level," Pat answered, a slight smile on her lips.

McMullen turned his attention to the morning of October 13,

1994, and a conversation Pat Goodman had with Reeves on the telephone.

"When I answered the phone he said, 'Patty,' which was my childhood nickname, 'I think I'm in trouble.' He was real breathless and he was on his mobile phone. You can tell by the sound. That's when he proceeded to tell me he had a visit from the officers the night before in his home," Goodman stated.

Reeves had told his sister that police officers had come to his home and he had refused to let them in the house.

"I said that was pretty stupid considering that if he didn't have anything to hide he should have let them in," Goodman said. "He said 'they ticked me off.' The word he used was 'pissed.'

"He asked me if I would go to I.H.O.P. with him and Theo. Theo had been with him, driving around all night long, and he was hungry."

Pat Goodman continued the explanation by saying she had a bad feeling about the meeting with Reeves and had left a note for her husband on the white message board at the back door of her house. Reeves had called again on his cellular and Goodman had met him in front of her house. He'd driven her and Theo to the restaurant in his truck.

"How did the defendant look that morning?" McMullen asked.

"He had huge circles under his eyes. He was shaky. His eyes were bloodshot. When we went into the pancake house we all sat down. He went and got a newspaper and started flipping through it. And I asked what he was looking for. He said, 'Well, I thought there might be something in here about Emelita missing.' "

"Had he turned in any kind of missing person's report?" McMullen questioned.

"No."

Goodman explained that Reeves told her at the restaurant that Emelita had just disappeared; he didn't know where she was. He had gone four-wheeling at Fort Hood with Theo.

"I thought that was kind of strange, because the man doesn't like dirt, and he would go four-wheeling?" The event seemed farfetched to Goodman. "For one of his trucks to get dirt on it would be kind of beyond comprehension.

"And then he said he had gone to buy a new couch. That was a little out of character, too, because furniture has never been his thing."

Jack Reeves sat quietly staring at his half-sister. His steely eyes reflected a mixture of sadness and anger at what he obviously considered betrayal.

"After I saw the couch, I said, 'My God, why didn't you call Gary or Randy to come help you?' " Goodman continued. "It was a huge sectional. He said he didn't want to bother anybody. But he had called Gary before at ten-thirty at night one time because his air-conditioner hose was leaking in the hallway and he didn't know how to stop it."

Goodman explained that Reeves told her that the dogs had chewed the sofa and he wanted to surprise Emelita with new furniture when she returned. Reeves had described how he had to tear the hide-a-bed out of the couch and rip the arms off in order to move it out. The witness remembered making the comment to Reeves that someone else could probably have used the sofa he had discarded.

Pat Goodman described her relationship with her half brother as casual—visits mostly limited to holidays. She had not seen or heard from Reeves from March 1994 until the day of Emelita's birthday in May. The siblings had run into one another by accident at a local donut shop and he'd called his half-sister that afternoon—just to talk.

"He asked if we were still looking for a pop-up camper," Goodman said, referring to the conversation she had with Reeves. "I told him no, we are putting Bengie in braces, that we couldn't buy a pop up. That we'd just continue making a tent city when we go camping. He asked if we would use one if we had one. I told him we couldn't afford one. And he said, 'Well, I just bought you one.' I told him we couldn't pay for it. He said, 'Well, I feel guilty because I have got this big fifth-wheel and you've only got tents.' "

Goodman went on to tell jurors that Reeves arrived at her house later with a check for the balance of the camper cost, less his initial meager down payment. Reeves told her not to tell Emelita about the camper because she would be mad. Then the next day he arrived back at the house with a broken finger. He claimed he and Emelita had had a big fight over the camper. The broken finger came when he attempted to block one of her punches.

Reeves had begun showing up at Pat and Gary's house with some regularity after Emelita's birthday. He would sit for hours and talk about Emelita—and sex.

Reeves claimed that Emelita had attempted to seduce his son Randy. He told the Goodmans that Emelita had heard that Randy had a "pretty one." She wanted to see for herself. According to Reeves, the term a "pretty one" originated with Myong, who had seen Randy in the shower one day. Reeves had related the story to Emelita, who then claimed she wanted to see for herself.

Reeves also told his half-sister about Emelita's lesbian relationships and that he didn't care as long as it didn't involve another man. He even liked to watch, he told her.

Reeves complained frequently about Emelita being gone at night all the time. He also complained that Emelita was unresponsive during their sexual relations.

"He said she just laid there and it really made him angry," Pat Goodman testified. "I told him that when you buy someone, you can't buy love. What did he expect?"

"And it was your understanding that Emelita was a mail-order bride, so to speak?" McMullen asked.

"Yes."

Under cross-examination Wes Ball insinuated that the Goodmans were jealous or envious of the gadgets, toys, big-screen television, stereo, and other material things owned by Jack Reeves. He produced federal tax liens against the Goodmans. Perhaps Ball believed financial jealousy would explain the hostility displayed by Pat Goodman toward his client. She denied the allegation, contending that the idea of taking the big-screen television from Reeves's home to hers was Randy's, and she was simply storing it for Reeves, as a favor.

Judge Morgan called for a short recess and excused the jury. As the fourteen members of the panel were filing out, Pat Goodman glared at Reeves and whispered the words, "You're sorry," with disdain. Reeves removed his glasses and shook his head at the remark. Wes Ball would later ask that the remark be stricken from the record.

On redirect McMullen asked Pat Goodman about money being sent to Emelita's family, and what Reeves had told her about it.

"He kept insisting that when he would talk to her family from overseas they said they were still getting money from Emelita, and he couldn't figure [it] out. You know, if she was alive what she was doing to earn that money? He said that she must be a call girl, because she had no Social Security number."

Before Ball excused Pat Goodman from the stand he had one last correction to make. "Do you know whether or not Jack needs glasses to read documents?"

"Well, he is over forty, I'm sure he might need glasses just to read," she conceded.

Wes Ball took the glasses from his client and approached the witness. "Is that a bifocal there at the bottom with the larger, increased magnification?" Ball asked, pointing to the clear lenses.

"That's probably about a two point seventy-five, something like that," Goodman answered.

"All right. So these aren't fake. These are corrective lenses, aren't they?" Ball prompted.

"They are reading glasses."

Jack Reeves had a scowl on his face as his half-sister left the witness stand. He had expected loyalty from his family.

The next witness called made Reeves no happier. His mood darkened as Tony Dayrit took the stand.

The window light behind Tony Dayrit made his black hair shine like onyx. He appeared calm and cooperative.

McMullen asked Dayrit to explain to the jury his relationship with a woman known as his fiancée.

"Before I came here, sir, I already got fiancée," Dayrit said, in a pronounced Asian accent. "I am already committed to this lady. So, I was thinking when I come back home to marry her."

"Have you married her?" McMullen asked.

"I did, sir."

"And you have a child; is that correct?"

"That's right. My son is ten years old now."

"So you have been in this relationship with her for a long time?"

"It was a long time, that's right," Dayrit acknowledged.

Dayrit admitted that he and Emelita would sometimes meet at the disco club and occasionally go to the park with Theo during his lunch break from work, but he adamantly denied any sexual relationship with Emelita. He was aware that Emelita had become smitten with him, and had told her friends that they were having an affair. But Dayrit steadfastly contended that he and Emelita Reeves were nothing more than platonic friends. He made light of the attraction the young Filipino woman had for him, and of her assertion that they were lovers by saying, "Sometimes Emelita lies."

Like Emelita's other friends, Tony Dayrit was always able to reach her at any time on her pager. Anytime except the night of her mysterious disappearance. At that point he had become concerned for Emelita. He had phoned Lynn Combs the following morning to check on Emelita.

Work records from National Semiconductor showed that Tony Dayrit didn't work October 10 through 13. However, Dayrit disputed the records and testified that he worked at the Lotus Restaurant October 10 and 11, and October 12 through 15 at National Semiconductor. He had not notified the payroll department of the discrepancy because he was unaware of the error. Arnel

Perkins, Dayrit's friend and coworker at National Semiconductor, would later verify Dayrit's work schedule.

In his continued effort to show cause to believe that someone other than Jack Reeves had been responsible for Emelita's death, Wes Ball questioned Tony Dayrit about the mysterious call from a Filipino man claiming to be Theo's father.

"He spoke in Tagalog. That was international language we use in Philippines," Dayrit explained. "He told me he was in town and was looking for Emelita and Mona, just to get that camcorder they borrowed from him."

Dayrit told the jurors that the man claimed to be Theo's father and that he planned to get an attorney to get custody.

"He said he was going to call me back just to have a drink with him, but he didn't call me back again."

Through redirect examination Andy McMullen made it clear that if Emelita had ever called Dayrit at home or at work that his phone number would have been available to anyone paying the bill. Furthermore, he emphasized that the mystery caller had asked only about Emelita and Mona, never inquiring about his alleged son, Theo.

Tony Dayrit was excused. As he walked from the cordoned-off court area, Jack Reeves's stare followed him though the swinging gate and out the double doors. From the angry expression on Reeves's face, he didn't believe Dayrit's testimony that the extramarital affair was a figment of Emelita's imagination.

With Randy Reeves's testimony, the prosecution introduced a photo of Emelita lying on the sofa Jack Reeves admitted removing on the night Arlington officers made their initial welfare check.

"Is this a true reflection as far as the size of that couch? That Emelita's body could pretty well be extended the full-length of that couch?" McMullen asked.

"Yes, sir," Randy replied.

Randy continued by stating that his father told him he had to remove the hideaway bed from the couch to move it out of the house, and that Randy later noticed the frame in his father's back-yard.

The photo image of Emelita stretched out on the sofa was an eerie representation to prosecutors, who believed that it was the container used by Reeves to dispose of his wife's petite, lifeless body.

"Did you have an occasion to talk to your father after the skeletal remains were found in Bosque County?" McMullen asked.

"Yes, sir."

"Did he tell you how he heard about those skeletal remains?"

"I believe he told me he had heard about it through Wes Ball," Randy said, looking toward the defense table.

"Did he mention any news coverage?"

"No, sir."

"What did he tell you about those skeletal remains?"

"He hoped it wasn't Emelita. A couple of days later he said he had never been to that side of the lake," Randy said nervously.

"Did he say that he couldn't camp on that side of the lake?" McMullen asked further.

"Yes, sir."

"And when he called you about those skeletal remains, did he make a statement to you that he was shaved, showered, and ready to be arrested?"

"Yes, sir." Randy Reeves shifted in his seat uncomfortably.

"And did he make that statement to you before he even knew whose skeletal remains they were?"

"Yes, sir," Randy said softly.

McMullen encouraged Randy Reeves to tell the jury that neither he nor anyone in his family had been to the Lake Whitney area after the discovery of Emelita's remains; that no one in the family knew exactly where the remains had been discovered; and at that time, it hadn't been positively determined that it was Emelita's body.

In response to questions posed to him by the prosecution,

Randy Reeves told the court that his father had replaced the carpet in his house.

"Did you tell him, 'Well, since Emelita's missing, Dad, you need to keep that carpet for law enforcement'?" McMullen asked.

"Yes, he said he didn't kill Emelita and there wasn't anything wrong with the carpet. He was having the carpet replaced because of dog stains and the dogs tearing it up. That was the only reason it was being replaced."

"Why was he cutting holes in the carpet before he had it removed?" McMullen asked.

"He said bugs were coming up through the foundation of the house and he needed to plug the holes," Randy answered.

It was Wes Ball's turn to ask questions. Ball established that Jack Reeves had indeed attempted to file a missing person's report, but Arlington Police declined to accept it because one had already been filed. Reeves's attempt was made on Saturday, October 15, 1994, four days after Emelita's disappearance.

Ball attempted to diminish the impact of Reeves's preparation for arrest by asking a series of questions that indicated that he himself had told Reeves that a warrant might be issued for his arrest. With the discovery of a body at Lake Whitney, Ball himself had told the defendant that he had been talking to the police concerning Jack Reeves surrendering himself if they had a warrant.

On redirect McMullen discussed Reeves's Ford dualy pickup.

"When your father saw a news account concerning Emelita's remains, did he make a statement to you about the dualy vehicle?" the prosecutor asked.

"Yes, sir. He said the Ford dualy would not fit in that area," Randy answered.

"Had he ever seen that area to your knowledge?"

"No, sir."

On recross-examination Randy explained further that the only news footage he had seen of the body recovery site was basically straight down on the grave. Very close-up footage, and of the grave site only.

Thankful that there were no further questions, Randy Reeves stepped down from the witness stand. As he had been from the beginning, Randy was torn between loyalty to his father and the truth as he knew it. He was glad his testimony was concluded. Relief flooded him.

The third day of the Jack Reeves trial was concluded. The prosecution had presented an additional nine witnesses.

"It's starting to come together," Assistant District Attorney Ben Stool said outside the courtroom. "There's been a huge amount of foundation to lay."

August 14, 1996

Gary Goodman, Jack Reeves's brother-in-law, took the stand for the prosecution on the fourth day of trial. McMullen questioned him concerning a phone conversation he had with Reeves after learning that a body had been found near Lake Whitney.

"Buddy Evans called me early that morning, and said, 'I think we found her.' Buddy Evans was the missing-persons detective with the Arlington Police Department. I said, 'Really? Has Jack found out?' Evans said, 'No, don't call him until after we have positively identified her.' He called me that afternoon and told us that the autopsy was going to be done the next day and that everything pointed to it being Emelita. Later that afternoon I called Jack and told him they'd found Emelita's remains in Lake Whitney. He says, 'It couldn't be Emelita, we didn't camp on that side of the lake.' Then he said he had already heard and that he was shaving, and showering, and getting ready to be arrested."

"Did you know if it was Bosque County or Hill County?" McMullen asked.

"Lake Whitney is all I knew," Goodman said.

"Had you heard any news reports about it?"

"There wasn't any news out at that point. None," Gary Goodman replied.

Under cross-examination Wes Ball brought out the man-to-man type of relationship between Reeves and Gary Goodman, and the fact that Reeves often talked with Goodman concerning his personal life.

"Toward September or October 1994, did Jack begin to come over frequently and want to talk?" Ball asked.

"Yes. He had several complaints," Goodman said. He expounded by telling the jury that Reeves was having difficulty in adjusting to being a father again. He'd complained that Emelita was having lesbian affairs, and that she was running around with her friends at night. Reeves also claimed that Emelita would be gone for days at a time.

"He told me, as long as she kept giving him sex, took care of the house and Theo while he was working, he was happy," Reeves's brother-in-law stated.

Gary Goodman had advised Reeves to keep a record of the times Emelita was absent for the purpose of winning custody of Theo if a divorce battle ensued. When Ball produced a ledger Reeves had maintained, indicating dates and times of Emelita's absences from the home, Goodman remarked that it appeared to have been written all at one time.

"The ink is the same, as well as the handwriting," Goodman said, suggesting that Reeves had not made notations as events happened, but rather wrote the ledger in one sitting.

Ball questioned Gary Goodman concerning the finances of Jack Reeves, and how Randy Reeves ultimately became responsible for his father's estate.

"Randy was trying to figure out whether he should bond his dad out. You know, he didn't really want . . . ," Goodman let the sentence fade away.

"In fact, did Randy seem more concerned about getting money out of Jack's name and putting it into his?" Ball asked.

"Absolutely."

"Wanting to know why Theo was named the beneficiary of Jack's CDs?"

"There was a big deal over that," Goodman remarked.

"In other words, Randy didn't appear very concerned about getting his dad out of jail. He was interested in the money stuff?" Ball prodded.

"Well, I'll put it this way; Jack still would be in jail right now if I hadn't been there," Goodman claimed.

Gary Goodman elaborated on the events that took place while Reeves was initially incarcerated, describing the burglaries of Reeves's house, and the distribution of Reeves's property to both the Goodmans and Randy.

"We ended up with a small portable TV that has a VCR in it. Jack told us to take that over to the house. Told us to haul the big-screen TV over there, because it wouldn't fit in Randy's apartment. He didn't want it put in storage. There was a lot of electronic stuff. The motorcycle, a Harley-Davidson, and a piano. We moved it all over to our house. Put it in the garage. We put the piano and big-screen TV in the house," Goodman said.

Goodman went on to tell the court that he had cleaned and repainted Reeves's home to get it ready for sale. There had been two separate contracts on the house, but because a potential buyer must be informed if a death, or in this case suspicion of a death, had occurred in a house, both contracts had fallen through. The bank was in the process of foreclosing.

On redirect McMullen asked Gary Goodman if he had any knowledge concerning Reeves setting Emelita up in an apartment of her own.

"He told us that he would pay Emelita thirty thousand dollars, and set her up in an apartment. She could be on her own after she got her Social Security card. The thirty thousand dollars was to get her up and going, to set up housekeeping, I guess. But he was not going to give up Theo," Goodman stated.

McMullen moved on to the recovery of the cellular phone.

"We went over to get the valuable stuff out of Jack's house, and put it in the garage. Randy was going to look for an apartment. We loaded things like leather jackets, electronics, ten to fifteen pairs of blue jeans he had never worn, lots of odds and ends. We moved it all into the garage," Goodman explained. "Jack called and said the phone was in the leather jacket in his closet. Well, the leather jacket had already been hauled out to the garage. We went out there and looked and that's where the phone was. I gave it to Randy and said, 'You need to notify the Arlington PD; they were looking for it. Let them know you have possession of it.' "

"So Jack Reeves knew where the phone was?" McMullen asked.

"Yeah. We never would have realized it. It was laying out there in the garage," Goodman said.

Gary Goodman's testimony was complete. He had remained calm, even during the embarrassing moments when the defense inquired about his personal financial situation. Ball had attempted to show the Goodmans as money-hungry relatives ready to feast off the remains of Jack Reeves's accumulated holdings. But Gary Goodman had held his own, denying allegations that he and his wife, Pat, had suggested to Randy Reeves that they divide Reeves's wealth once he was incarcerated.

The prosecution presented testimony and manufacturer's specification literature that proved that both of Jack Reeves's vehicles would have made it through the narrow clearing leading to Emelita's shallow grave. The testimony effectively discredited statements made by Reeves to his family members that his truck would not have been able to get through the brushy area.

Since the time of Emelita's disappearance, Reeves had claimed that his Filipino wife must be alive because she continued to send money to her parents in the Philippines. District Attorney McMullen dramatically disproved the theory by introducing into evidence bank videotapes of Reeves making the transactions himself.

In other testimony, employees of Wilson's Leather store in the Parks Mall in Arlington, Texas, described their encounter with Jack Reeves.

Melissa O'Hara described her first encounter with Jack Reeves. He had gone into store, demanding a refund of the down payment Emelita had made on a leather jacket the day of her disappearance. Reeves had claimed that his wife had left him and was not coming back. O'Hara told the jurors that she explained to Reeves that just because Emelita was gone, didn't mean she wouldn't still want her layaway. She informed Reeves that she could not return the payment. He got very upset and demanded the money back. He had told O'Hara that it was his money that Emelita had used to purchase the jacket in the first place. O'Hara continued to refuse payment, informing Reeves that she had to give Emelita an opportunity to come in and pick this layaway up or pay on it.

"So then what happened?" McMullen asked.

"Well, then he asked me, what would happen if she never came back in? I told him we would return it to stock. He asked me what would we do with the money. I told him it would just be put in our credit memo. And he said, 'What would happen if she's dead?' " O'Hara stated.

The eyes of some jurors widened at the implication Jack Reeves had made to the attractive young store clerk only days after Emelita's disappearance.

"If she's dead?" McMullen repeated, as if he hadn't heard the words the first time. But he certainly had heard, and he wanted to make certain the jury had heard, as well.

"Yes."

"That's what Jack Reeves said?" McMullen asked a second time, for emphasis.

"He said, 'What if she's dead?' " O'Hara answered. "He kept insisting she was not coming back. He told me that she was in an alternative lifestyle and that she was not coming back."

A refund was eventually made to Jack Reeves on November 14, 1994, one month after his wife's disappearance.

The prosecution had presented a total of thirteen witnesses during the fourth day's proceedings. They had followed the course they had set at the beginning of trial. They had laid an impressive foundation of circumstantial evidence. It was time to bring in the big guns. It was time for Evans and Le Noir to face Jack Reeves in court.

Twenty-three

August 15, 1996

Buddy Evans sauntered to the witness stand with confidence. The nervousness he had felt in the Coryell County trial was gone. He and Le Noir had done their job—and had done it well. They had helped to prove Jack Reeves guilty of Sharon's murder, now they would help put the finishing touches on the case against Reeves for the death of Emelita.

The dark-haired, youthful-faced Evans described to the court the first meeting he and Detective Le Noir had with Jack Reeves at the Arlington PD.

"It was on the twentieth of October in 1994. Mr. Reeves voluntarily came up to the Arlington Police Department to speak with me and Detective Le Noir about Emelita Reeves being missing.

"We met with him in the juvenile division where there's a large conference room. Detective Le Noir conducted most of the interview with Jack Reeves. Mr. Reeves voluntarily gave a written statement to us. After the statement was given, Mr. Reeves was given the opportunity to review the statement and make any changes that he wanted to make. He requested a copy of that statement. There's a copy machine inside the conference room, and Detective Le Noir got up and made a copy, while I stayed at the conference table with Jack Reeves. We were conversing back and forth when Reeves made an unsolicited statement." Evans cast a quick look at Jack Reeves. "He said, 'If you find her body at Lake Whitney, are you going to blame me?' " Evans reported as he looked at Reeves.

Reeves looked down, avoiding eye contact with one of the two men responsible for his day in court.

Jurors remained void of expression, but spectators in the courtroom mumbled amongst themselves. Why would Reeves mention finding his wife's body at Lake Whitney less than ten days after her disappearance?

"And what was the occasion of the other statement that he made, which was similar to that statement?" McMullen asked.

With an attitude of confidence, Evans adjusted his metal-rimmed glasses slightly before responding to the prosecutor's question.

"On the twenty-fifth of October, 1994, Jack Reeves contacted Detective Le Noir and said he had some evidence or some things that he believed might help locate Emelita or might help us with the investigation regarding Emelita. On that day, about noon, he came to the police department. He had his youngest son, Theo, with him, and we met him in the little conference room up on the third floor of the police department. At that time he presented us with what is more commonly referred to as dildos or sexual-type material that represents a penis, which a person would use in order to gain sexual excitement. He advised us that they belonged to Emelita and we might be able to use them in locating her," Evans said, again looking at the defendant, who quickly turned away from Evans's judgmental gaze.

Many of the retired spectators, who had been attending the trial for purely entertainment reasons, gasped at the notion of Reeves taking a dildo to the police station. The conservative senior citizens were obviously offended by talk of such private matters.

"At that time we continued to talk to Mr. Reeves," Evans continued. "Detective Le Noir basically ran what we call a bluff in which he stated that a body—he didn't say what body—but a body was reported to have been located by an unknown person.

Basically, that's all he said. He didn't give where it was located or who it was. Mr. Reeves asked if it was Emelita and was she found at Lake Whitney."

On cross-examination Wes Ball asked Evans if Jack Reeves had not given the detectives other materials at the same time the sexual items were presented to them. Evans answered in the affirmative, stating that he had also brought makeup containers, which Reeves believed might reveal the fingerprints of his wife.

"And did y'all also, after running the bluff about a body at Lake Whitney, install on Mr. Reeves's automobile a tracking device?" Ball asked.

"Yes."

"And was part of the bluff to see if, by making some claim about somebody finding a body, to then use this tracking device to see where Mr. Reeves might go?"

"Yes."

"Suffice it to say, following that bluff Mr. Reeves did not make his way to Lake Whitney based on y'all's monitoring of the tracking device, did he?" Ball asked.

"No."

Ball also questioned Evans concerning the wooded area behind Reeves's house, an undeveloped area that Reeves had also made comment on in reference to the possibility of a body being found, and him being blamed for its existence. Evans testified that, based on Reeves's comments, the wooded area had been searched. The search had proved futile.

The second bluff, pertaining to the carpet at the Reeves home, was addressed by the capable defense attorney.

"To the best of your knowledge, did the officers that had the residence under surveillance, did they see the carpeting being taken away from the residence?" Ball asked.

"I don't believe they did. I don't think the surveillance was run for a period of time and that's probably when the carpet was being removed," Evans answered, explaining the intermittent surveillance of Reeves's house.

During redirect, McMullen continued to address the sexual references made by the defendant during questioning.

"Would Mr. Reeves go off and talk to you about what his preferences were as far as sexual gratification?" McMullen asked Evans.

"He was very proud of the fact, and stated numerous times of his sexual prowess, how when he and Emelita would have intercourse, that he would let her have four or five orgasms and then basically he would finish. He talked about that quite extensively. He talked about, for whatever reason, that his father had a penile implant," Evans responded as Wes Ball stood to object based on relevancy.

A few snickers could be heard from the gallery, and several red faces surrounded by halos of gray were scattered about the courtroom.

Spectators quickly quieted as the jury listened attentively to Evans describe the day he, Dr. Howard, and the Goodmans took young Theo Reeves to the grave site of his mother.

"I guess the first initial thing was when we pulled up to the site and exited the vehicle," Evans began his explanation. "Obviously, sometimes in a new surrounding or foreign surrounding, a young child would not want to stray off too far from the people that had custody of him. In Theo's case, he immediately took off going everywhere. Talking. He knew about the water. . . ."

Ball immediately objected. The court had ruled earlier, out of the presence of the jury, that anything Theo said to the officer would be considered hearsay in court.

During the objection Evans peered at Reeves, who once again turned away to avoid eye contact. *He's a coward,* Evans thought. *He likes to control the conversation, to dictate where he wants things to go. He is frustrated because he can't control what's happening right now.* Evans suppressed a smile. He turned his attention back to the prosecutor and to the jury, who would make the determination as to the worth of their case.

"Was there a ramp or a pathway that led from the scene surrounding the grave site down to what was a creek, or creekbed?" McMullen asked.

"It was a dry creekbed," Evans replied. "I guess it's Cedron Creek. There is a makeshift ramp. I guess it's just gravel and rock where you could actually go down to the creek level, possibly to put a boat in there."

"Did Theo lead out and go down that ramp?"

"Yes."

"And in the course of going down that ramp, did Theo warn you of something?" McMullen asked, setting Evans up for a dramatic response.

Tears filled the eyes of the female jury foreperson as Evans painted the horrifying picture of four-year-old Theo warning the adults to beware of the "big hole" in the area of his mother's shallow grave. Evans watched the faces of the seven men and seven women turn from calm to righteous indignation. He was holding the jury spellbound with his testimony, and his words appeared not only to anger the jury, but the defendant, as well.

Jack Reeves glared at the jury foreperson, seemingly disgusted by her emotional display. She returned his cutting gaze.

Wes Ball, the spokesman for Reeves, had underestimated Buddy Evans. Ball had focused his attention, his preparation, on Tom Le Noir, the detective he considered to be in command of the investigation. Evans was apparently considered no more than Le Noir's flunky, his errand boy. But what Ball had obviously failed to recognize was that the missing-persons detective, drafted into homicide, had been a capable dominant force in the Reeves investigation.

Evans felt good about his testimony and later remarked that he had hammered Ball in the Bosque County trial—because Ball hadn't expected it.

Before Tom Le Noir was called to the stand, Cristi Barr was summoned to the courtroom. Barr, Emelita's cousin, was asked questions about Jack Reeves's request for her and her husband, Ron, to have Emelita's younger sister come to live with him. Barr explained that Reeves wanted another Filipino woman, but because of Theo he said it would be best to have someone from Emelita's family, a blood relative.

Barr was further questioned about a portion of a home VCR tape that had been aired on Channel 8 in Dallas. Debbie Reeves had testified earlier that she had seen the news segment featuring a story about the discovery of Emelita's body at Lake Whitney. On the tape was a shot of a young woman Debbie believed to be Emelita. The date on the bottom of the home tape was December 1, 1994, a month-and-a-half after Emelita's disappearance.

Debbie had told both her husband, Randy, and Jack about the video segment, which included an unknown man. The airing of the program had fueled Reeves's contention that Emelita was still alive.

Cristi Barr was brought to the witness stand to explain that the woman in the videotape was another of her cousins, who lived in another state. She explained that when reporters from Channel 8 asked the Barrs for photos of Emelita, the 1994 Christmas video was mistakenly given.

Mary Stewart, an attractive, blond-haired Channel 8 field reporter, later testified that she was uncertain from the beginning that the image on the tape was that of Jack Reeves's wife.

"I have never believed it's Emelita Reeves," Stewart testified. "That story was done in my absence by an editor who normally doesn't handle my stories. It was an accident that that three-second clip was put in there."

Ms. Stewart further explained that she had told defense attorney Wes Ball, not once but twice, that the person in the clip was not Emelita Reeves.

As the name of the next witness was called, the muscles on the back of Jack Reeves's neck tightened. His shoulders grew rigid and his jaw taut.

Detective Tom Le Noir walked through the swinging wooden gate, which cordoned off the principals of the trial from the spectators. He strolled with confidence, his head held high, shoulders back. As he gave a passing glance toward Reeves, a faint smile crossed the detective's face.

McMullen began by letting the jury know a little about the lead detective on the Reeves case.

"Detective Le Noir, just briefly, would you tell us about yourself?"

"Well, I'm a police officer with the Arlington Police Department. I am presently assigned to the homicide division. I have been assigned to the homicide division for approximately twelve years. Prior to being in homicide I worked narcotics. Prior to that, I was a patrol officer. That is where I initiated my career. I became a police officer in 1980. I'm coming up on my seventeenth-year anniversary with the police department," Le Noir said proudly. "I have a bachelor's degree from the University of Texas at Arlington, and I conducted my graduate studies at Texas Christian University."

Not even Wes Ball could refute the experience Le Noir brought to the case.

Le Noir explained that he became involved in the investigation of the disappearance of Emelita Reeves after being requested to review the initial incident report. He had then contacted Jack Reeves.

Le Noir related to the jury that Reeves indicated that he wasn't concerned that his wife was missing because she lived a questionable lifestyle and was known to be gone for days at a time. When Le Noir had asked about what type of vehicle Emelita drove, Reeves told the detective that the Pathfinder had been recovered.

"You don't need to worry about her, she'll be back this weekend, I'm sure," Reeves had told Le Noir.

Le Noir attempted to make eye contact with Reeves throughout his testimony, but the defendant always diverted his attention to his attorney, papers on the table, or an unknown spot on the far wall.

McMullen asked what approach Le Noir used when first meeting Reeves face-to-face.

"There are several different investigative techniques," Le Noir said. "There's the shotgun approach, which I do not use. That is where something happens, foul play occurs, and you just start looking at everybody. I utilize what is called a process of elimination. Rather than trying to prove somebody *did* do a crime, you work on trying to prove that they were *not* responsible for that crime. In doing so, it's a process of elimination and you eventually obtain the evidence and the probable cause that you need to focus your attention of suspicion."

Le Noir had the jury's attention. Most of the rural county residents had never seen a detective except on television. Le Noir's explanation of the investigative process fascinated them.

"Why did you think that you had a crime at that point?" McMullen asked.

"Several reasons. Obviously the disappearance. That's why the homicide division becomes involved. Anytime you have anyone who has disappeared, and can't be accounted for and there's no reason or rationale for their disappearance you have to suspect that there's probably foul play involved," Le Noir responded.

Le Noir explained that homicide shares the responsibility of the missing person with the missing-persons division. He'd contacted the National Criminal Information Center, as well as the Texas Criminal Information Center, to send out the description of Emelita Reeves.

"What it does is it provides information to law enforcement all over Texas and the United States that if anyone came across Emelita Reeves, or anyone that looked like her or matched the description, they would know to ensure her safety and to detain her. Or, if a body is found, to contact us," Le Noir explained in detail.

As to why Le Noir and Evans, detectives from two separate departments, were joined to conduct the investigation of the disappearance of Emelita Reeves, Le Noir said, "Our policy at the police department is that anytime a different division, be it auto theft, robbery, missing person, or any other division in the department, if they are involved in an investigation that results in death from foul play, it is immediately under our scrutiny and the supervision of the homicide division. However, we always investigate with the particular unit simply because we are dealing with areas of their expertise."

During the course of the first interview with Reeves, Le Noir recalled that the defendant commented that he didn't mind Emelita having lesbian affairs; as a matter of fact, he would enjoy watching. But he said he would definitely not tolerate her having an affair with another man. In the same interview Reeves had expressed concern that Emelita was going to take Theo from him. He indicated that he would not give up his child and he would do anything that it took to keep Theo with him.

McMullen moved on to the written statement made by Reeves during that same initial interview.

Le Noir pointed out discrepancies in the statement.

"In the first paragraph of this statement the defendant states that Emelita left their home to go to Dita's house. He identified Dita Hayes as the party that Emelita had gone to see. However, in the third paragraph of this statement, he states he didn't know where she was," Le Noir said.

Another discrepancy was Reeves's claim to have seen the police officers at his front door the night of Emelita's disappearance. However, Le Noir pointed out, the front door is not visible from the garage windows.

Reeves had also told Le Noir that on that same evening the only vehicle in his garage was his Harley-Davidson motorcycle. Yet the two uniformed officers who arrived at the Reeveses' house noted a utility-type vehicle parked in the garage.

"During the course of you providing Mr. Reeves with a copy of his written statement, did he make a verbal statement?" McMullen asked.

"While I was making the copy I heard Mr. Reeves make a statement that if Emelita is found, or if her body is found at Lake Whitney, was he going to be blamed," Le Noir responded.

"Was that statement made in response to any kind of question?"

"That was off the wall."

McMullen questioned Le Noir about the bluffs used during his investigation.

"It's an investigative technique. That's simply a means of seeing what kind of reaction that you can get from someone, seeing how they react to what you say to them. That is the sole purpose for that. It has absolutely no scientific meaning or development behind it. They were just two techniques I used to talk to the defendant, just to see how he would react to me," Le Noir explained.

"One of the things we talked about was the carpet in his house. The defendant was very adamant in letting me know there were no bloodstains in that home. I explained to him that bloodstains are not the only way to find out how people are killed and how they die. There are different types of trace evidence. Simply because someone didn't bleed, doesn't mean they weren't killed. And that's when I told him there was a type of DNA that we utilized. That once a person dies and their body begins to decompose, DNA basically embodies itself into the carpet. That's not factual in any capacity, but I told him we had means and methods of extracting that DNA and comparing it to the deceased person. The defendant wanted to know if and when the body was found, could we tell how she died. He was very concerned about that and wanted to know if we could find out exactly how she was killed. I told him there were several factors involved. I said it would also tell us if she was sexually assaulted."

"What did he say?" the prosecutor asked.

"He said that he had sex with her right before she left and he was concerned that he might be blamed for some type of foul play. He wanted to make sure that I knew he had intercourse with her at the time of her disappearance," Le Noir said.

"How long after this conversation was it that the carpet came out?"

"I believe the surveillance team saw it within twenty-four hours of our conversation."

McMullen pursued the second bluff run by Le Noir.

"I told the defendant that I had information from Crime Stoppers that a body had been found. I made it very clear. I said I can not tell you this is or is not Emelita. I'm not going to tell you that, but we have information that a body has been found. I told him that we were going to get with the informant and have the informant set up cones where this body was found so that we could locate it through aerial surveillance and at that point in time we could find out who this person was.

"Mr. Reeves's response at that point was, 'Is it Lake Whitney?' I told him I can't tell you that. We don't know. We don't want to discuss that right now. Then his second response was, 'Am I going to be blamed?' "

The jury listened intently. This was the second time Detective Le Noir had told them that Jack Reeves made reference to Lake Whitney in their discussions.

Reeves continued to watch the jury with interest. His stare often rested on the attractive face of the jury foreperson.

Le Noir told the jury that there had been three possible locations where they believed Emelita's body could be found: behind the defendant's house because the large area was engulfed in mesquite trees; somewhere at Fort Hood, based on the defendant telling them that he had gone four-wheeling in the area the morning of his wife's disappearance; and, of course, Lake Whitney.

Le Noir produced documents that indicated that Jack Reeves had taken his Dodge truck to be washed on October 13, 1994, and that the Nissan Pathfinder had been washed and detailed twice before Reeves took it to the police department for inspection. The detective also explained to the jury the manner in which Reeves exited the Pathfinder when he brought it to the PD. He pointed out the seat position, the steering-wheel tilt, and Reeves's inability to lock the doors or set the alarm.

McMullen asked Le Noir if he noticed anything in the house that would cause a person to disassemble a couch to get it out of the house, and yet not disassemble another couch to get it into the house. Le Noir answered no, explaining that the width of the doors were the same going in as going out.

"What did your study of cellular phone records produce?" McMullen asked.

"It revealed evidence that there were not periods of time greater than a few hours—but no periods of time certainly greater than twenty-four hours—that there was not communication between Emelita and the defendant," Le Noir reported. "There was continuous communication between the numbers associated with the defendant and phone numbers associated with Emelita and her friends, which indicated that there was never a long period of time that she was unaccounted for or disappeared."

Le Noir continued by saying that the phone records indicated that the only time she had left and was not in communication with Jack Reeves was since the time she disappeared and had never been seen again. He added that, for a three-month period, sixty-three percent of Emelita's phone calls were to the defendant. Contrary to what Reeves had told Le Noir during interviews, except for the night of her birthday Reeves had always known where Emelita was.

"And during the time of her disappearance, what did you learn from the phone records?" McMullen asked.

"They very accurately accounted for and corroborated what witnesses had told me regarding Emelita's whereabouts and the chronology of her whereabouts the day leading up to her final destination at the residence on Iberis Drive," Le Noir said. "What they also revealed, was that on October eleventh, 1994 at eight-thirty-one P.M., she made the last recorded phone call. It was to the residence on Iberis. After that, there are no phone calls made until October fourteenth, 1994. Those calls related to phone calls that I had evidence the defendant made to persons listed on the phone bill printout."

Le Noir added that, at no time did Jack Reeves indicate to Tom Le Noir or Buddy Evans that he was in possession of the cell phone and pager belonging to his wife.

"You made inquiries to the INS before the remains of Emelita Reeves were found, did you not?" McMullen asked in an attempt to show the jury the thoroughness of the detectives's investigation.

"Yes, sir. We did a very thorough background check on Emelita to see if she was even in existence in this world. It was so detailed—I don't mean to sound tongue in cheek—but so detailed that we would know almost anything unless she was living in a cardboard box underneath a bridge. We covered every area that you could cover to see if she was existing in this world, and that went nationwide," Le Noir said with a degree of exasperation in his voice.

Jack Reeves was getting restless. Le Noir could see him wiggling in his seat and continually whispering to his attorney. Le Noir knew he was getting under Reeves's skin. He recalled his conversation with Wes Ball before trial began, warning the confident defense attorney that he would have trouble controlling Reeves in court by himself. Ball had thought he was up to the challenge. *I bet he's changed his mind,* Le Noir thought with a repressed snicker.

"Did you have an opportunity to appear at a court proceeding and testify as a witness, with the defendant present in court, regarding the distance from the trailer park on Lake Whitney to the location where the remains were found in Bosque County?" McMullen asked.

Le Noir watched Reeves's reaction. The question obviously angered him.

"Yes, sir. I said it was across the lake, not far, just a couple of miles, but they wanted to know specific travel routes. We had measured that travel route, and I gave a mileage of seventeen point eight miles from their campsite to the burial site," Le Noir said, keeping his eyes on Reeves.

"Did you observe a reaction?" McMullen asked casually, knowing the impact of the question.

Le Noir took a moment to recall his previous testimony. He had approximated the distances, both across the lake and around the perimeter. In the hearing Le Noir had stated the span across Lake Whitney, from Reeves's camp to the grave site, was approximately four to four and a half miles. He testified the outer distance was about fifteen miles. Now Le Noir had the precise measurements.

"I observed two reactions. The first was when they asked me a correlation between the two sites. . . . when I said two miles the defendant became visibly upset. He was speaking to his attorney. He was moving in his chair. That was when Mr. Ball objected and asked if I could tell the court specifically. I gave the mileage, seventeen point eight miles.

"I was looking directly at the defendant. He was acknowledging, yes," Le Noir said, staring at Reeves.

Jack Reeves was true to his pattern of behavior. Again, just as Le Noir had described in the previous court hearing, Reeves was upset, moving in his chair, and talking to his attorney.

Before Andy McMullen could get another question out of his mouth, Wes Ball angrily and loudly said to his client, "Would you shut up?"

The courtroom was silenced. All eyes were on Wes Ball, whose frustration with his client had been released in open court. McMullen was speechless, Le Noir burst out laughing, an embarrassed Ball snickered, and even Judge Morgan laughed out loud.

The stoic prosecutor didn't miss a beat, he turned back to his witness and continued with his questioning.

"I would like to talk to you about the other persons that are significant in this matter and ask you about what work you have done in the process of elimination," McMullen stated. He then asked specifically about Monalisa Pate and Tony Dayrit.

"I have a protocol I follow," Le Noir explained. "First, I try to determine the relationship between the person who is being accused and the deceased. Mona and Emelita were friends. They were lovers. They were having an affair. Second, I ask, what is the relationship? The relationship between Mona and Emelita was friendly. I look for a history of violence. There was no history of violence between Mona and Emelita. No history of any violence. I look at police reports, files, criminal histories, background checks. We looked not simply in Arlington, or in Tarrant County, but any location where Mona has been."

Le Noir told the court that after completing the protocol on both Mona Pate and Tony Dayrit, it was determined that there was no evidence to support either of them as a suspect in Emelita Reeves's death.

At 4:35 P.M. Judge Morgan called court recessed for the day. Andy McMullen had covered considerable ground. The following day he would wrap up the state's case.

August 16, 1996

Detective Le Noir found himself in an all-too-familiar place—the witness stand against Jack Reeves. He had looked forward to testifying, but as the week had drawn on, he was ready for the case to go to the jury and a verdict rendered.

Wes Ball, Le Noir's old schoolmate, stood before him, ready for cross-examination. Le Noir admired Ball, but he wasn't about to give him a hole through which Reeves could crawl.

After a few brief questions about Miranda warnings and witness statements, Ball moved on.

"Did Mr. Reeves tell you that if Emelita comes back she may try to take Theo away with her?" Ball asked.

"Yes, sir," Le Noir answered concisely.

"Did he tell you that he even changed the locks on the house?"

"Yes, he did."

"And I think he also told you that he was going to either change the title or sell the Pathfinder, is that right?"

"Yes, either sell it or give it to Randy," Le Noir said.

Wes Ball was attempting to make the actions of his client in the days and weeks immediately following Emelita's disappearance appear as normal as possible.

"Four-wheeling is off-road driving. Would it be your understanding that four-wheeling would probably get a vehicle dirty?" Ball asked.

"Common sense would dictate. Of course, that depends on the condition of the earth. Is it wet; is it dry; is it hard; is it soft? There're a lot of variables there."

The records of the Colonial Car Wash in Arlington, Texas, had already been entered into evidence by the prosecution. The records showed that Jack Reeves had brought his Dodge Ram in to be cleaned on October 13, 1994. Ball contended that it was a routine habit of Reeves to have his vehicles washed and cleaned at least five to seven times a month, and that the car wash October 13 was nothing more than routine maintenance. Ball also saw nothing unusual or contrived that Reeves had the Nissan Pathfinder cleaned before placing it on the market for sale.

"When he said he had washed the vehicle, I just told him that once the vehicle is washed it obviously damages any type of evidence that we want to try to look for. It damages the integrity of any type of search," Le Noir stated.

Ball reminded the detective that Randy and Debbie Reeves had requested the vehicle be impounded and checked out at the time it was found in the HyperMart parking lot. Le Noir admitted that, if he had been on the case at that time, the car would have indeed been impounded, but it just wasn't done at the time. He did, however, have the vehicle processed when Jack Reeves brought it to the police station. Nothing of evidentiary value was found.

"Were you aware that there were some gloves seized, I think brown, from the storage shed that was in the rear of the lot on Iberis?" Ball asked.

"Yes, sir."

"Did you make any decisions to have those analyzed by any scientific technique or turned over to any crime laboratories?" Ball questioned.

"I made a decision to preserve them until we had evidence to do some type of analysis. The medical examiner, and the lab and forensic specialist, and I discussed it after Emelita's body was found. We agreed that there was absolutely no trace evidence to compare to those gloves," Le Noir explained.

Then Ball took Le Noir back to the pretrial hearing when he claimed to have observed a reaction from his client in regard to the distance from the campsite to the location where Emelita's body was found.

"Do you know what conversations Mr. Reeves and I might have been having during testimony at that hearing?" Ball asked.

Tom Le Noir knew where Wes Ball was headed. He planned to claim that Reeves's reaction to his statement that the distance between the campsite and the burial spot was two miles was actually a reaction to a question he himself had asked his client. But it wouldn't work. Le Noir was a highly trained, observant police officer. He told Ball that he heard what he had said to his client in court, that Ball had not written Reeves any notes, and that Ball's attention had been on his cross-examination, not his client. Furthermore, Le Noir stated that cocounsel Chris Thetford was massaging Reeves's shoulders in an attempt to calm him down.

After an extensive review of the cellular phone records, Ball asked two final questions.

"In regard to the house on Iberis, was there any evidence of a forensic nature to show that there was any homicide in that house?" Ball asked, looking Le Noir in the eye as he waited for his answer.

"No, sir."

"In regards to the location where the skeletal remains were found in Bosque County, Texas, was there any forensic evidence that links those remains to Jack Reeves?" Ball asked.

"No, sir."

Ball passed the witness.

McMullen had a few minor clarifications from prior testimony to cement his strong circumstantial case, then Tom Le Noir was excused. Twenty-two months of work and two days of testimony were complete. Now all the normally hyperactive Le Noir could do was wait. Wait for the defense to present its case, and for the jury to reach a verdict. Le Noir was uncharacteristically subdued.

At 1:05 P.M., Andy McMullen, district attorney for Bosque County, stood tall before the court and announced, "The state rests, Your Honor."

Twenty-four

With the jury at recess, Wes Ball approached the bench.

"Your Honor, at this time the defense would move for an instructed verdict of acquittal. The State of Texas has failed to prove by evidence beyond a reasonable doubt the offense of murder."

"Okay," the judge said casually. "That motion is denied."

At 1:15 P.M., ten minutes after the state rested its case, the Bosque County jury returned to their seats. Without making an opening statement, Wes Ball began his brief defense by calling David Kulesz as his first witness.

The board-certified family law attorney had represented Jack Reeves in his divorce from Emelita. He stated for the court that Jack Reeves had appeared at his office and had related that his wife had disappeared and that he was concerned she would reappear and try to take their child. Under Texas law there is no such thing as an application for separation, thus giving equal rights to a child to both the father and mother. Kulesz said that the only alternative in protecting Reeves's parental rights was to file a petition for divorce, along with a temporary restraining order.

"There is language in the divorce petition that says something like 'discord and conflict of personalities.' Can you explain why that would appear?" Ball asked.

"Texas is a no-fault divorce state, and so the general pleading in starting a divorce is that the marriage has become insupportable because of discord and there's no chance of reconciliation. That's probably in virtually every petition that's filed in the State of Texas," Kulesz elaborated.

Kulesz continued to explain Texas divorce procedures by stating that there was an attempt made to serve Emelita Reeves with notice of divorce, but because she was unable to be found, a public notice was placed in *The Record* newspaper. The temporary restraining order automatically ran out fourteen days after issue. Kulesz stated that he had asked the court to extend the restraining order for an additional fourteen days because they couldn't locate Emelita. The court had complied.

An attorney ad litem, Mrs. Dupont, had been appointed to represent Emelita in her absence, a procedure common in such cases. A final decree was quickly granted, and Jack Reeves was given permanent custody of Theo.

Andy McMullen approached the divorce attorney with some degree of irritation. Kulesz had failed to respond to a subpoena issued by the Bosque County prosecutor in reference to his file on the Reeveses' divorce. Kulesz handed McMullen the file from the witness stand. McMullen took a few minutes to review it.

The file showed that Reeves had first seen Kulesz on October 25, 1994, and that within twenty-four hours a multi-page divorce petition had been filed.

McMullen ask Kulesz to read aloud a letter dated February 10, 1995, written by Mrs. Dupont to Kulesz.

"On February first, 1995, I spoke with Petitioner, Jack Wayne Reeves," Kulesz began, "to discover what knowledge he had of where Respondent could be located. Mr. Reeves indicated to me that his wife had run away and that he was afraid she would come back and take their minor child. Mr. Reeves told me that the last time he saw his wife was on Tuesday, October eleventh, 1994. Mr. Reeves stated that she left that evening to visit friends. Mr. Reeves stated that the following day he left for a camping trip to Lake Whitney and was not concerned that his wife had not returned, as she often spent several days with her girlfriends. Mr.

Reeves does believe that his wife is still alive and that she may return and try to take away their minor child."

According to the letter Mrs. Dupont wrote Kulesz, Reeves claimed to have left to go camping on October twelfth, a direct contradiction to the date of October 13 given police investigators and state park records. The date of October 12 had been incorporated as a statement of evidence in the divorce proceeding and presented as evidence in Reeves's criminal trial. Investigators believed it was Reeves's way of manipulating the timeline to his own benefit.

The second witness called by the defense was Shawn Parker, a metroplex locksmith. Jack Reeves had requested Parker change the locks on the Iberis Drive house during a phone call to Parker's office on October 18, 1994, at 3:41 P.M. When asked the reason Reeves gave for changing the locks, Parker replied, "He said he was changing his locks because he found out his wife was sleeping with another man and a woman. I assumed he was changing the locks so his wife or people that she associated with couldn't get in."

Parker told the court that Reeves had said that his wife was cheating on him with another man, but failed to mention that she had disappeared. Parker, who was paid $127.98 for the lock changes, remembered his conversation with Reeves as being unique, because Reeves appeared more upset at his wife's alleged affair with the man than the woman.

The final defense witness to take the stand was Bruce Cummings, investigator for the defense. The focus of Cummings's testimony was on the Channel 8 news clip, at one time presumed to be of Emelita Reeves.

Cummings testified that he had taken a copy of the tape to Wichita Falls in an effort to have Cristi and Ron Barr identify the woman on the tape, represented by the news station as Emelita.

"How long was your meeting with Mr. Barr at his residence?" Ball asked.

"Probably thirty seconds," Cummings responded.

McMullen approached the bench for cross-examination. McMullen asked Cummings if he had not already been advised by Wes Ball, before being sent to Wichita Falls, that Channel 8 had already advised him that the woman in the video was not Emelita Reeves. Cummings admitted that he had.

"And how long have you known Channel eight's position, that it was not Emelita Reeves, prior to the video being played to the jury?" McMullen asked.

"Oh, I probably wouldn't have known that until the latter part of 1995," Cummings said.

"The better part of a year?" McMullen asked, a bit of surprise in his voice.

"I'm not sure. I have known for a long time. Yes, sir."

Cummings told the court that he had pursued the identity of the woman in the video at the insistence of Jack Reeves, who told him he believed it was his wife on the tape.

Once again, Reeves had attempted to manipulate his own defense team to his advantage.

McMullen asked Cummings if he had had an opportunity, during his investigation, to talk with Reeves concerning contracts between Reeves and a publication known as *Cherry Blossoms*.

Cummings said he had not.

At that point, McMullen read portions of a letter found in the home of Jack Reeves during the evidentiary search. The form letter, authored by Reeves, was evidently mailed to prospective new wives whose photos and addresses appeared in the pages of *Cherry Blossoms* magazines earmarked by Reeves.

"Dear 'blank,' Hi, I saw your picture in the 'blank' issue of *Cherry Blossoms*," McMullen read. The prosecutor then asked Cummings to read the last paragraph of the first page.

"I'm a Christian man and I do not believe in divorce. My marriage lasted for seven years and I divorced my wife because she was a tomboy. She deserted my son and I, so I had to file for divorce to get custody of my son. His name is Theo, and he is a very wonderful young man and I love him very much. I am a devoted family man and I really tried to make my previous marriage work. I was unable to do so because of her desire for other women," Cummings read.

"According to that letter, it was the lesbian relationship that drove him to divorce. Is that correct?" McMullen asked.

"That's what this paragraph says," Cummings commented.

When the state had concluded its questioning of the defense investigator, Wes Ball rose.

"The defense rests, Your Honor," Ball said.

The entire defense of Jack Reeves lasted one hour and seven minutes, in which they presented a total of three witnesses.

The jury was dismissed for the weekend.

August 19, 1996

Andy McMullen began his closing arguments.

"Ladies and gentlemen of the jury, the purpose of this presentation is to go over the evidence with you. In a circumstantial evidence case such as what we have here, it is important to establish that the evidence points to the guilt and establishes beyond a reasonable doubt the accused's guilt. I'm going to move directly into the evidence after I express to you my sincere thanks for your work, your interest, your attentiveness in this case.

"What did the picture of Emelita on the couch, Mrs. Dupont's report, and the statement of evidence that said that Jack Reeves went to Lake Whitney on October the twelfth, 1994, have in common?

"The answer is: How did Emelita's body get to Lake Whitney. And the purpose of this photograph is to show that Emelita's body fits perfectly on that couch—a beautiful couch.

"Why would anyone cut the arms off a beautiful couch, or tear the fabric? They would cut them off to fit them in the back of a Dodge Ram. Why would the inside of the couch be taken out? The mattress? It's because, with those items out of the interior of the couch, Emelita Reeves's body would fit in that couch and could be transported to Lake Whitney for burial.

"There are inconsistencies in his [Reeves's] statements. First, he tells his son, Randall, that he reassembled the couch. He tells his half sister, Pat, that he didn't reassemble the couch.

"Randall testified that his father was a regular customer of Levitz, who would have delivered the new sofa. Yet, when police officers appeared on the scene, he was moving a new sofa into the house.

"He told the Goodmans he hadn't slept in forty-eight hours, and that's to explain why on the twelfth of October he took that couch, after he had modified it to fit in the back of his Dodge Ram, and went to Lake Whitney. That's why he began to tell people a dualy wouldn't fit in that area. He was trying to throw people off, because he used the Dodge Ram.

"How do we know it was the Ram? Because he called his sister the next morning, upset, nervous, he hadn't slept, but he washed that Ram before he went to see her.

"What do we know about Emelita's last days? We know she had lunch with friends, that she had been crying, her face puffy, bloodshot eyes. Jack Reeves had pulled her hair, he had choked her. She was determined to divorce Reeves. She planned to take Theo and the dogs. But Jack wanted Theo, and he was going to do anything it took to keep him. None of her friends are able to reach her later that evening.

"The police arrive, they see the defendant crouched down in the garage. The defendant becomes angry at the mention of Emelita's name. Three times he denies them access to the house. He appears nervous.

"The next morning he calls Pat [Goodman] and wants her to meet him at the International House of Pancakes. The first thing he says to her is, 'I think I'm in trouble.'

"Jack showed no concern for Emelita's welfare. He showed no concern when her car was found. Jack had the keys to Emelita's car with him at Lake Whitney.

"What was the relationship of Emelita and Jack Reeves? She had married him out of a financial obligation to her family. He was totally in control of her. When she was three months pregnant he sent her to the Philippines, where she stayed until Theo was seventeen months old.

"On her last birthday they had a physical altercation.

"Jack tells officers that the pager and cell phone are with Emelita, but the cell phone is found in Jack Reeves's jacket at his house.

"Jack called Emelita names—lesbian, whore.

"We know Jack Reeves was familiar with Lake Whitney. And so when he heard the remains were found, he advised his son, and then his brother-in-law, that it couldn't have been Emelita, because he didn't camp on that side of the lake, the dualy wouldn't fit there. He said he showered, and shaved and was ready to be arrested.

"Randy found his father cutting up the carpet on October thirteenth. Then Reeves had the carpet removed.

"We know who was buying the money orders, shown by the bank's videotape, in Emelita's name.

"We know the two rings friends said Emelita always wore were found at the house on Iberis.

"While Jack's telling his lawyer he's afraid she's going to come back and take Theo, he's demanding money back from Wilson's Leather Store and he's selling her vehicle.

"Tom Le Noir testifies in a court proceeding, and looks right at the defendant. He describes the reaction Reeves had to his testimony. . . .

"He gives detectives inconsistent statements pertaining to where Emelita was the night officers arrived at his house.

"He gives an off-the-wall statement to Evans and Le Noir that, if they find the body at Lake Whitney, are they going to blame him. He again mentions Lake Whitney in response to the bluff of a Crime Stopper tip.

"Cristi Barr told you that Jack Reeves wanted her to talk to Emelita's younger sister, Marisa, to see if she could come to live with him in America.

"Gary Goodman told you that both of Theo's car seats had come to him from Jack Reeves. That's important because, although Emelita's car always had a seat in it for the child, when the vehicle was found there was no car seat.

"Shawn Parker told you that Jack Reeves told him his wife was involved with another man. Jack Reeves consented to his wife having romantic relationships with other women, but could not tolerate it if she was having a relationship with another man.

"I've tried to go over the evidence hurriedly. I'll have an opportunity to respond after Mr. Ball's statements," McMullen finished. He returned to his seat at the prosecutor's table.

"Ladies and gentlemen," Ball began, "I want to thank you for the patience and attention that you've shown. I know you have, because many of you have taken detailed and copious notes.

"I want to say one thing, the tape with the video of December first, 1994, I'm convinced, after hearing the testimony of Mrs. Barr, that's not Emelita Reeves. We had no way of knowing that when we sent our investigator out to the Barr household and they wouldn't talk to us. That's cleared up, forget about that tape."

Nice move, Wes, Le Noir thought from his front-row seat in the courtroom. *Ask them to forget that you knew that wasn't Emelita, and yet you still sent your investigator to check it out.*

"There is something called the presumption of innocence, and the burden of proof the state must meet before they are entitled to a conviction," Ball continued. "No person may be convicted of an offense unless each element of the offense has been proved and established beyond a reasonable doubt.

"Now, Mr. McMullen, when he started out his argument, showed you this photograph and talked to you about a scenario with sofas in the back and bodies being concealed. Where's the proof of that? That's speculation. It has to be proved beyond a reasonable doubt, not speculation.

"Now, what have you heard in this case? Well, I may insult Mr. Reeves a bit, but can you think of a more dysfunctional household or dysfunctional marriage than the one that was between Jack and Emelita Reeves?

"Jack's a weird guy. Jack's a paranoid guy. Jack's dysfunctional. There isn't any question about that. Those are not the elements of the offense. I believe you don't like Jack Reeves. That's not one of the elements of the offense.

"The elements of the offense are set out. Did he intentionally or knowingly cause the death of Emelita Reeves? That's what they have to prove beyond a reasonable doubt. There is nothing in these instructions that, if you find Jack's a weird guy, strange guy, nervous guy, paranoid guy, then he's guilty. That's not our law."

Predictably, Wes Ball attacked the character of the dead victim. Emelita had come to the United States to live the good life. She ran around at all hours. She told lies. She had male and female lovers.

"They want to show Jack as a cold, callous guy because he files a petition for divorce, he haggles over jacket money. Does Jack really want her back at home in the marriage? I think not," Ball told the jurors.

During Ball's arguments, the jury foreperson and Reeves continued to lock eyes. Le Noir watched with interest. He shook his head slightly, convinced that Reeves still believed he could wave his manipulative wand and come out the victor.

Ball continued to talk about Emelita's lifestyle by mentioning the man from New York that had called Tony Dayrit and claimed to be Theo's father. No wonder Jack Reeves called Emelita bad names, Ball declared.

On her habit of disappearing for days at a time, Ball said, "What do we mean by disappear? Completely vanish or spend the night over at someone's home? There is no information that Jack said she just completely vanishes. She says she's going off with somebody, and she's gone two or three days."

Ball began putting suspicion on others. He reminded the jurors that Mona [Pate] stated that she and Emelita planned a long relationship together, but then there was Tony [Dayrit].

"Mona told you she didn't want anybody in the way of her

and Emelita, including Tony. She might have been jealous. She knew about Tony. Mona was a spurned lover."

Ball again questioned the work records of Tony Dayrit in an attempt to cast doubt as to his work schedule at National Semiconductor.

"And can I prove that Mona did this, or can I prove that Tony did this? No. And it's not my obligation to prove anything. It's their obligation to prove beyond any reasonable doubt the defendant, and no other, caused Emelita's death. I submit to you now, you can at least consider these matters," Ball said.

"Was there a vehicle in the garage?" Ball asked. "I don't know. I know Officer Hirschman didn't see any vehicle in the garage. If the vehicle was a van or Suburban, Detective Le Noir changed it to the same color, make, model."

Ball reminded the jurors that the first officers on the scene saw no signs of foul play, and that Reeves told them he was moving a sofa. That was consistent with Reeves's picking up a sofa at Levitz.

"Jack ought to be customer of the year for Levitz Furniture and Colonial Car Wash," Ball said, tongue-in-cheek. "Because you have seen documents that he had ten transactions at Levitz during that time period. And he used Colonial Car Wash services at least six to seven times a month."

Ball was ready for another attack—this time on Pat Goodman.

"You are the sole judges of the credibility of the witnesses, and the weight to be given their testimony and what you are asked to do [is] to look at the demeanor of the witnesses.

"Are they here to tell you what the facts are, to let the chips fall where they may? Or do they have a position? When Pat Goodman walked into the courtroom and was given the oath, she didn't say 'I do'; she said 'I certainly do.' She said the man with the fake glasses, she had to be admonished by the judge as she left to be excused. She looks at the defendant and says in the microphone, 'You're sorry.' You can use that to judge her credibility. She's consumed with hate. She's not here to tell the truth; she is here to advocate a position."

Ball moved on to Randy Reeves. "He retrieved the cellular phone. What's interesting is he didn't say Jack said, 'Hide it, don't give it to the police, do away with it, smash it, throw it away.' Jack gave him no such instructions whatsoever."

Ball attributed Reeves's comments to Randy and the Goodmans about being ready to be arrested, to Ball's own counsel with the defendant concerning the accusations being pointed at Reeves and his possible arrest.

The coy defense attorney reminded the jury that Randy Reeves told them that Jack often bought cashier's checks in the name of Emelita Villa, because it was easier for them to be cashed by her family in the Philippines.

"There is no physical evidence at the residence to show that anything in the nature of foul play occurred," Ball told the seven men and seven women. He added, "If you commit murder, what do you do to hide it? You fake grieving, you put up a front. You wouldn't engage in erratic behavior; you would shed crocodile tears. Jack's conduct wasn't grieving, it was consistent with a husband who found out about his wife and that thing about the man, and it was good riddance."

Ball wanted the men and women of the jury to consider Evans's testimony in regard to Theo as a stretch.

"They want you to draw an inference because Theo sees a hole and seems at home in the woods that he's been there before. Come on. I submit to you that's the stretch they want to make so you will find the defendant guilty. I submit to you, you won't do that. You won't make that stretch."

On Le Noir, his words were conservatively biting. "He's a professional witness and advocate," Ball stated.

Ball began wrapping up. "The state has not proved the defendant, Jack Reeves, has ever been in Bosque County other than for court appearances. The state has not proved there was any homicide in Arlington, Tarrant County, Texas. They have proved Jack's weird. They proved that there are inconsistencies, but that does not equal the elements of murder, ladies and gentlemen. This is your decision, and your decision alone. I can't prove somebody else did it, but they have to prove that he did it, and no one else in this world, beyond a reasonable doubt. There's no witness that says he killed her. There is no confession he killed her. There is no scientific evidence that he killed her. And all of that, ladies and gentlemen, adds up to a reasonable doubt. You know, somebody might say, 'Well, let's find him guilty anyway, because he's inconsistent.' Have the courage to see that reasonable doubt, and vote not guilty, because I submit to you, the state has not met its burden. They have done a fine job and they have presented you a lot of evidence and a lot of witnesses about a lot of things that circle around the issue, but they have not proved the elements of murder beyond a reasonable doubt, or that this Defendant murdered Emelita Reeves.

"Thank you for your attention and patience. Thank you."

Wes Ball's job in the guilt and innocent phase of the Reeves murder trial was over. He sat down next to Reeves and waited to hear the prosecution's final remarks.

"Ladies and gentlemen, in closing, there are friends and family of Emelita who have waited patiently for this day," Andy McMullen said. "For it to come to a jury to consider all the evidence. Law enforcement has done all it can do. The Arlington Police Department has done a fine job. The Bosque County Sheriff's Department has done a fine job, so have the Texas Rangers. I have done the best I can do to bring you all of these witnesses and this evidence for you to consider. Ladies and gentlemen, the family simply waits for justice.

"I ask you for a verdict of guilty based upon the evidence that points to one man seated right there," McMullen said as he pointed to the defendant. "Jack Reeves." Reeves scowled at the impressive orator though narrowed eyes.

"All of the evidence taken together points to one man, and only one man, who had the connection to the location, who had the connection with the property that was found after the crime to tie him to this case. Only one man who made the statements that were inconsistent and incriminating to tie him into this web of murder. Thank you."

It was over. The major hurdle for the state had been jumped.

Judge Morgan excused the two female alternates and instructed the remaining seven men and five women to adjourn to the jury room for deliberations.

The time was 10:32 A.M.

Witnesses, family, and friends mingled with a number of reporters while they waited for the jury to return. No one knew how long the jury would be out. It was hard to gauge what a jury would do.

James Vaughn, the ailing father of Sharon Reeves, descended the steps of the old Bosque County courthouse via a small chair mounted on an electric track. His weak legs were shaky beneath him as he stood. Vaughn and his son, Larry, had come to the Bosque County trial in part to see Jack Reeves pay for yet another young woman's death, and in part in memory of Sharon.

Pat and Gary Goodman stood on the courthouse lawn and answered questions from members of the press.

Emelita's close-knit group of Asian friends waited together in the warm August sunshine just outside the double glass doors.

After hearing more than sixty witnesses and reviewing more than two hundred pieces of evidence, one hour and seventeen minutes after the twelve jurors entered the jury room—they returned to the courtroom with a verdict.

Judge Morgan addressed the audience before asking for the verdict. "I don't want any outcry," the distinguished judge said, "If you can't control your emotions, you need to get on out of the courtroom before the verdict is read."

Jack Reeves stood and faced the jury. All of his fifty-five years showed in his face. He looked tired, haggard.

Judge Morgan read the verdict handed to him by the jury foreperson. "We, the jury, find the defendant, Jack Wayne Reeves, guilty of murder as charged in the indictment. It's signed by Marla Jill Hutyre. Any reason the court should not accept the verdict?" Judge Morgan asked.

The pale-faced Reeves looked at the floor and shook his head. Then, looking up at the judge, he said, "I didn't do it, Your Honor."

"No, Your Honor," Ball answered, ignoring his client's comment.

Judge Morgan dismissed the jurors until one o'clock when they would return to hear arguments for penalty.

Tom Le Noir and Buddy Evans heaved huge sighs of relief. Their case had proven solid. But the two dedicated detectives weren't ready to celebrate. They couldn't celebrate until Jack Reeves was assessed a penalty worthy of his crime.

At 1:02 P.M. Andy McMullen addressed the jury for the final time.

"Ladies and gentlemen, thank you very much for your verdict. A lot of work has gone into the case. I am very gratified and humbled by the verdict that you have returned.

"I think the facts of the offense itself are sufficient. You have tables that I suppose are objective scientific tables that you can use. I am looking at the life-expectancy table. Emelita Reeves at age twenty-seven, as a female in the all races category, had fifty-two point seven years left to live. Just as important, Theo had fifty-two point seven years to know his mother, and neither of those will come to pass. That man," McMullen said, pointing to Jack Reeves, "seated right there, is what caused that not to come to pass.

"Theo knew more than a hole—more than one hole. By your verdict you have found, I feel, substantial evidence that Theo was there at the time of the burial. You have evidence of his delayed development, and to what extent that contributed, I suppose we'll never know.

"But one day he will know he was present when his father killed his mother, and when his father buried his mother. He will know about how the dogs dragged her out of the ground. He'll know about the freshwater snail removed from her head. And her family will know. They will know what happened to their daughter who came out of obligation to her family to better their condition in the Philippines and entered into this marriage.

"This man," McMullen again pointed to Reeves, "to save his own neck, blamed it on hardworking, decent people. To save his own calculated, cold-blooded neck, so you have that to consider.

"And ladies and gentlemen, as a law enforcement officer for Bosque County, there's something else that I ask that you consider. Do people from the Metroplex area come and try to hide their crimes in Bosque County because we don't have the resources to fight criminals like they do in the Metroplex? I think a message needs to be sent to them that we're not going to tolerate it. If they think they can get away with crimes by hiding their criminal evidence in Bosque County, they've got another thought coming. We will not tolerate it.

"Ladies and gentlemen, thank you."

Andy McMullen had sent a powerful message to his constituents.

Wes Ball stood and walked the few feet from the defense table to the jury box.

"Ladies and gentlemen, you have worked hard and long, and you have reached a decision, and I am not going to quarrel with your verdict. You now have another job to do, and that is to decide what the appropriate punishment is. The legislature says you can sentence a defendant found guilty of murder to as little as five years, or as much as ninety-nine years, or life.

"Why is that? Because the facts in each case are different.

"We can assume that Jack and Emelita stood in front of a Catholic priest in Cebu City and they took vows, such as forsaking all others. I submit to you they didn't take any vows forsaking all others, except Mona or Tony.

"Emelita came to the United States and misrepresented herself to Jack because she wanted to better her financial circumstances for her family. She enjoyed the things that he had. She went out while Jack was home with Theo. There's no evidence Jack is out running around on Emelita, that Jack's not keeping that vow of forsaking all others. Emelita's doing that. She made that choice.

So we know this is not a stranger-on-stranger crime, for which the ninety-nine years or life end of the punishment range would be appropriate.

"You might consider that the phone message left on Emelita's answering machine by Tony may be what set things off. You can consider that.

"Jack Reeves is fifty-five years old. There's something in the court's instructions about parole law. The defendant will not be eligible for release until he has served a flat one-half of the time period imposed. The judge, however, has instructed you that you are not to base your punishment decision on those rules.

"But Jack Reeves is fifty-five years old, so a sentence of any term of imprisonment beyond the bare minimum is essentially a life sentence for him. I would ask you to consider that," Ball continued.

"I ask you to look at the facts, the circumstances, what Emelita was doing, how that marriage had really degenerated into nothing, what she was doing at night, and calling her friends, and driving around, being on the cellular phone, discoing while Jack was at home taking care of Theo. I would ask you to look at the low end of the punishment range, because Jack's fifty-five and those circumstances, that crime-of-passion circumstance, is certainly present in the evidence. Thank you."

Andy McMullen had the last word, and he made certain he made the most of it.

"Mr. Ball talks about vows. I suppose those were the vows that Jack Reeves broke in 1988 when he got a divorce from Emelita.

"And when Jack Reeves, in January, responds to his *Cherry Blossoms* magazines, he writes a letter and says, 'I do not believe in divorce,' and on the last page of his letter he said 'I am a marriage-minded man and I am looking for a life partner.'

"In Emelita's case, it was a partner for life—for her life.

"And, ladies and gentlemen, there he goes again. Somebody's got to stop that man," McMullen said, again pointing to Reeves. "How do you stop somebody like that? You stop them by never letting them get out. The way you satisfy yourself he will never get out, to get back in this kind of conduct, his partners for life, is to return a verdict of ninety-nine years. He'll never get out, and he'll never get his form letters going again for Filipino women; for his partners, for their lives.

"We have to think about society, and in this case the greater world society when we know who the victims are going to be. They are going to be Filipino women. We have to stop him, and by your verdict I ask that you say, 'Jack Reeves,' " McMullen again pointed at the defendant, " 'you're wrong, you did it.' "

Unexpectedly, Jack Reeves uttered a childish, "Did not!" toward the prosecutor.

"Jack Reeves, no more," McMullen added.

At 1:21 P.M. the jury retired to deliberate the sentence of twice-convicted murderer Jack Reeves. Twenty-five minutes later they emerged with the maximum sought by the prosecution.

Jack Wayne Reeves was sentenced to ninety-nine years in the Texas prison system, and a ten-thousand-dollar fine. He would be required to serve at least fifty years of that sentence.

Emelita's family and friends restrained their exuberance, but the broad smiles that shone on their faces reflected the pleasure they felt with the sentence.

Tom Le Noir leaned against one wall of the courtroom as he quietly observed the happy faces of the people he had come to know and like over the past twenty-two months. Then he noticed a juror moving toward him. *I wonder what's on her mind,* Le Noir thought as he watched her cross the floor. He turned to Mary Stewart, the Channel 8 reporter, and Sandy Gately, district attorney for Coyell County, and commented, "I think I have a juror mad at me. I was a bit aggressive, a little confrontational. My God, she's going to come over here and kick me. She'll probably say something like we convicted him in spite of you."

Sandy and Mary laughed at Le Noir's nervous chatter.

"I'm serious," he assured them, only half joking.

He took a deep breath, stood straight, and braced himself for whatever was coming.

This could be ugly, Le Noir thought.

To his surprise, the woman stuck out her hand and took Le Noir's, shaking it as she spoke. "I just want to thank you," she said sincerely.

It was an experience Le Noir had never had in his twelve years as a homicide cop. No juror had ever thanked him for his efforts. He felt a warmth he had never experienced after a trial.

As Le Noir and Evans faced reporters outside the courthouse, Le Noir remarked, "The story pretty much comes to a close right now. This is what we've been working for, for two years."

Jack Reeves was quickly whisked away to a waiting sheriff's car.

In response to Reeves's continued denials, a reporter shouted, "Who do you think killed her?"

Reeves angrily pointed to Lynn Combs standing on the courthouse lawn.

"That lesbian lover of hers!" an enraged Reeves barked.

"Burn in hell, Jack! Burn in hell!" Combs shot back.

"You killed her!" Reeves retorted.

But it was Jack Reeves who had been found guilty of killing Emelita by twelve good-and-true jurors. And Jack Reeves would probably never leave prison alive.

Epilogue

The Tenth Court of Appeals for the State of Texas affirmed the convictions of Jack Wayne Reeves for the murders of both Sharon and Emelita Reeves. Jack Reeves is currently serving concurrent sentences in the Gurney Prison Unit of the Texas Department of Criminal Justice, Tennessee Colony, Texas. The fifty-seven year-old Reeves will be eligible for parole in 2046.

After careful review of the drowning death of Myong, it was determined that there was insufficient evidence to warrant further investigation. Reeves still maintains his innocence in the deaths of both Sharon and Emelita.

Wes Ball diligently represents Reeves in his higher court appeals.

Detective Tom Le Noir continues to work in the homicide division of the Arlington Police Department.

"Everybody was against me when this thing started," Le Noir said after the trial. "But once things began to turn, everyone came around." Le Noir maintains that Buddy Evans, Dave Berry, Sandy Gately, and Andy McMullen are true heroes of the Reeves convictions.

Buddy Evans has transferred from the missing person's division to work as a liaison between the police department and the Arlington Independent School District. He is currently investigating gang-related activities. Buddy Evans is a natural for working with kids.

Former district attorney Sandy Gately is now in private law

practice in Gatesville, Texas, as is Andy McMullen in Bosque County.

James Vaughn, the father of Sharon Reeves, died shortly after the Bosque County trial. Some say the ailing Vaughn's desire was to stay alive just to see Jack Reeves brought to justice. His wish was granted.

BOOK YOUR PLACE ON OUR WEBSITE AND MAKE THE READING CONNECTION!

We've created a customized website just for our very special readers, where you can get the inside scoop on everything that's going on with Zebra, Pinnacle and Kensington books.

When you come online, you'll have the exciting opportunity to:

- View covers of upcoming books
- Read sample chapters
- Learn about our future publishing schedule (listed by publication month *and author*)
- Find out when your favorite authors will be visiting a city near you
- Search for and order backlist books from our online catalog
- Check out author bios and background information
- Send e-mail to your favorite authors
- Meet the Kensington staff online
- Join us in weekly chats with authors, readers and other guests
- Get writing guidelines
- AND MUCH MORE!

Visit our website at
http://www.pinnaclebooks.com

TRUE CRIME AT ITS BEST
FROM PINNACLE BOOKS